Penguin Books

A Job to Live

Shirley Williams was elected to the House of Commons in 1964 as the Labour Member for Hitchin and became Parliamentary Secretary to the Ministry of Labour in January 1966. In 1967 she became Minister of State at the Department of Education and Science, and from 1969 to 1970 was Minister of State at the Home Office. Between 1970 and 1974 she was opposition spokesperson for social services, home affairs and then prices. In 1974 she entered the Cabinet as Secretary of State for Prices and Consumer Protection, becoming a Privy Councillor, and in 1976 became Secretary of State for Education and Science and Paymaster-General. She was a member of the National Executive of the Labour Party from 1970 to 1981. In March 1981 Shirley Williams, with Roy Jenkins, David Owen and William Rodgers, launched the Social Democratic Party. In November of that year she became the first elected Social Democrat MP when she won a by-election at Crosby, Merseyside, a seat she represented until the General Election of June 1983. She was elected as the Party's first President in 1982 and was re-elected in 1984.

From 1979 until 1985 she was a research fellow at the Policy Studies Institute. She was a Visiting Fellow at Nuffield College, Oxford, from 1968 to 1975, Fellow of the Institute of Politics at the Kennedy School of Government during 1979–80, Godkin Lecturer at Harvard University and Rede Lecturer at the University of Cambridge in 1980. She has received many academic honours, including doctorates from the universities of Leeds, Southampton, Bath, Radcliffe (USA) and Leuven. She is currently a consultant on employment and technology for the OECD and a member of the faculty of the International Management Institute at Geneva, Switzerland.

Shirley Williams's earlier book, *Politics is for People*, was published by Penguin in 1981.

Shirley Williams

A JOB TO LIVE

*The Impact of Tomorrow's Technology
on Work and Society*

Penguin Books

For John and Eileen,
in gratitude for a lifetime's friendship

Penguin Books Ltd, Harmondsworth, Middlesex, England
Viking Penguin Inc., 40 West 23rd Street, New York, New York 10010, U.S.A.
Penguin Books Australia Ltd, Ringwood, Victoria, Australia
Penguin Books Canada Ltd, 2801 John Street, Markham, Ontario, Canada L 3 R 1 B4
Penguin Books (N.Z.) Ltd, 182–190 Wairau Road, Auckland 10, New Zealand

First published 1985

Made and printed in Great Britain by
Richard Clay (The Chaucer Press) Ltd, Bungay, Suffolk
Filmset in 9/11½pt Monophoto Plantin Light by
Northumberland Press Ltd, Gateshead

Contents

'...the entire experience of mankind demonstrates clearly that useful work, adequately rewarded in some combination of material and non-material things, is a central need of human beings, even a basic yearning of the human spirit.'

E. F. Schumacher

Acknowledgements

This book is one of a series of publications arising from a study of job generation supported by the Monument Trust and conducted jointly by the Policy Studies Institute (of which I was a Senior Research Fellow from 1979 to April 1985) and Imperial College, London. The other titles in the series, which are to be published by the Policy Studies Institute, are *Waste: A Study of Efficiency in the Sewerage Industry*, by Dr Jeremy Turk, Professor Leo Pyle and John Fox, and *Less Fuel, More Jobs: The Promotion of Energy Conservation in Buildings*, by Dr Mayer Hillman and Dr Alan Bollard. We are indebted to the Monument Trust for their support and encouragement.

While I am solely responsible for what is written in this book, I owe a great deal to many friends and colleagues who have given me the benefit of their knowledge, their opinions and their constructive criticism. John Spencer, Anthony King and Richard Layard read the book all through in an early draft, John Kenneth Galbraith and David Yonkelovitch in a later one, and their comments were very valuable. Ezra Vogel looked at the chapters on Japan; William Spring and Douglas Caulkins at the many sections referring to the United States. Umberto Colombo was the source of several illuminating ideas for the chapters on small business networks and jobs for the future, as were Paul Doty and James Alty for those on artificial intelligence and the use of expert systems, and Dr Janet Vaughan on the health consequences of unemployment. Richard Neustadt and Paul Sieghart were very helpful on the chapters concerned with information, surveillance and democracy. I have spent many useful hours discussing small business and local employment initiatives with Christopher Brooks of OECD and I am grateful to him and to Tony Fidgett for statistical data. Faye Duchin, Charles Jonscher, Howard Rosenbrock, Sara Morrison and Len Grice produced helpful amendments on the sections describing their own work; Jim Northcott and Norman Evans, two colleagues at the Policy Studies Institute, have contributed greatly to Chapters Seven and Sixteen respectively, while Richard Davies has given me great support throughout. I have discussed the theme of the first part of the book with Fritz Scharpf, whose thoughts on economic policy are always stimulating and perceptive. Finally, I have gained greatly from contacts with the faculty and students of Grinnell College, Iowa, especially Bob Gray and Steve Adams, and with friends in the Kennedy School at Harvard University.

Jane Ward, Margaret Sampson and Mark Bostridge have laboured over the language, the references and the presentation of this book, and to them also it owes its existence.

Introduction

I started work on this book in 1980, as unemployment began its inexorable rise in much of Western Europe. The work was repeatedly interrupted by the demands of politics, and in particular by my eighteen months as Member of Parliament for Crosby, yet was given a sense of urgency by what I learned in that time. In Merseyside, one of the poorest parts of the United Kingdom, the desolation and waste caused by mass unemployment are visible and tangible. So is the rotting of the economic fabric that cries out for work to be done. So is the decay of social standards: the high level of petty crime, the growing drug problem, truancy and casual violence, the bitterness of political polarization. This is a region in pain, where it is hard to believe anybody cares.

Emotional appeals will not alter the minds of those in authority, and slogans carry no weight against an intellectual establishment in which monetarism remains the dominating school of economic thought. Its protagonists have argued that there is no alternative to the Government's policies, and that those who suggest there is deceive themselves by resurrecting the failed policies of the past. Those policies had mixed results but were by no means unmitigated failures, on the basis of such criteria as growth, investment, the trade balance or the unemployment rate. But that is to challenge the central orthodoxy. Many distinguished economists have done so: in the United States, for example, Kenneth Galbraith, James Tobin and Rudolf Dornbusch; in the United Kingdom, James Meade, Richard Layard and Amartya Sen, to name only three among many. Their objections have been disregarded or dismissed.

I decided to look at what other countries have done, to see why Japan and Sweden have such low levels of unemployment, how West Germany has kept youth unemployment down to the same level as adult unemployment, and how the United States succeeded in bringing unemployment down from 11 to 7 per cent in only two years. Practical men and women might dismiss even the most powerful intellectual arguments: surely they would have to take seriously the evidence from other countries?

My investigations started when I chaired a series of OECD examinations of national youth employment policies in the United States, West Germany, Denmark and Ireland. They provided my fellow examiners and myself with a unique opportunity to question those who made policy and those who were affected by it. I saw something of the West German apprenticeship system and of the Irish industrial training programme. I went to Canada to hear at first hand of their experiments in work-sharing. In Japan, I learned about lifetime employment and the use of on-the-job training and transfer to ensure that skills are constantly up-dated. In Scotland, which can tell the most encouraging story of economic renaissance to be heard in Britain, I saw what can happen when the public and private sectors work together, and when research in the former is developed into marketable products by the latter.

As I explored the macroeconomic arguments and the microeconomic measures, it became clear that the recession and restrictive financial policies bear a large share of responsibility for mass unemployment. An increase in government borrowing used to finance projects where the cost per job is low, like many in construction and conservation, could transform the employment prospects for the young and the less skilled. The additional demand created by one or two million more people in work would benefit the private sector, and the beneficial effects would spread throughout the economy. The Government is rightly concerned about inflation, but the experience of other countries indicates that economies working as far below capacity as Britain's is today can expand substantially before setting off inflationary pressures. An effective incomes policy would allow reflation to go further and unemployment to decline faster than would be wise if no such policy existed.

But the recession and monetarist policies are not the only causes of unemployment today. The other main cause of the unemployment I saw was a structural mismatch. Many men and women had skills that modern technologies had made obsolete, while many vacancies remained unfilled for lack of the new skills required. Outstanding firms like IBM and Marconi told me that they had good jobs going unfilled, for the lack of young men and women trained in electronics and in electrical or mechanical engineering. Small firms were hunting for people with experience of microelectronics, because they could see that their futures depended on adopting new technologies. The irony was that the desperate search for those with relevant skills and knowledge coincided with the highest unemployment among young people in Britain's history. The missing factor was appropriate and sufficient education and training, and that in turn demanded a transformation of attitudes and a willingness to break out of the formal patterns of the past. Britain's economic decline relates directly to inadequate investment in manufacturing and inadequate investment in the economic infrastructure, but, most of all, to inadequate investment in human resources. Still directed to the academic achievements of a small élite, Britain's education and training systems have as yet created neither the high general level of skills and knowledge that accounts for the economic success of West Germany and Japan, nor the high proportion of graduates that fuel the innovation and enterprise of the United States.

The scale of the mismatch between old skills and new needs shows that the industrial world is moving towards a second Industrial Revolution, a revolution based on information technology. The movement from one kind of industrial society to another is not a steady progression, but a quantum leap, like the change from feudal agriculture to manufacturing industry concentrated in the cities. The relics of feudal Britain, the half-timbered houses, the cathedrals and castles, remind us of a vanished society. The empty factories of Merseyside and the desolate mills of Yorkshire and Lancashire are, similarly, monuments to a fast-disappearing industrial past. Some countries failed to manage the difficult transition from feudalism to industrialization. Spain and Portugal suffered a rapid decline from the great heights they attained in the sixteenth and seventeenth centuries. So did Turkey. In a time that the French historian Fernand Braudel describes as a passage between epochs, the United States and Japan seem to be managing the transition from the industrial society to an information-based society with ease, while Europe flounders. Among the European countries, Italy has proved the most adaptable, responding with a mixture of creativity and enterprise, and by-passing the obstacles thrown up by the institutions of the past. West Germany, the most successful industrial European economy, has used the new technologies in its industry without making any substantial changes to its institutions. It remains to be seen whether that will be enough for success in the new era. The Federal Republic's institutional framework is in any case relatively new, having been reconstructed after the Second World War, and that may prove to be a substantial advantage. British industry and British institutions have adapted only slowly to the new information revolution, though British customers are very much aware of microelectronic products and services.

As I observe my own country's rough and dangerous passage across the gulf that separates the old Industrial Revolution from the new, I see it being pulled apart. In one Britain the new plants and offices, clean and shining, rise from lawns and flower-beds. Those who work in them continue to live in one of the most unspoiled settled environments in the world. In the other Britain, the scars of the old Industrial Revolution remain unhealed. Unwanted young people hang around the littered market-places and grimy terraces. Their rejection will not go unmarked. Beneath the surface apathy, resentment is welling up. The mounting toll of violence on the football terraces and in the colliery villages is met by more stringent laws and better-armed policemen, suppressing the symptoms of a country in crisis. What is not tackled is the crisis itself.

The new industrial epoch need not mean mass unemployment, although for the first time the professions will be affected as well as white-collar and blue-collar jobs, as 'intelligent' computers complement and compete with human knowledge and human expertise. New technologies do destroy jobs, but they create others, as the chapter on jobs for the future indicates. Some of those new jobs will be in small businesses, which are exploiting their flexibility and their good industrial relations to move into niches in a fast-changing market; the flourishing of small businesses and of local employment initiatives is described. Other new jobs will go only to those with advanced education and sophisticated skills. Education will determine a country's success in the new epoch; two chapters deal with education and training.

Incomes policy is an essential element in any sustained programme to reduce unemployment, for the demands of organized labour can otherwise divert additional money pumped into the economy into higher wages. Fiscal policy has to complement incomes policy by ensuring that additional money is not siphoned off into tax-cuts for better-off people either. An incomes policy can only be sustained if there is a reward for restraint; in the chapter on incomes policy, profit-sharing, wider share ownership and a different structure of remuneration in which weekly or monthly wages would be only a part of the total are briefly examined.

The industrial relations that underpin an incomes policy are also essential to the successful exploitation of information technology revolution, as the chapter on men, machines and management indicates. The rewards of innovation and effort depend on management and labour cooperating to ensure the success of their common enterprise. Working relationships are based on teamwork, not on hierarchical management structures, which are unacceptable in better-educated societies. Human resources are valued, and people are encouraged to contribute suggestions, criticisms and ideas, as described in the chapter on Japanese attitudes. The industrial relations needed to sustain incomes policy, without which an employment programme can be at best only a very limited one, are the industrial relations needed to make an information-based society successful too.

The political institutions of a country reflect its economic structure. Britain's political institutions have the rare distinction of surviving over three centuries unbroken by civil war or revolution. That period spans the transition from an economy based on crafts and agriculture to one based on manufacturing industry, and includes the whole of the first industrial era, from its rise to its decline. But the transition from that industrial society to the new epoch is proving very difficult for British political institutions to manage. Information technology flourishes on a free flow of information. Britain has a tradition of secrecy, of control over information by the executive that goes back centuries, and presents a major obstacle to the advent of an information-based economy. The challenge new technology poses to democracy will not go away, however. The democracies will need to think carefully about the implications of using command systems dependent upon artificial intelligence to make decisions. It is the essence of democracy that the people are consulted through the representatives they elect. No one elects a computer, yet up to now legislatures have not discussed who programs them, who chooses the experts whose knowledge is embodied in the software, and on what assumptions expert systems are being devised.

It may seem a long journey from unemployment to the effect of new technology on political institutions, but they cannot be separated. This book falls into two parts. The first is largely about unemployment, ways to create jobs and the changes in them required by the advent of information technology. There are grounds for optimism about the prospects for jobs, especially in local employment initiatives, and in a new partnership between the private and public sectors. There is hope too in the strong demand for highly skilled and highly qualified people, provided that that demand can be met.

These growth points are hampered, however, by institutional structures that do nothing to encourage them. The need for institutional change is what the second part of the book is about. Centralized government, jealous of devolving power to regional and local authorities, discourages local enterprise and small business. Confrontational industrial relations sour the climate for innovation and enterprise, as do ideological objections to the public and private sectors working together, as they do so successfully in Japan.

Because politicians determine the ruling ideology, because they control official information and decide what resources should go into education and training, the final chapters deal with political institutions. To preserve democracy in an information-based economy, they should be decentralized, flexible and open. If they do not embody safeguards for democracy, they may become centralized, secretive and oppressive, using information technology to make autocracy efficient. The choice will be determined by the respect paid by those in authority to the individual human beings that compose society. A society that cares little for the human waste of unemployment is unlikely to care much for the fulfilment of individual aspirations and the expression of individual values. Industrial societies have become transfixed by their own scientific and technical achievements; how those achievements should be used in the service of human beings is discussed hardly at all. We press on with arms races that serve no purpose except to increase our capacity to destroy one another, not twice or three times over but ten or twenty times over. We pursue aggressive industrial and agricultural technologies based on heavy capital investment in Third World countries whose fragile social fabric is unable to bear the strain, and tears apart. Iran and much of black Africa are testimonies to that. We consume fossil fuels and forests, and we destroy fertile soil at a rate that threatens the survival of the human species even without war.

Yet the new technologies can help us to move away from the dependence on energy and scarce raw materials of the first Industrial Revolution. They can harness human wisdom and knowledge to the survival of the planet. They can enhance the lives of men and women or they can blight them. The choice is ours, and it is what this book is about.

PART ONE

ROUGH PASSAGE

'Unemployment is bound to remain high
and bound to be slow coming down.'

Sir Geoffrey Howe, 1983

'Gizza Home, Gizza Job'

Graffito on wall of
tower block, Moss Side,
Manchester, 1983

1 The Dole Queues Lengthen

'It is suggested that many young people already living will never have paid employment of the traditional kind.'

Scottish Council for
Community Education, 1981

Unemployment is the most serious domestic problem facing the countries of the West. In Britain, every poll over the past two years has listed unemployment first among all the problems the country confronts. There is ample justification for this public concern.

In Western Europe, one person in nine is out of work. Among young people under twenty-four, the rate of unemployment is two to three times higher than in the rest of the work-force: in France and Britain, one in four of them are jobless, in Italy and Spain more than one in three. Over 40 per cent of the unemployed are under twenty-five.[1] Furthermore, unemployment lasts a long time for many people in Western Europe: nearly three fifths of Britain's 3·2 million unemployed, and two thirds of the unemployed in France have been out of work for over six months; around two fifths of those in both countries have been without a job for over a year. An underclass of young men and women with few, or inappropriate, skills is emerging. They are members of a deprived generation, born in the post-war 'baby boom' years, educated in overcrowded schools and now struggling to find work in a sparse job market at a time of low growth.

After the Great Depression of the inter-war years and up to the late 1970s, Western Europe, with the exception of Southern Italy and part of Iberia, economically backward regions, experienced neither long-term unemployment nor mass unemployment among young people. The high levels of unemployment experienced in the older industrial cities of the United States, particularly amongst their black populations, were once alien to the experience of post-war Europe, but today such levels are commonplace. They are spectacularly high among young people in the most recently established European democracies – Spain, Portugal and Greece – and among those from ethnic minorities.

The Safety Net

Does unemployment matter?

Most unemployed men and women today receive unemployment benefit or welfare payments that are supposed to assure a minimally decent standard of living. In Western Europe, benefit is usually paid for the first twelve months of unemployment at a rate, depending on family circumstances, of about two thirds of the claimant's earnings when in work. But thereafter, in most countries, the unemployed become dependent on various forms of welfare payment, and their position can deteriorate sharply. A recent OECD (Organization for Economic Cooperation and Development) study compared the income of long-term unemployed individuals and families in several countries with a 'standard income': that of a married couple with one earner on average pay and two children. The study showed that, in Britain, single people are worst off. They can expect a quarter to a third of that average wage, while couples with two children get between two thirds and three quarters. In West Germany, the low paid suffer most. Families whose benefit payments start at half average pay, made up to 61 per cent by family allowances, fall back to 37·6 per cent of average pay after a year of unemployment. The position in the United States is worst of all, indeed dreadful, with low paid families with two children getting 29·2 per cent of an average wage once unemployment benefit runs out. That is poverty by any standard. The OECD report concluded, with that organization's customary restraint:

> The results of this analysis stand in stark contrast to the popular belief that a spell of unemployment has little personal financial cost. While this may be true of very short spells, it is not true of longer spells. It is difficult to escape the conclusion that existing social security arrangements may be deficient in protecting the unemployed, and in particular the long-term unemployed, from economic hardship.[2]

In many American states, the financial provision for the unemployed is inadequate to maintain even a minimally decent standard of living. After twenty-six weeks of benefit, families whose heads are unemployed are dependent on welfare (which varies between states from $90 to $200 a week for a family) and on food stamps.[3] An unemployed person without a dependent family is not entitled to welfare at all. For many, the loss of a job is a passport to poverty. Poverty and malnutrition in the United

States have become much more extensive recently, following a twelve billion dollar cut in Federal spending on food stamps and child nutrition programmes between 1982 and 1985. 'Hunger is a problem of epidemic proportions across the nation,' concluded the Physicians' Task Force on Hunger in America; 'up to twenty million citizens may be hungry at least some period of time each month.'[4] Other evidence bears out the physicians' findings. Infant mortality in the United States is no longer in a decline but has levelled out at about 10·9 per thousand, a high figure by the standards of other well-off nations. In areas of very high unemployment, like Harlem, infant mortality is more than twice the national average; other factors such as poor housing contribute. Diseases of malnutrition like kwashiorkor, the scourge of Africa, are re-emerging in the poorest districts of the United States. A minority is in acute need, locked into a Third World microeconomy in the richest country in the world.

The Sole Consequences

Whether welfare benefits are adequate to maintain a decent standard of living for unemployed families or not, the unemployed still suffer from boredom, bitterness and loss of self-respect. The boredom produced by aimless days, without structure, can finally kill the desire to *make* anything happen. 'Further rejected job applications, lack of day to day structure and continuing boredom had led in many cases to a feeling of apathy which affected any enthusiasm for tackling problems,' was how a study of unemployed school-leavers in Scotland summed it up.[5]

Earnest advocates of self-instruction and constructive leisure pursuits as solutions to the boredom of unemployment underestimate its corrosive effects. It is hard to maintain motivation and drive when nobody needs you, and nothing more clearly demonstrates rejection than failed applications for jobs. There are people, in Merseyside and elsewhere, who have applied for hundreds of jobs and have been offered few or no interviews. The sense of failure brought by rejection after rejection sours their enthusiasm. But by and large, these young men and women are characterized by apathy rather than anger. Many drift into drug-taking. The rate of drug offences among unemployed youngsters is particularly high, in spite of the difficulty of raising money to buy drugs.

Drug abuse is even more widespread than official figures suggest. The number of drug addicts registered with the Home Office increased four

times over between 1970 and 1983, and in one year, 1982–3, the number
of officially recognized young addicts increased by 50 per cent; but a
recent *Lancet* article concluded that the number of regular users of
addictive drugs exceeded by five times or more the Home Office notifica-
tions and that the divergence between the official figures and the real
ones is widening: 'Thus while Home Office figures show a four-fold
increase in total prevalence from 1970 to 1983, the real change may be
closer to a ten-fold rise. The main part of that rise appears to have
occurred since 1978.'[6] Official figures kept by Merseyside police for
drug offenders showed a three-fold increase between 1974 and 1983,
from 307 to 913. More frightening still was the thirty-fold increase in
heroin offenders between 1981 and 1983, from twelve to 373.[7]

It is hard to believe there is no association between increased drug
abuse and the massive unemployment in the region. In some districts
of Birkenhead, a Liverpool suburb, being unemployed is the norm, to
have a job is exceptional. On one big housing estate, in 1984, only two
people were employed. 'I've stopped going down to the Job Centre,'
said one man. 'I don't know anyone who's in work,' said another. Four
hundred parents on this Birkenhead estate confessed that at least one of
their children was a drug addict.

Not all drugs that cause addiction are illicit like heroin and cocaine.
Solvent abuse – glue-sniffing – is common among those without the
money for drugs or alcohol; in some inner city areas, it is endemic among
school-leavers who cannot find jobs. Its physical consequences can be
severe and irreversible. Tranquillizers have become a way of life for
many unemployed people trying to cope with their depression. A
Birkenhead general practitioner expressed his anger in dramatic terms:
'I resent being used as an instrument of government to anaesthetize the
frustrations of the unemployed.'[8]

The evidence for other forms of social breakdown is inescapable. In
Britain, 43 per cent of the 25 to 44-year-old age group who are unemployed drink heavily, compared to 28 per cent of the employed.[9] These
miserable statistics are mirrored throughout Western Europe. The
International Labour Organization has charted the increased incidence
of heart disease, depression and other illnesses among the unemployed.
Furthermore, among the long-term unemployed the will even to live
weakens. The British medical periodical the *Lancet* reported the results
of a longitudinal study which explored reasons for above-average mortality among certain groups of the population. Even when the tendency

of people with low incomes and unskilled jobs to die earlier on average than those with high incomes and professional jobs is taken into account, it remains the case that mortality is 20–30 per cent higher among the unemployed and their spouses than among the employed. In the restrained language of science, the *Lancet*'s contributors wrote:

Previous studies have suggested that stress accompanying unemployment could be associated with raised suicide rates, as were again found here. Moreover, the mortality of women whose husbands were unemployed was higher than that of all married women ... and this excess also persisted after allowance for the socio-economic distribution. The results support findings by others that unemployment is associated with adverse effects on health.

Furthermore, the research showed that mortality rates among the younger unemployed (the 25–54 age group) rose proportionately more than rates among workers approaching retirement who lost their jobs, reaching 170 per cent of the average for their income and age group. In plain language, prolonged unemployment kills people who would otherwise be alive.[10]

Though large-scale manifestations of violence and rebellion have been rare among the unemployed, riots have occurred in recent years in Berlin, Zurich, Liverpool, Manchester, London, Amsterdam, Frankfurt, Paris, Lille and elsewhere. Sometimes specific local issues have set them off, but the immediate causes have been inflamed by a sense of alienation among young people, and notably unemployed young people, from the political and social establishment. And not only among the young is there unrest: the anger unleashed at Algerian and other North African immigrants in France, and condoned by M. Le Pen's Far Right and M. Marchais' Communist Party alike; the long, dour dispute over working hours between Germany's metal workers' union and the employers; the savage confrontation between pickets and police over many months in the coalfields of Derbyshire and Yorkshire – all are evidence of societies under a strain that is exacerbated by the fear of unemployment.

These events are evidence too of a breakdown of the consensus between the democratic political parties, and between management and labour, the consensus which provided the foundation for the years of economic growth during the 1950s and 1960s. Although there were instances of disruption during those years – the student revolution that swept Europe and the United States in 1968, fuelled in part by revulsion against the war in Vietnam, as well as strikes and industrial disputes –

leading politicians and the powerful industrial organizations had common objectives and shared similar goals. One of them was full employment. With the decline of consensus, political attitudes have become polarized and there is profound disagreement about society's priorities. Those on the political Right believe the conquest of inflation should take precedence over full, or even high, employment; those on the Left believe the opposite. Societies become unsettled and restless as they are pulled between these two poles.

Apathy, ill health and social unrest are not the only prices to be paid for mass unemployment. There is also a direct price in terms of lost output and the burden of financing benefits.

In Britain, in 1984, the cost of each person on the dole was £5,000, and that did not include loss of tax revenue and national insurance contributions. When these are taken into account, the cost of unemployment rises to £6,500 a head: at least £19·5 billion nationally at 1984 prices.[11] Huge sums are being spent simply on maintaining an income for the unemployed, while the scope for useful work, to our towns and cities, in our environment and for the more vulnerable members of society, is immense. The unemployed have been left to rot, whatever the physical and psychological costs to themselves and to society. Political imagination ought surely to be able to match the dole queues to the work that needs to be done. But, apart from a few Government schemes, such imagination has not been evident.

Fibs, Lies and Damned Statistics

Some men and women work in the unofficial economy. They are 'on the black': paid in cash or kind, their wages go unrecorded. Some of them draw unemployment insurance or benefits; they are fiddling the system. Others do not draw benefit, and will therefore not be registered as unemployed. Whether drawing benefit or not, they do not pay taxes or social security contributions on their unofficial incomes.

The faster the growth of the unofficial economy, the greater the burden of social security contributions. In Italy, where estimates of the output of the unofficial economy range from a quarter to a third of the gross national product, social security contributions from employer and employee combined are equivalent to over half a worker's wages. Few other European countries would approach those levels, but the unofficial economy is nevertheless expanding rapidly everywhere. This expansion forces up the level of contributions paid by those in regular jobs. While the unofficial economy provides a source of occupation and extra income for a proportion of the unemployed, it also erodes the foundations of the welfare state and may compel governments to transform the means by which public services are financed.

The unofficial economy has another less immediately obvious consequence: it weakens respect for the law and for good civic conduct. 'Fiddling the system', however, is not confined to the unemployed. Governments are adept at the game as well.

Official unemployment figures in most European countries are based on the numbers of people claiming unemployment benefits, while in the United States the rate of unemployment is based on responses to a monthly sample survey of 60,000 households. However, the United States has a second measure of unemployment which is much more like the European method of assessment – the insured unemployment rate: that is, the number of jobless people entitled to claim insurance benefits. In the past ten years, total unemployment (based on the sample survey) and insured unemployment (based on benefit entitlement) have diverged sharply. A recent Brookings paper showed that, while the *insured* unemployment rate in the United States was only 2·6 points lower than the *total* unemployment rate in 1975, by 1982 the divergence was 5 points – the difference between 4·7 per cent and 9·7 per cent.[12] If one goes back before 1975, the correlation of one rate to the other is even closer; in the 1950s, the total unemployment rate and the insured unemployment rate were almost identical, the difference between them rarely exceeding 1 per cent.

One reason for this recent divergence is the change in the composition of the labour force. Prime-age men (24–55) now represent a much smaller proportion of the total labour force than they used to, yet they continue to be disproportionately represented among the insured unemployed. This is because the greatly increased number of married women in paid work and the many young people among the unemployed are rarely eligible for the benefit their husbands and fathers are entitled to, and therefore do not appear among the statistics of the insured unemployed.

But, at best, that explanation accounts only in part for the increasing disparity between total unemployment and insured unemployment between 1975 and 1982. The main reason is a simple one: because Congress has tightened up the rules, far fewer Americans are eligible for benefit. In addition, benefits are now taxed, which makes them less attractive to the unemployed in higher income groups – for example, the wives of well-paid men.

The difference between the total unemployment rate and the insured unemployment rate has another consequence which in turn operates to widen the gap between the two even further. Benefits can be paid in certain circumstances to the unemployed for an additional thirteen weeks, financed half from federal funds and half from state funds. The trigger for these extended benefits is the insured unemployment rate, which must exceed either 5 or 6 per cent, the exact threshold depending upon state law. Because so many unemployed people are ineligible for benefit, even states with total unemployment rates of 10 per cent or more fail to reach the required threshold; their unemployed citizens do not get extended benefits. They then count for the total unemployment rate but not for the insured unemployment rate, because they run out of benefit entitlement. As the gap widens, the long-term unemployed fall through it.

The combined effect of all these factors was remarkable. In November 1982, only 48 per cent of the American unemployed were receiving benefits compared to 78 per cent in 1975.[13]

While these statistical calculations mean that there is a great deal of poverty and hardship among unemployed Americans, especially in the old industrial and mining areas of the Middle West and the Appalachians, they do not conceal the *number* of people unemployed and looking for work, for they are shown up in the sample census.

It is in Western Europe that the real levels of unemployment have been hidden.

The Hidden Unemployed

Western European governments have found it difficult to create the economic conditions in which there will be enough jobs to absorb the unemployed. Employment has grown very little in the past five years, and in a number of Community countries it has actually dropped. It has proved easier to manipulate unemployment figures downwards by a series of administrative measures than to find real jobs for people on the dole.

To take the case of Britain, in May 1982 the Department of Employment changed the basis on which it calculated unemployment, from counting those who registered as unemployed to counting those who claimed unemployment benefit. Because the social insurance system still treats married women as dependants of their husbands, any woman whose husband was employed or drawing unemployment benefit ceased herself to count as unemployed unless she was insured in her own right; most married women were not. This nominal change reduced female unemployment by 19·3 per cent – the difference between the old figure and the new figure, taking an average over the six months from May to October 1982 in which the Department of Employment calculated both officially. Between 200,000 and 250,000 people disappeared from the unemployment figures as a result of this change alone.

A second substantial group was removed from the unemployment figures after 24 November 1981. Older workers, men over sixty, who had been employed and in receipt of supplementary benefit for over twelve months could draw the higher, long-term rate of benefit payable if they no longer registered as unemployed. The year-on-year figure shows that 98,000 of these older men disappeared from the unemployment statistics between June 1983 and June 1984.

Without these administrative changes unemployment in Britain in January 1985 would have been not 12·9 per cent, but over 14 per cent, and even that figure does not take into account discouraged workers who don't bother to register because they see little hope of a job.

By keeping the unemployment figures at a lower level in these ways, governments provide a placebo for public concern. The Press and the public accept statistical manipulation to an amazing extent, and soon forget how far the real position is distorted. But governments do not wholly escape the consequences, for the 'Catch 22' effect is that any upturn in employment has a disproportionately small impact on the unemployment figures. Unregistered workers come out of the woodwork to take many of the jobs. It is difficult to be precise, but it is estimated that, because so many job-seekers are not registered as unemployed, three jobs or more have to be created to take two people off the official unemployment register. The same is true of the United States, where four million jobs were created in the calendar year 1983 but unemployment fell only from 10·7 per cent to 7·8 per cent of the work-force, a reduction of 2·2 million. Governments find themselves chasing their own tails: the difficulty of getting unemployment down has been aggravated by their own statistical manipulations.

2 Unemployment: Why Does Society Acquiesce?

'I see one third of a nation ill-housed, ill-clad and ill-nourished.'

Franklin Roosevelt, Second Inaugural
Address, January 1937

Why do European societies acquiesce in these terrible levels of unemployment – indeed, sometimes even accept them as beneficial?

There are several reasons.

The Employed are Alienated from the Unemployed

Class divisions in Europe have run along occupational lines, with the traditional professions like medicine and law at the top of the hierarchy, technical and white-collar occupations in the middle, and unskilled labourers and service workers at the bottom. Now there is a new division between the employed and the unemployed which cuts across social distinctions. To be employed is to see one's real income rise, albeit modestly, and to enjoy a better standard of living. To be unemployed is to see one's real income fall, to add to the pain of rejection the difficulty of maintaining one's old life-style on a sharply reduced income.

Unemployment in the Great Depression struck at a working class which shared similar occupations and life-styles. In the 1930s, the workforce on both sides of the Atlantic was largely blue collar and largely male. Women represented only a quarter of those in paid employment, and were concentrated in traditionally 'feminine' occupations like domestic service, clerical work and the clothing industry. Unemployment was an experience shared by working-class communities, binding them together in common poverty and a common way of life. In Europe, working-class solidarity was the bedrock of the socialist and Communist parties – the British Labour Party, the German Social Democrats, the French and Italian Communist parties were all closely associated with the industrial trade unions.

That solidarity survived the Second World War, but began to weaken as the nature of the labour-force changed out of recognition. The trebling of standards of living in the thirty years between 1948 and 1978; the change in occupational structures towards a majority of white-collar, technical and professional jobs; the increased proportion of women in the paid labour-force – these factors all contributed to the transformation. The employed, at least in Western Europe, improved their real earnings steadily throughout the 1970s. Between 1973 and 1980, real earnings in Britain went up by an average of 4·1 per cent a year.[1]

Organized workers improved their job security through laws that required compensation for redundancy, restrictions on dismissal and, in some countries, negotiations with workers' representatives before anyone could be laid off. In certain trades, particularly the professions, entry requirements became tougher; formal qualifications were introduced for many jobs, on top of the traditional requirement for craftsmen/women of a completed apprenticeship. Until the recession became very severe, slimming down staff numbers was accomplished largely by 'natural wastage', which meant that no-one was forced to leave a job; voluntary retirement and a suspension of recruitment achieved the necessary reduction. 'Proper' jobs, full-time traditional jobs, turned into zealously protected quasi-monopolies of the employees, and overheads for their employers. The losers were part-time workers, the young and those who, like many married women, moved in and out of the formal labour force. Often, those lucky enough to be employed did not want to be told about those without jobs.

While those employed in traditional blue-collar or white-collar jobs strengthened their defences and improved their material position, the unemployed became poorer. Faced with demands for more public expenditure on the one side and pressure for reduced taxes on the other, some European governments cut unemployment and welfare benefits. In the Netherlands benefits have been frozen; in West Germany pensions are no longer fully indexed. Earnings-related unemployment benefit in Britain was abandoned in 1982, and conditions for supplementary benefit were tightened up. In the United States, entitlement to extended benefits was made subject to the most stringent conditions in 1981, including barring anyone who could not show evidence of 'a systematic and sustained effort to obtain work'. Officials administering welfare programmes were under pressure to make savings wherever they could.

Those suspected of 'fiddling the system' were pursued with renewed energy.

Subtly, the political climate changed. Conservative economists identified inflation as the enemy, and blamed it on high wage demands and excessive public expenditure. The unemployed became less objects of pity than objects of contempt or criticism. 'They could get a job if they wanted to.' 'Life's too comfortable for them to bother.' 'Why don't they get on their bikes?' In some business and political circles, it became fashionable to eschew sympathy and compassion. Life, it was said, is a hard, competitive game. No firm could afford to be lumbered with unnecessary workers. Industry needed to become leaner and fitter to compete against newly industrialized countries. If unemployed people really wanted jobs, workers should accept lower wages. Indeed the classical economic argument, that every market achieves equilibrium between supply and demand at a particular price, was used to show that there could be full or nearly full employment if workers would accept lower real wages. But since social benefits are a floor below which no sensible person would accept paid employment, the second stage of the classical economic argument was that social benefits should also be cut.

It can certainly be argued that a badly paid job is better than penury. Governments on both sides of the Atlantic believe that part of the answer to unemployment lies in a rapid growth of low-wage jobs, and that this may entail a reduction in social benefits. But the trouble with looking to low-wage jobs as the solution to unemployment is that they are usually low-skill jobs. Neither employee nor employer has much incentive to improve productivity by training in new skills or by operating more efficiently; the economy gradually slips into producing low-technology goods and services. Domestic demand will not be buoyant, and exports will be concentrated on intermediate products. As the country concerned competes with the rest of the world in these intermediate markets, the pressure to lower costs will increase. It will be argued that benefits must be reduced further because there is not enough incentive to work. It is true that high wages combined with low productivity can price people out of jobs. But improving productivity and the quality of goods are more promising ways of competing than cutting wages and reducing people's standard of living, policies which implicitly condone economic decline.

The Politicians are Remote from the Distressed

Arguments of the type outlined above – which like so many arguments in classical economics assume that the human being can be treated as 'economic man' and is not a political, emotional and holistic being – would be less easily accepted by the political leaders of the West if they were more aware of how their electors lived. Television and terrorism, a strange combination, have divorced and isolated modern political leaders from the lives of their people, and particularly from the lives of the poor and deprived. The campaign trains of Franklin Roosevelt and Harry Truman, the open-air meetings addressed by Gladstone in the Lothians or Lloyd George in the Welsh valleys, were in another world compared to the controlled television Press conferences, the carefully engineered and produced visits, or meetings with invited audiences which constitute political communications now.

Though political leaders rarely plunge into the most depressed or turbulent regions of their country, on the rare occasions that they do, it is clear that they are shocked by what they see. Michael Heseltine was so moved by his brief period as Minister for Merseyside, one of the most depressed regions in the United Kingdom, that he fought in the Cabinet and beyond, against great resistance, for additional resources for the region. Similarly, Patrick Jenkin was horrified by deteriorating housing in the North-west of England. Across the Channel, Giscard d'Estaing visited the homes of workers in humble jobs. But despite such examples there is a pervasive sense that the political class is out of touch, and that political leaders move among the rich and powerful who finance their appearances and support their increasingly expensive campaigns. They neither see nor know what is happening in Harlem and Saint-Denis, in Liverpool and Appalachia.

'Nothing can be done anyway'

One reason for the acquiescence of today's societies in mass unemployment that should not be underestimated is the belief that unemployment is inevitable and that none of the policies intended to deal with it has been successful. This profound scepticism extends to the unemployed themselves; an *Economist* survey recorded that over half the unemployed people interviewed believed that nothing could be done to get them jobs.[2] They accepted the argument so frequently advanced by the

Government led by Margaret Thatcher that 'there is no alternative' to monetarist policies.

This attitude of resignation is far more widespread in Western Europe than in North America. Europe, unlike the USA, has not been successful in creating new jobs (though the USA itself has had little success in the old industrial areas). Employment has grown only slowly, or in some countries even fallen, while unemployment has risen. Workers have been laid off in the old industries, especially steel and shipbuilding, and only a relatively small number of new jobs have so far emerged in new industries such as microelectronics. Jobs created in services have been lowly paid, and many are only part-time. Forecasts of future unemployment remain stubbornly high, showing a further increase and no prospect of substantial improvement. The OECD estimates that European unemployment will reach $20\frac{1}{4}$ million in the first half of 1986, one and half million more than in the first half of 1984.[3] Medium-term projections for Britain by independent research bodies show unemployment continuing to rise in the next two or three years.[4]

American commentators are biting on the subject of Europe's decline. In an article entitled 'A Continent stews in its own economic juice', a reporter on the *Wall Street Journal* wrote that 'Europessimism has become an epidemic infecting all the continent'.[5] *Forbes Magazine*'s chief European reporter commented in July 1983, 'There is an aura of twilight about Europe.'[6] Nothing that has happened since has made any reconsideration of these conclusions necessary. Europe's unemployment has gone up month by month, while that of the United States has fallen dramatically.

The Consequences for Inflation

The obvious way to lower unemployment in any economy is to stimulate economic growth. It does not matter so much whether the stimulus comes from tax-cuts, private investment or public expenditure; it will increase aggregate demand, and that in turn will generate jobs. 'Despite the dire science fiction prophecies that accompany every period of high unemployment, revival of aggregate demand has always created jobs in numbers vastly beyond the imaginations of the pessimists,' wrote the American economist and Nobel prize-winner James Tobin in an essay on the significance of macroeconomic policies for unemployment.[7] Tobin pointed to the remarkable American achievement which created six million new jobs in eighteen months and brought unemployment tumbling down, 'a classic, well-timed Keynesian anti-recession fiscal policy'.

The United States' administration may not have intended to embark on such a policy, which fitted ill with Republican pronouncements about stern financial rectitude and the moral obligation to balance the budget. Two other objectives advanced in the 1980 Presidential election campaign in practice took priority. One was the supply-side conviction that tax-cuts would create increases in output and productivity which would more than compensate for the initial decline in tax revenues. The other was the commitment to a large increase in the defence budget. The coincidence of tax-cuts and a bigger defence expenditure produced a massive budget deficit in 1983, and that deficit in turn had the effect Keynes would have predicted on unemployment.

European governments have been more cautious and more orthodox than the Reagan administration. Their primary objective has been the reduction of inflation. To this one end, the West German Government and the British Government have reduced public investment, restrained spending on public services year by year and raised the overall burden of taxes and social insurance contributions while modestly reducing personal income tax rates. The net effect has been to contract the budget deficit. One would normally expect that deficit to increase in a recession, owing to higher expenditure on unemployment benefit and welfare payments on the one hand and reduced tax revenues on the other. Indeed, if the increased spending on unemployment benefit is taken out of the calculation, both the Federal Republic and the United Kingdom would have had budget surpluses in 1983, 1984 and 1985. In other words, the governments took more out of their economies than they put in. These macroeconomic policies deepened the effects of the recession and dampened the modest recovery which began in 1983. That modest recovery itself owed little to European fiscal and monetary measures. It was engendered by American growth, which opened up opportunities for exports from the European countries and Japan.

The dilemma in European economic policy is plain. On the one hand, the United States is criticized for its huge budget deficits, expected to run at 185–187 billion dollars a year until the end of the decade. That deficit forces up interest rates world-wide, with serious repercussions for investment and for the servicing of international debts by Third World countries. On the other hand, European governments unwilling to adopt even modest expansionary fiscal policies depend upon the United States to act as the sole engine for growth in the West. Unless there is a reversal of these contractionary policies, Western Europe is doomed to high unemployment that structural measures on their own can only moderate but never cure. European unemployment will get even worse if the United States corrects its own destabilizing deficit without a compensating European expansion.

An Unnecessary Sacrifice?

What has not occurred in the United States, however, is the renewal of inflation that conservative economists predict is bound to follow a deficit-financed expansion. Prices in the United States in 1984 were increasing slightly less rapidly than in 1983; forecasts indicate only a small rise in inflation, of 1 or 2 per cent a year.

At first sight this is puzzling. Control of inflation has been given priority over all other economic objectives by several large European countries, a control exercised by limiting the quantity of money in the economy and by keeping down public expenditure. Inflation rates have come down in almost all Western European countries, some being cut by half or more. But success in the battle against inflation has been achieved at a heavy cost. Economies are running well below capacity. The incentive to increase productive capacity is therefore low, and investment, both public and private, fell in the recession of 1979–83 in most of the member-states of the European Community. In Britain, private investment dropped in absolute terms below the 1979 level of £30·5 billion in every year up to 1984. Investment in manufacturing fell by 30 per cent between 1979 and 1984, even though 1984 was the best year since 1980. Public sector investment fell in 1981 and 1982, by over a quarter from its 1979 level of £13·3 billion, recovering to £12 billion, still 10 per cent down, in 1984. Even excluding receipts from sales of council houses, public sector investment in 1984 was well below annual expenditure in the 1970s. The American experience raises the question: has Britain's sacrifice been unnecessary?

The question cannot be answered yet, because American unemployment has not fallen to the level identified in 1980 by the United States Council of Economic Advisors as that at which inflation begins to accelerate. The argument is that if unemployment falls below a certain level, say 6 or 7 per cent, demand for labour will push up wage rates,

Table 1: Gross Fixed Investment

	Total	Public Sector	Private Sector	Manufacturing
	National Accounts Definitions (£ million, 1980 prices)			
1975	41,808	17,207	24,476	6,779
1976	42,434	17,155	25,172	6,470
1977	41,323	14,934	25,172	6,774
1978	42,938	13,615	29,323	7,220
1979	43,868	13,301	30,567	7,496
1980	41,609	12,248	29,361	6,471
1981	37,928	10,251	27,677	4,852
1982	40,468	10,261	30,207	4,685
1983	42,013	11,547	30,466	4,619
1984	45,259	11,974	33,285	5,257

Source: National Institute of Economic and Social Research.

Note: Alternative definitions of gross fixed investment take into account the sale of public assets. On these definitions, public investment fell less dramatically, private sector investment improved less. 1984 figures are:

	Total	Public Sector	Private Sector	Manufacturing
	National Accounts Definitions (£ million, 1980 prices)			
1984	45,259	13,094	32,165	6,142

creating inflationary pressures. If unemployment is above that level, the existence of unused resources of manpower will keep wage rates, and hence inflation, down. American experience suggests that there is now so much slack in Western economies that considerable expansion can occur before inflation takes off again.

European electorates, however, have been so badly burned by the experience of double-digit inflation that they seem ready to accept high unemployment and near-stagnation rather than risk a return of inflation. One misleading phrase may have helped to persuade them: 'squeezing inflation out of the system'. The phrase is misleading because inflation will return once there is rapid growth and lower unemployment unless the system itself – corporate institutions, large companies with large plants, industrial relations based on confrontation, and inflexible management hierarchies – is drastically altered. Suffering the pains of recession will not cure inflation without such a transformation. The 'system' in Western Europe, and particularly in Britain, is inflexible. This is not because Europeans are inherently less creative or less hardworking than Americans. After all, in the three decades after the war, the European Community countries outperformed the United States in growth and in productivity. It is fashionable in the United States at present to regard Western Europe as a geriatric economy, but that goes against the facts. The European Community has the same problems as those regions of the United States in which traditional manufacturing industry, sometimes called 'smokestack industry', was most strongly established. The Middle West and Pennsylvania, with their dependence on heavy industries like steel, engineering and cars, resemble the Ruhr, the Pas de Calais and the North of England. Northwest Europe was more industrialized than the United States; it is therefore difficult for new enterprises to find greenfield sites, or to escape from the regulations and trade union wages and conditions of the old industrial areas to economically undeveloped areas like those in the American South and West. The American 'rust-belt' is as familiar with the storms and strains of making the passage from one industrial epoch to another as North-west Europe is; it is with this 'rust-belt' that comparisons ought therefore to be made.

The British experience of the 1970s was one in which inflationary pressures were contained by a whole spectrum of incomes policies, some statutory, some voluntary, all of which broke down after a few years of operation. On two occasions, in 1974 and 1979, governments lost office because of a direct confrontation with the trade unions over pay. The electors in 1979, aware of the threat to the body politic, accepted economic policies that curbed inflation and constrained trade union power through mass unemployment, since incomes policies had evidently not been successful. Yet paradoxically it is mass unemployment itself that now threatens social cohesion and well-being.

Mass unemployment makes workers suspicious of change, and particularly of technological change. The transformation involved in the switch from a wartime to a peacetime economy was achieved with relative ease after the Second World War, because unemployment was, and was perceived to be, a temporary phenomenon. Once General Marshall's tentative proposals of June 1947 had been converted into detailed plans for European recovery in 1948, demand was no problem. American credit and multilateral funding arrangements financed an economic recovery that lasted for nearly thirty years.

The passage from an industrial mass production economy to an information economy demands no less a transformation than a passage from a wartime to a peacetime economy. But the bitterness, suspicion and self-protection engendered by high unemployment do not produce a climate conducive to an easy passage.

Making Industry More Efficient

Is there any way out of the dilemma of being compelled to choose between higher unemployment or higher inflation? Conservative economists advocate a decline in the unit cost of labour, which means that labour becomes more competitive with capital, and industries in Europe more competitive with industries elsewhere. Unit costs can fall either because wages drop or because productivity increases; both are advocated. Trade unions respond by opposing wage cuts. In the short run jobs may be created, but in the long run, they argue, lower wages will reduce effective demand, leading to a further contraction in the economy. Their opposition is made all the stronger by their need to fight to keep their members. The recession has cut union membership, and the unions are now in a defensive mood.

Improved productivity is an easier route to follow. Responsible trade union leaders recognize that some of the fruits of increased productivity should go to reward the owners of capital as well as the labour force. They are entitled to argue, however, that higher productivity is not wholly dependent on harder work. More investment and better investment increase the productivity of labour, yet that decision is not one labour is able to make. It should be remembered that closing down inefficient firms or plants increases the productivity of those that remain; the impressive record of increased productivity per man-hour in Britain between 1980 and 1983 almost certainly owed more to the effects of the recession in destroying inefficient firms than it did to better and more intelligent use of capital and labour in firms right across the board.

Consistently improved productivity will take time to achieve. It requires good management, up-to-date and appropriate machinery, and realization of the potential of human resources. Europe's managers cover a wide spectrum, from the excellent to the awful. Business and industry have not been high in the pecking order of careers chosen by able young people. Much of Europe's unused capital is obsolete and was designed for old technologies. Bringing it back into use would increase capacity but might well lower productivity. As for human resources, they have been notoriously undervalued in the old industrial countries apart from West Germany and Sweden. To become competitive, Europe will have to change both its attitudes and its institutions. Industrial relations based on outdated class antagonisms; education systems devised for a small élite; political structures that control the flow of information and limit discussion – these are not conducive to the emergence of modern economies capable of competing with the United States, Japan and South-east Asia. If our economies are not competitive, we cannot hope to employ our people. And if Europe cannot steer through the rough passage between the industrial revolution and the new knowledge-based society, what the French historian Fernand Braudel called 'a passage between epochs', it may find itself washed up on that unexplored new shore, its social and political structures battered and broken.[8]

Some of the institutional changes we need to make are explored in later chapters. The unemployed, however, cannot wait for a generation of reform. There are policies that can be adopted immediately to improve their chances of getting work. The first set of policies are microeconomic schemes that can be adopted without fundamentally altering the cautious economic policies of European governments. The second, an incomes policy, would allow governments to embark upon expansionary economic policies without fear of inflation, provided of course that it was adhered to.

3 Microeconomic Schemes: Putting Benefits to Work

'It would be desirable to use in some measure the Unemployment Insurance Trust to assist training and retraining.'

The Human Resources Report of the White House Conference on Productivity, 1983

Since the Great Depression governments have operated directly on unemployment through publicly financed schemes which provide jobs in public works or conservation, labour-intensive sectors which interfere little with the normal operation of the labour market. During the Carter administration in the United States, public works schemes were substantially expanded, and so were Federally aided training schemes for unemployed young people. In Britain, a guarantee of either training or work experience was given in 1977 to young people under the age of eighteen who had been without work for six months or more. Four years later, as youth unemployment continued to rise, the Youth Opportunities Programme evolved into a Youth Training Scheme open to all unemployed sixteen-year-olds, offering them a year of combined work experience and basic training. In 1984, the Youth Training Scheme alone absorbed over 350,000 young people aged sixteen and seventeen, most of whom would otherwise have been unemployed. Various kinds of public works programmes were devised for the long-term unemployed, such as the Community Programme, which had 130,000 places until it was expanded in March 1985. Wages are limited to £63 a week, which means that all but the lowest paid can only work part-time. Nevertheless, the scheme has been useful in rehabilitating men and women who have lost the habit of work.

Job release schemes, under which older workers retire early to enable the unemployed to succeed them, have been adopted in several European countries. Workers can usually only retire under these schemes a few years earlier than the statutory retirement age, and there are strict limits on what they can earn without losing benefit, which is usually at a rather higher rate than the retirement pension. It is possible, rather than going into full retirement, for an older worker to reduce his or her hours by

39

half, thereby receiving half the job release benefit, provided that a half-time job is then made available to an unemployed person.

The impact of publicly financed employment schemes on unemployment has been substantial, accounting for nearly half a million people in Britain in 1984, according to Department of Employment estimates. Sweden has been even more ambitious, with its extensive publicly financed job creation and training programmes. In January 1984, Sweden introduced a new scheme for young unemployed people which provided them with paid work equivalent to the benefit they would otherwise be entitled to from the state. This idea, of a work guarantee rather than an income guarantee, is attractive. A work guarantee mobilizes for useful community purposes the large sums of money now effectively locked up in funds for income maintenance. It enables unemployed men and women to maintain or reacquire habits of work and to keep their self-respect. Young people are at least assured of a part-time job instead of the heartbreaking trek from one work experience project or training scheme to another, without ever having a 'real job'.

The obstacles to work guarantee schemes are so great, and the opposition to them so powerfully organized, that they have only operated in heavily circumscribed ways. The minor obstacle is in finding and administering the work itself. The major, related obstacle is that unemployed people may be substituted for workers who already have jobs or who would be offered them in the ordinary labour market if the work guarantee scheme did not exist. The trade unions are deeply suspicious of such schemes, believing that they will deprive union members of their jobs and undercut wage rates agreed through collective bargaining. They were unenthusiastic about the work guarantee for young people in Sweden; similar schemes suggested in private discussions by governments in Britain were strongly opposed by the unions who were fearful for their members' jobs and pay.

Benefits for Training

There are other variations on the theme of mobilizing unemployment insurance for creating and saving jobs as well as for maintaining income. Benefits can be paid to unemployed people while they retrain, provided the courses are approved. This is already happening in Sweden and West Germany and in several American states. Legislation passed by Congress in 1970 permitted workers enrolled in training courses 'with the approval of the state agency' to continue to receive unemployment benefits, though the benefits cannot be used directly to pay training costs. Claimants who take training courses under the new United States Job Training Partnership Act continue to receive benefit. The difficulty arises from the requirement that, to receive benefit, unemployed people must be available for work. In Britain, where there is a similar condition, unemployment benefit or supplementary benefit cannot be paid to people on full-time training or education courses, though they may receive a training allowance while on a training course. A rather awkward compromise enables unemployed people who study for under twenty-one hours a week to continue to draw benefit.

Offering training as an alternative to unemployment, and not just for young people, is a policy that is rapidly gaining support. Trade unions are beginning to bargain for training funds which can help redundant workers while they learn new skills. Modest payroll taxes have been imposed on employers in California and Delaware to finance training for 'dislocated workers' and to assist the transition from school to work. Much interest has been shown in a scheme proposed by Pat Choate of TRW Inc. for an individual training account (ITA) to which employers and employees would contribute, receiving tax relief on their contributions. The ITA would provide funds for retraining; any part of it that was unused could be credited to an employee's retirement account.

Work-sharing

An ingenious way of mobilizing unemployment insurance to save jobs is work-sharing, or short-time working. Work-sharing averted nearly 35,000 lay-offs in Canada in 1983, according to an evaluation made in March 1984. Under this programme, the available work is shared out among the same number of employees, who reduce their hours to match the decline in demand for their products. Benefit is then payable in strict proportion to the loss of working time. If the work-load falls by 20 per cent, the hours of employees will fall correspondingly, and they will be paid 20 per cent of unemployment benefit in lieu of their lost wages. The workers succeed in keeping their jobs, although there is some marginal loss of earnings. The employer avoids redundancy costs and keeps a skilled, experienced work-force in operation. The painful social consequences of prolonged unemployment are thus avoided.

The scheme does have its drawbacks. Much the most important is that it may delay the necessary structural and technological change. This objection does not hold water in so far as the scheme is directed to avoiding cyclical unemployment, the loss of jobs in a temporary recession. The European Community's similar short-time scheme, which compensates workers for part of their loss of wages consequent upon short-time working, is intended for firms suffering a temporary setback, though that is not always easy to define.

Short-time schemes involve some increases in administrative costs and in social security contributions if entitlements, for instance to pensions, are not to be affected. The Canadian authorities estimated the incremental costs of the scheme at $29 million out of the $83·1 million paid out in unemployment benefits to work-sharers in 1983. No estimate was made of the additional social costs of the 35,000 people who would otherwise have been made redundant.

Work-sharing was initially opposed in Canada by the trade unions, but proved so popular with their members that the union leaders had to change their position. Work-sharing schemes on which ballots were cast at plant level attracted the support of an overwhelming majority, whenever the alternative was redundancy for part of the work-force. Older workers positively welcomed the additional leisure.

A different form of work-sharing has been successfully worked out by a British company, GEC. The firm, which regularly offered scores of jobs to young engineering workers, found that during the recession the applicants exceeded the places available. The firm was concerned at the very high level of youth unemployment in the neighbourhood of its plants at Aycliffe and Coventry and decided it could help alleviate the problem by filling each vacancy with two people instead of one. So starter-jobs at the GEC plants in Aycliffe and Coventry, which make telecommunications equipment, were split between two young people. The new recruits each receive half the weekly wage and work half the normal hours. The other half of their time is spent in training and further education, though that is not compulsory. Each worker is available to fill in for his or her job-partner in the event of illness, an arrangement which has resulted in the jobs being manned virtually 100 per cent of working hours. An unexpected benefit of the scheme arose when the firm was able to give an immediate response to a surge in product demand, by switching its ready-trained job-sharers to full-time work for a few months. There can be no more effective way of doubling output without increasing unit costs!

In a few cases the partners needed a short overlap to hand over, and in some activities where the work-load is uneven – as in a wages office – the hours were arranged so that both partners were present to cope with the peaks. The firm reckons that the savings resulting from such flexible working arrangements balance any additional administrative costs.

For the young people the scheme has obvious attractions. In addition to a wage well above what they could get from supplementary benefit, it provides them with training in a real working environment alongside adults. After eighteen months of job-sharing, GEC puts them at the head of the queue for full-time jobs, so that there is an excellent prospect of a long-term career with the firm. Those who do not get a full-time job with GEC are in a very good position to get jobs with other firms, for they can offer experience as well as skills. The state also benefits by saving one supplementary benefit for each job shared.

There are many ways in which shared starter-jobs can be encouraged. The Government can pay half a training allowance or partial benefit for the balance of the week, or can bear the social security costs of the second employee. At a time of unemployment combined with skill shortages, the sharing of starter-jobs is a strongly positive policy response.

The Unemployed Go into Business

Unemployment benefit is being ploughed into the creation of new businesses too. A scheme called *Chômeurs Entrepreneurs*, designed to capitalize unemployment insurance in order to make an initial investment in a new business, has proved successful in France. Unemployed men and women who want to establish their own businesses can draw in advance the benefits to which they would be entitled for six months, using the accumulated sum for investment or as collateral for borrowing. Sometimes a group of workers made redundant by a factory lay-off or closure will pool their unemployment benefits to create a fund to establish a workers' cooperative, or even to buy up their old plant. For workers eligible for unemployment insurance the maximum is £3,000, for those no longer eligible, having exhausted their insurance cover, the maximum is £800. Since the scheme began in 1979, 170,000 new enterprises have been established (up to the end of 1984), providing on average 1·6 jobs. It has proved to be a successful low-cost way of generating employment.

A British scheme also uses unemployment benefit for new businesses, but it differs from the French scheme in that it does not permit benefits to be drawn in advance. Would-be businessmen and businesswomen are maintained for up to twelve months while they establish themselves, at the rate of £40 a week. Piloted in 1980 and made nationally available in 1982, the scheme has attracted 149,000 unemployed people. Of the businesses established before 1982, two thirds were still trading three years later, a high figure by small-business standards. Each business averaged 1·5 jobs. More remarkable is the reversal of financial flows from unemployment insurance funds. In the first year, unemployed would-be entrepreneurs cost £2,690 net each, this sum mainly comprising the benefit paid to them while they were establishing themselves. In the second year, as revenues began to come in to the new businesses, the net cost fell to £650. In the third year, as the new businesses became viable, there was a gain of £3,000 per person, from profits, tax revenues and social security payments, net of all expenditure by the public authorities. In other words, the elusive goal of mobilizing unemployment benefit to create employment and thereby to save money had been achieved.

It is necessary to add a caveat. The French and British schemes for transforming unemployed men and women into entrepreneurs perform another function, that of legitimizing businesses being run in the unofficial economy. No one can say what proportion of the businesses accredited to the schemes in fact existed before any application for support was made. People making money out of 'moonlighting' or doing jobs on the side may turn those marginal occupations into legitimate businesses if their regular jobs disappear. But even if this is an element in the success of these enterprise allowance schemes, it does not matter. A successful method of reincorporating the unofficial economy itself contributes to the reduction of official unemployment.

The various government employment schemes which I have described are only the most innovative among many. Some countries offer subsidies to employers to take on the long-term unemployed, or bear the cost of national insurance or social security contributions for an additional worker. There are all sorts of ingenious ideas.

When an economy is running well below capacity and has large numbers of people unemployed, the argument for sharing out the work is very strong, provided it is not used as a way of slowing down structural changes. Work-sharing is a good way of coping with short-term cyclical fluctuations. Where an industry is in secular decline because of technological advances or changes in market preferences, there is a sounder case for helping individual workers to adjust through grants for retraining, or through early retirement if they so wish, than there is for subsidizing the industry itself. Where there is unemployment among young people despite skill shortages, shared starter-jobs combined with training, as in the GEC example, can open the way to permanent jobs once the young person has both experience and skill. Like the schemes for setting up suitable unemployed people in business, these approaches have proved themselves to be constructive and viable. Work guarantees are more controversial, yet they do oblige the authorities to look round for work which needs to be done. If the amount earned is limited to what a person would draw in benefit with the addition of a sum to cover normal transport and working expenses, and if the minimum union rates for the particular job are respected, there should be no undercutting of the ordinary labour market. One can understand unions being fearful; but schemes can be devised to calm their worries. What must be stated, loud and clear, is that a guarantee of some paid work, even for only fifteen or twenty hours a week, which offers unemployed people the chance to earn their benefit if they so wish, would counter the demoralization of long-term unemployment. The choice must be for the individual, for he or she has contributed to an insurance benefit which is a right, not an act of charity.

Whatever measures are taken, there is a paradox at the heart of the unemployment insurance system. Unemployment and other welfare benefits paid to insured employees are financed by taxes on labour, for the contributions paid by employers and employees are based on the number of people employed and on what they earn. Labour as a factor of production is more heavily taxed than capital or raw materials. The better the provision made by the welfare state, the greater the financial burden carried by labour. The way out of this dilemma is to use unemployment benefits to create jobs and to share the financing of the welfare state between all the factors of production, thereby reducing the disproportionate burden carried by labour.

Financing the welfare state with a turnover tax which takes into account all the factors of production is a necessary reform which would benefit employment, though it cannot be achieved quickly, and offers no immediate hope to people out of work now. Microeconomic schemes may help them. A more fundamental approach, however, is to create the conditions for economic expansion without inflation. The only way to make such an expansion possible, short of major institutional changes, is to pursue some form of incomes policy.

4 Incomes Policy

'There are only three possible approaches to inflation. One is to continue indefinitely with high unemployment. Another is to botch up a centralized incomes policy on a temporary basis. And the third is to have a permanent decentralized incomes policy, based on the incentive principle. The last offers us new hope.'

Richard Layard, *More Jobs, Less Inflation*, (1982)

Economic expansion without inflation can be achieved if incomes policies are adopted and adhered to. Incomes policies rarely reduce wages, but they prevent them from going up as fast as the unrestrained use of bargaining power would allow. They have another beneficial consequence: they distribute the gains from growth more evenly between industries and services with great bargaining power and those without. In a modern industrialized economy, bargaining power is related to the strategic position labour holds in any given industry. Centralized, capital-intensive industries with high levels of organization such as domestic oil production and refining, electricity generation and chemicals, offer the most powerful bargaining positions. Labour in such industries tends to be highly paid, for the cost of any disruption is very great compared to the cost of higher wage settlements. Unions in labour-intensive industries with a high level of organization and substantial capital investment per head – coal-mining, car manufacturing, engineering and steel, for example – used to be in a strong bargaining position, but this has been undermined by declining competitivity in the international market. Unions in decentralized or dispersed industries – like construction – or in those with a high level of female, part-time or unskilled labour – like the distributive trades and textiles industries – have weak bargaining positions.

Incomes policies, especially those based on some sort of national norm, favour the weak against the strong. That is one reason why they break down. Strong unions realize they could do better in a free market; skilled and highly productive people resent the narrowing of differentials between themselves and the unskilled.

It is sometimes argued that incomes policies obstruct quick responses to changes in labour market requirements. They are indeed likely to slow down such responses, but they possess the great advantage of

47

enabling the wider national interest to be taken into account. The winners in the free collective bargaining game are the strong, the scarce and the well-organized. The losers are the weak, the unorganized and the unemployed. It is simply fraudulent to equate free collective bargaining with the cause of the unemployed and the underprivileged, as some left-wing politicians do. That could only be the case if unions accepted the unemployed as members and bargained on their behalf, and if unions represented the whole labour force and not sections within it.

An institutional answer to an institutional problem, incomes policy seeks to redress the balance between the interests of the employed and of the unemployed. It is, however, for the reasons already given, an unstable solution on its own. What can be done to underpin an incomes policy and make it more successful?

In the short run, an incomes policy can be sustained by tax measures, used as a sanction against breaking the agreed norm. The most carefully worked-out proposal is that of the economist Richard Layard, for an inflation tax. If income increases were to exceed the norm worked out on the basis of what the economy can afford without inflation, the excess would be heavily taxed.[1]

An inflation tax could be an effective sanction for an incomes policy for a year or so. In the long run, however, changes would need to be made in the framework of collective bargaining to reduce the pressures on incomes policy which have broken through it in the past. Those changes would involve moderating the role hourly or weekly wages play in the bargaining objectives of free trade unions.

Wider Bargaining Aims

If wage increases are the only or by far the most important yardstick of a union's efficiency, unions competing among themselves for members will find incomes policy destroying their *raison d'être*; this will hit effective unions more than ineffective ones. Incomes policies work better where unions have wide bargaining aims. Unions are more likely to survive and flourish in any case, as industrial structures change, if they bring their bargaining aims into line with their members' needs. Those needs are not only for good wages, but also for employment security (*not* job security, which is an obsolete objective in a fast-changing economy). Employment security means the right to up-date one's skills, to retrain, to enrich the quality of one's work as new technologies are introduced, to acquire greater control over one's own working life, to be informed and consulted. The most effective European trade unions, like the Japanese unions, have widened their bargaining aims far beyond the old objectives of higher wages and shorter hours, though those remain important. Wider bargaining objectives can be pursued while an incomes policy is in being; their pursuit provides a valuable function for union officials and shop stewards.

Profit-sharing

The other way to underpin incomes policy, even to supersede it to some extent, is to design a system of remuneration and reward of which hourly and weekly wages are only a part. In Japan, as much as two fifths of a person's annual remuneration can come from a year-end or twice-yearly bonus based on the performance of the company. The employee therefore identifies closely with the company, for his or her own reward will directly reflect the company's results.

What is particularly relevant about profit-sharing is that it acts to maximize employment. In a recent book, *The Share Economy*, Martin Weitzman, Professor of Economics at the Massachusetts Institute of Technology, argues that under a profit-sharing system firms have an incentive to expand employment until the extra cost of the last worker to be employed is equal to the extra revenue he or she earns.[2] If the market is growing, the firm will take on more workers. If it is contracting, the firm can cut prices instead of output, sharing the decline in profit with its employees. They may lose pay, but they will not lose jobs.

Obviously profit-sharing systems are not suitable for all firms or all sectors of the economy. They could be misused by public or private monopolies, and their relevance to public services is limited. Furthermore, where unions are well established there may be resistance to replacing wage bargaining with profit-sharing. But part of a worker's remuneration could continue to be paid as a basic wage. Unions could then divert bargaining power to improving profits and gaining a fair share of them. Employees themselves, especially if they were given access to more information about company finances, would come to appreciate the need for part of a company's profits to be invested in its future growth and development. In the long run, participation would replace confrontation, and the pressures on an incomes policy from inflationary wage demands would lessen. Professor Weitzman claims that profit-sharing could lead to resumed non-inflationary growth. It is not, he argues, on 'the lofty, antiseptic plane of pure macroeconomic management', but in 'the muddy trenches of micropolitical reform' that solutions are to be found.

In contrast to Japan, Western countries have been singularly slow to develop profit-sharing, though those companies that have introduced it, like I C I, have good records of industrial peace and cooperation.

Incomes policies have been resented because the long-term benefits of income restraint have traditionally gone to shareholders. Even when dividend restraint has been adopted too, the capital values of shares have appreciated as profits have risen. Profit-sharing would overcome this difficulty too. It could be the key to maximizing employment and resuming growth.

Protection

Those who reject incomes policies or policies to reduce or stabilize unit labour costs, yet who want to bring down unemployment, are driven towards protection, at least in the short term. To become more competitive, the country concerned needs to adapt and modernize. As that cannot be done quickly, advocates of protection argue that while it is being implemented existing jobs in uncompetitive industries must be protected.

The combination of recession, new technologies and the rise of the newly industrialized countries has been so traumatic for traditional smokestack industries in Europe and North America that politicians have found it difficult to resist demands for support and protection. Support for industries has taken the form of subsidies or government finance of one kind or another. Huge sums have been poured into steel, shipbuilding, railways and car manufacturing on both sides of the Atlantic. Sometimes restructuring or rationalization have been conditions of government help, as with the wool industry in Britain or the steel industry in France. In recent years, the accent has moved towards support for individuals rather than industries suffering the consequences of international competition or technological change.

Such consequences are different both *within* and *between* industries. The overall effect of change or of competition on an economy may be positive, while the consequences for particular communities or sections of a community may be negative. Microelectronics, for instance, will increase the productivity of both capital and labour, and therefore the wealth of the community. But whole sections of society – clerical workers, foremen, single-skill craftsmen – are likely to find themselves without a job meanwhile. The majority of winners can compensate the minority of losers and still enjoy a net benefit. Compensating individuals, by supporting them while they retrain or by making up their lost income, is more satisfactory than subsidizing or protecting whole industries or firms, because the latter course freezes the market into the patterns of the past. Such moves can only be justified if the industry is uncompetitive for reasons that are temporary or relate to a period of bad management in a particular firm.

Protection carries its own penalties. Once established it is hard to remove, especially where the industry or firm protected wields political clout. If it is not removed, the industry is likely to become less and less competitive, and consumers will pay more than they need to. The British experience of Imperial Preference shows how a system of protection can weaken management and undermine product quality: if goods and services can be sold anyway behind a tariff wall, why bother to improve them?

There is a more brutal argument against protection in an international market as competitive as it is today: it is the high probability of retaliation. Kant's categorical imperative* applies with great force to the world of international trade. The strongest economies, like that of the United States, may get away with specific protectionist measures, but even then the risk of retaliation is strong. Weak economies cannot hope to act in this way unless they are accepted by their trading partners as 'basket cases' needing exceptional treatment to survive. The European Community, whose members find it difficult to agree on common trade policies, has been engaged in a number of conflicts with the United States, especially over the Common Agricultural Policy. Europeans in turn have criticized American measures to protect steel and to curb exports of high-technology products to the Soviet bloc. The First World is more protectionist than it pretends, and there is a real danger that the reduction of tariffs achieved by successive rounds of negotiations under the General Agreement on Tariffs and Trade will be reversed.

* Kant's formulation may be loosely defined as: So act that the maxim of your action can be willed without contradiction as a universal law; to put it another way, to ask oneself of every projected action: 'What would happen if everyone acted in this way?'

New Jobs or No Jobs

Countries can cling to the old industrial regime; they can shore up old industries, protect their markets, reduce their living standards and cut their wages in order to do so. But the refusal to change will be very costly, for the real choice is likely to be between new jobs or no jobs. Technological change will not be halted. It will advance where it is welcomed, and the countries where it advances will win markets from those which resist it. Welcoming technological change does not simply mean opening frontiers; it means a society whose political institutions, industrial relations and education systems are capable of responding to the needs of a new epoch. 'The Europeans,' wrote an American journalist, 'whatever their skills and their past accomplishments, are falling behind in a world where the old technologies count for less and the new technologies count for more.'[3]

Living in a scientific age, we are all conscious of the impact of inventions. Our parents' lives were shaped by the motor car and the telephone, our own by television, jet aeroplanes and telecommunications. The inventions of the eighteenth and nineteenth centuries – the steam engine, the railways, the Bessemer converter – brought the first Industrial Revolution, and changed the nature of society. The methods of production – the factory, specialization of labour, the assembly line – determined economic relations and thus the new industrial class system. Since that first Industrial Revolution, inventions and innovations have changed particular industries dramatically, and in some cases new industries have been born. Many of today's jobs – television repairmen, computer programmes, laser technicians, transplant surgeons – did not exist a generation ago; and some of the jobs that existed then – stenographers, shipwrights, blast furnace men – have disappeared for ever. Incomes policies ease the process of transition from old industries to new ones, and can minimize the impact on unemployment by making it possible for governments to stimulate economic growth without risking inflation. The transition itself is inevitable, for the new technologies are already here.

5 The Information Technology Revolution

'The sense was present – and still is – that in Western society we are in the midst of a vast historical change in which old social relations (which were property-bound), existing power structures (centred on narrow élites, and bourgeois culture (based on notions of restraint and delayed gratification) are being rapidly eroded. The sources of the upheaval are scientific and technological. But they are also cultural, since culture, I believe, has achieved autonomy in Western society.'

Daniel Bell, *The Coming of Post-Industrial Society*, (1974)

The family of new technologies, with microelectronics and its associated software at the centre, is, like the steam engine, horizontally pervasive. It is not a set of discrete inventions, of individual new processes or products. Everything will be affected: every industry, old and new, private services, social services, education, government – nothing in society will be untouched. That is why we are looking not at a single major invention but at a new epoch, the dawn of the information society.

The first Industrial Revolution altered economic relations and class structures. It required a new education system: universal and compulsory elementary education – in a word, literacy. The achievement of basic education and of literacy in turn made it easier to extend voting rights to the whole adult population. Management structures and trade unions evolved from the relations established in the production of goods. Company structures were hierarchical. Labour's functions became specialized, and work was broken down into repetitive tasks. Managers made the decisions and workers obeyed them.

All these familiar structures, some of them embodied in powerful institutions, are changing as a result of the new information revolution. The winners in the world will be those who manage to make changes quickly and reasonably smoothly. The losers will be those who fail to make the changes soon, or at all.

One important reason why information technology is so pervasive is that it is not constrained by particular requirements of process or scale. Mass production – the assembly line – required large markets and economies of scale to be profitable. So did specialization of labour. By contrast, microelectronics can be used in mass production and also in making customized individual products, in large-scale and small-scale processes alike. It is as relevant to small businesses as to large ones; for microelectronics means not only artefacts, but also a language and a system which permeate all industries and all services.

New Technologies

Microelectronics is the best known of the new technologies. The term embraces microcomputers, control systems, robotics, processes like computer-aided manufacture and design and computer-aided inspection, and products like calculators and video games. Its close relation, telecommunications, is an older technology. The combination of the two, sometimes called informatics, or *télématique* in French, constitutes the basis of the information revolution, the linking of computer power with telephone or satellite networks. The elements of that revolution – the telephone and the micro computer – are already familiar to millions of people in the Northern Hemisphere. Naturally, young people feel more at ease with them than older people. The dominant position of older people in decision-making roles in industry and government has been one reason for the relatively slow diffusion of microelectronics in many traditional industries.

There are other new technologies that will have significant effects on the economy. Biotechnology, based on the manipulation of genetic material made possible by Crick and Watson's cracking of the genetic code, DNA, in 1953, will have far-reaching implications for chemicals, food processing, agriculture, medicine and waste disposal. Biotechnology may provide answers to the depletion of fossil fuels, by using biomass as a renewable source of energy. It may also provide the answer to the plight of a planet in which population is outrunning resources, and cultivable land is diminishing fast, by providing high-yielding plants and by converting hydrocarbons into proteins. Laser technology, as well as being important to the defence industries, is used in medicine for advanced surgery, and in engineering for metal fabrication and the shaping of materials. Like biotechnology, laser technology has vast potential, only a small part of which has been realized to date.

Less dramatic but equally important are the new materials, some of them by-products of space research, together with new methods of processing and shaping them. Powdered metals are compounded into parts; thin metal slices are banded together, forming light but sturdy components which greatly economize on raw material inputs. An ever-growing range of synthetics replaces more and more natural products, animal, vegetable and mineral. Industrial ceramics are capable of withstanding much higher temperatures than the hardest metals. New glues and resins bond as effectively as welded or bolted parts.

Adopting New Technologies

The speed at which the new technologies are adopted will determine the pattern of employment in the future, and will also determine its level. Countries slow to adopt the new technologies will find their technology trade balance moving into deficit. This is already happening to the European Community; imports of microelectronic products far exceed exports, and the balance is likely to continue to deteriorate throughout the 1980s. The speed of adoption is, however, itself determined by the availability of people capable of understanding and using new technology. If men and women with the appropriate skills are not readily available, firms will not know how to use microelectronics effectively. They will stay with obsolete technologies, and their labour requirements will be directed towards traditional skills. But these are the very areas where competition from newly industrialized countries is fiercest. Hence the constant pressure to reduce costs and lower wages. Advanced countries can only stay advanced by demanding – and providing – standards of skill and of education that enable them to remain in the forefront of technology.

Let us look first at the rate at which new technologies are being adopted; then at the new jobs they are likely to create, and the old jobs they are likely to destroy. We can thus get some idea of the gaps to be filled and the changes in education and training needed to fill them.

The rate of technological change differs from country to country and between industries and firms, the most important variable for the last of these being size. Some indication of the speed of adoption is given in two recent studies: one of Japan, believed to be the most fast moving economy in this respect, the other of Britain.

Japan in the Vanguard

According to a survey conducted by the Japanese Ministry of Labour in 1982, 59 per cent of Japanese manufacturing firms had introduced microelectronics into their products or processes or both. Among large firms, with over a thousand employees, the proportion was 96 per cent, among small (100–300 employees) only 51 per cent.[1] In other words, while non-awareness, or at least non-adoption of new technologies is not exclusive to small firms, it is very much concentrated in that sector. There are no technical reasons for the distinction. Microelectronics, unlike earlier industrial technologies, can be used in batch production or even for customized products, because of its adaptability and flexibility. To quote another Japanese study, 'on the production line, microelectronics has made it possible to automatically produce a small amount of many kinds of products.'[2] The Ministry's survey gave firms' own reasons for not adopting microelectronics, or for inadequately exploiting it once introduced. The most important reason, given by nearly half the respondents (all medium and small firms), was the lack of programmers and operators able to understand the new systems. The second most important reason was the initial cost of introduction and the continuing cost of maintenance. Small firms do not have easy access to capital, and they will not move until the market compels them to do so. Small Japanese firms are often used as regular subcontractors to large firms, and the large firms may be willing to lend them money. But there is evidence from Japanese research that large firms that have introduced microelectronic processes bring back some of their subcontracted work to the parent company. This helps large firms to meet their commitments to Japan's lifetime employment system, which holds good only for them and not for small firms.

The production process itself has been most affected by microelectronics. The complexity of assembly has so far limited use of the new technologies there. Only 48 per cent of Japanese firms used microelectronics in assembly, and in most the use was only for particular and not all assembly operations. Just over half the firms used microelectronics in inspection, a tribute to the concern of Japanese industry with quality.

The use of new technologies is particularly marked in certain industries, above all in industries which have established leading positions in international markets, such as cars, electrical and electronic machinery, and machine tools. In all three, penetration of microelectronics exceeded

70 per cent. Even more significant, in a whole range of industries not normally associated with leading-edge technology, like furniture, paper manufacturing and printing, as well as iron and steel and metal fabrication, it exceeded 50 per cent.

Robots

Striking as they are, these figures do not convey the vigour and energy of Japan's technological revolution. Take robots, for example. In 1982 there were some 40,000 programmable robots at work in the automobile industry alone. Between 1978 and 1982 Japanese manufacturers delivered 87,938 robots, three quarters of them to three industries; plastic processing, electrical engineering and automobiles. Production of robots is growing at a colossal rate, and their value is expected to have nearly quintupled by the end of the decade, from 107·8 billion yen in 1981 to 520 billion yen in 1990. Robots are becoming economically more attractive as their prices fall – in some cases by as much as 30 per cent in 1983 alone. An arc-welding robot can now be bought for about twice the annual wage of a skilled man, and, unlike him, the robot can work virtually continuously, bringing an annual return on outlay two and a half to three times higher than its human equivalent.

Production forecasts show an increase from 22,000 robots a year in 1981 to 85,000 a year in 1990. Only about 14 per cent of Japanese robots are exported, usually under joint arrangements with foreign companies; but there should be no problem about domestic demand, which is very strong, matching this high rate of expansion.

It is not only the amount of Japanese advanced technology that is impressive; it is also its quality and scope. The industrial robot, defined as a mechanism which has flexible motor functions analogous to those of a living organism (usually, though not always, a human being), is being overtaken by the intelligent robot which combines these functions with the capacity for recognition, judgement and learning – in short a robot that will be able to determine its own actions. In 1978, 86 per cent of Japan's robot output was of robots whose actions were controlled in a fixed sequence, or by manual manipulation as an extension of human muscle power. Four years later, these two relatively primitive forms of robot constituted only 40 per cent of output by volume, 15 per cent by value. 'Playback' robots, capable of repeating any operation once they have been instructed, and variable sequence robots, (described in

Chapter Ten below), robots for which instructions can readily be altered and which are particularly useful for batch production, amounted to 44 per cent. Output of 'intelligent' robots was in the same period growing fast: from 3 per cent to 8 per cent by volume, and from 11 per cent to 14 per cent by value. The intense Japanese interest in intelligent systems is exemplified not only by the fifth-generation computer, but by learning robots as well.[3]

Japanese laboratories are working hard on these new generations of robots, and there was a sharp increase in patents for robot development in 1982. By the early 1990s Japan expects to manufacture intelligent robots for use in dangerous environments such as nuclear power plants and the deep ocean, and in unpleasant or harmful working conditions. Others will be used for heavy work on construction sites such as tunnelling and scaffolding. In the second half of that decade, robots will be mining coal, felling trees and doing domestic tasks in houses and hospitals. The development of sensory capacities, such as 'seeing' and 'touching', one of the most difficult problems of robot technology, should have advanced considerably by 1995.

Flexible Manufacturing Systems

Another rapid growth area is flexible manufacturing systems (FMS), linking numerically controlled machine tools, robots and computers in a single package. FMS reduces manufacturing time dramatically, and cuts both labour and material costs. In October 1982, 203 such systems were in operation throughout the world, including 60 in Japan, 44 in the United States, 35 in West Germany and 10 in the United Kingdom.[4] But many more systems have been introduced recently in Japan, and the number in existence there is probably over 200. Some new systems are so sophisticated that they can be integrated with computer-aided design at one end and computer-aided inspection systems at the other – not just unmanned factories, but unmanned manufacturing. Multinational companies with plants overseas can link separate computerized systems together, determining a complete program from a single centre.

Japan is also working in linking FMS systems with laser cutting and machining. At Tsukuba such a plant is being built, capable of machining and assembling in highly complex processes. Advanced technology is also being applied to clothing, a traditional industry, feeding computer-aided designs into computer-controlled machines that use lasers to cut cloth and an automated sewing system to produce the garments.

Japan is in the vanguard of new technology, as these examples show. But more fundamental to Japanese success than the technologies themselves are the attitudes of Japanese men and women.

6 Japanese Attitudes

'We have come to see that Japan's startlingly rapid development owes at least as much to the peculiar characteristics of Japanese society and culture ... as to the country's specifically economic techniques.'

Martin Wiener, *English Culture and the Decline of the Industrial Spirit, 1850–1980*, (1981)

I have described Japanese developments at some length in order to give a picture not of the distant future, but of the next ten or fifteen years. Japan is driven by its awareness that its population is ageing and that the proportion of retired people to those in work is growing. Participation in higher education has risen very rapidly indeed, but even so skills, especially blue-collar skills, are in short supply. There is no great pool of unemployed people to draw on, since Japanese unemployment is below 3 per cent of the labour force. But a different spectre has haunted Japan – its dependence on the rest of the world for the essentials of life: food, raw materials and energy. The two oil price shocks of 1973 and 1979 galvanized the Japanese into the sustained pursuit of higher productivity in manufacturing, enabling them to maintain their position in highly competitive international markets. Their export successes have persuaded them that they can buy what they need, and can pay for what they buy.

Higher productivity was achieved in the past by careful attention to human relations and human capital as well as to plant and equipment. Japanese companies were able to engender loyalty in their employees because they valued them and demonstrated their commitment to them. Recent dramatic improvements have flowed from Japan's enthusiastic reception for the new technologies. Nor has ideology stood in the way. Private corporations, trade unions and government share and promote the same objective; that of Japan as the world's leading knowledge-based society.

Shared Objectives

Japanese governments, despite their stated belief in the free market, give a great deal of support to technological development and this support is not an issue of political controversy in Japan. About 5 per cent of the value of sales of goods is ploughed back into research and development in manufacturing industry (excluding investment in advanced design and production systems). The Government directly supports a great deal of research and development in universities and in its own institutes. The number of laboratories engaged in robotics alone increased from forty-three in 1974 to 153 in 1982; and of these, seventy-five were in the public universities. The Government also supports, by 100 per cent grants, work on advanced applications of microelectronics and robotics in private-sector companies. Companies work closely with MITI, Japan's trade ministry, on agreed major projects for which detailed plans are made and timetables laid down, showing what is to be achieved at every stage. The best-known instance is the fifth-generation computer, but it is far from being an isolated example. Commentators from outside Japan have pointed out that the process of consultation involved in these long-term strategic plans is the most valuable single element, worth more than the plans themselves.

Government-backed loans and grants encourage new technology too. Both central and local government make grants to any company installing automation systems or computers. Loans are available for buying or leasing robots, and tax write-offs may be shortened as a further incentive.

Trade Unions

Japanese trade unions do not oppose the advent of microelectronics, but they monitor developments carefully, to ensure that displaced workers are transferred to new jobs and if necessary retrained. They insist on full consultation and information about new investment and changes in working methods, and they negotiate guarantees that earnings will be maintained or increased as microelectronic equipment is introduced. A survey by JEWU–Denki Roren (the federation of electrical machine workers' unions) revealed that two thirds of their local branches had instituted consultation with management when microelectronic equipment was introduced in the work-place; others agreed to consultation at national level.[1] The attitude of JEWU can be viewed as giving a cautious welcome to the new technologies, on the one hand because the unions share the anxiety about the consequences of an ageing workforce, on the other because they recognize that 'the decreasing effect on employment caused by microelectronics has been mitigated by increased production volume, product diversification, job transfers and regulations of the labour union'.[2] But the anxiety is certainly there. The federation's guidelines flatly enjoin member unions 'to reject any ME project and suspend it, if it were to give any direct impacts upon employment accompanying any tangible dismissals'.[3]

The reconciliation of union opposition to redundancies with government and management support for the fastest possible introduction of microelectronic systems is possible only because of Japan's outstanding ability to produce and sell more and more of its manufactured goods, especially in world markets.

The Ministry of Labour survey showed that the number of workers decreased in 38 per cent of the firms surveyed that had introduced microelectronic equipment. In over half these firms, the decline was more than 10 per cent. Only 4·5 per cent of firms increased their workforce, but that figure does include a few large firms with over a thousand employees which increased employment by more than 50 per cent. Japan has gained more jobs from new industries selling electronic goods and information technology hardware than she has lost from the introduction of microelectronic processes in traditional industries and services.

Many firms that brought micro-electronics into manufacturing processes were able to absorb displaced workers by increasing output. These firms raised their production by 56 per cent in the five years 1976 to 1981, while their work-forces declined by less than 3 per cent. The firms that failed to introduce microelectronics or showed no intention of doing so raised output by only 20·5 per cent in these years, and lost 14 per cent of their work-force.

So the inference from Japan's experience is clear. Blocking the new technologies destroys jobs: the alternative to new jobs is no jobs. But the new technologies do reduce the need for labour. It is huge increases in output and sales, many of them exports, that have enabled Japan to maintain full employment.

This conclusion is borne out by work from the Japan Institute of Labour on movements of employment among industries between 1970 and 1980.

Looking at the industries which were able to increase worker numbers over the 1970–80 period, it is noteworthy that the increase was usually facilitated either by an expansion in final demand or by a combination of this factor and others. In other words, employment increase was in one way or another related to an expansion in final demand.[4]

To this, James Tobin and his fellow Keynesians would doubtless say 'Amen'.

Some workers are directly employed in making microelectronic hardware and in designing microelectronic software, and employment here has burgeoned. In the five years 1976 to 1981, employment rose by a net 11·4 per cent in firms producing microelectronic equipment, and by 48·7 per cent in those making integrated circuits.

Japan's success in the new products associated with the information revolution challenges even the position of the United States. American manufacturers have become significant importers of semiconductors and electronic components, importing in 1984 three billion dollars in value more than they exported. While the United States has the lion's share of computer sales – four fifths of the international market – more and more of their components are made in Japan or in the newly industrializing Asian countries. Asian domination of the consumer market for electronic goods (other than personal computers) and of the market for office machinery is an accomplished fact. In 1984, the United States approached a ten billion dollar trade deficit on the former, and exceeded a two billion dollar deficit on the latter. The overall United States trade deficit on electronic high technology was $6·8 billion in 1984.

The international competitivity of Japan, and specifically its domination of the world market for sophisticated electronic equipment, has thus far offset the employment consequences of the technological revolution, which has advanced so much further in Japan's manufacturing industries than in those of Europe. Whether Japan can maintain that remarkable record despite further advances in the automation of manufacturing remains to be seen, and must be questionable. Even in Japanese manufacturing, the most impressive and efficient sector, many older workers are unproductively employed. The Japanese use the term 'window-watcher' to describe them, people for whom jobs have been created to preserve status and save face. The use of such devices may have preserved Japan's full employment despite the technological revolution. What Japan has not escaped are the effects of that revolution on the composition of the labour force, as distinct from its size.

The Losers

Two sections of the labour force in Japan have suffered disproportionately: the middle-aged and women. Workers over fifty, and many over forty, do not find it easy to adapt to microelectronics. Their skills may be obsolete or inappropriate. Those trained in a single skill are particularly at risk, since the skill may no longer be needed at all in the production process. Skilled machinists, for example, are not in demand. Their jobs have been taken over by numerically controlled machine tools, and more recently by robots and lasers. Fewer craftsmen are needed, unless they can be retrained for maintenance and monitoring work. Four times as many Japanese firms reduced their demands for skilled workers as increased them. Three quarters of the firms reported that their older workers had adjusted poorly to the new technology.[5]

Given the demand for workers able to adapt readily to new skills, it is not surprising to learn that firms increased their proportion of young workers. In Japan older workers are more highly skilled than younger ones because skills are learned on the job, and some of those skills will become obsolete; older workers are traditionally much more highly paid than young ones.

Less predictably the ratio of male to female workers increased. One reason for this may be found in the almost insatiable demand for technicians and technologists and for graduates in science and engineering; in Japan, as elsewhere, those who qualify in these fields are overwhelmingly male. Another cause is the declining demand for traditional office and secretarial skills; women are beginning to be trained in the new technologies, but at modest levels of skill.

Japan's lifelong employment system applies to the employees of large reputable companies. Many small firms act as a buffer to the large firms, receiving subcontracts in boom times and seeing them disappear in bad times; they also act as an employment buffer. In some cases, workers no longer needed in the big firms find less well-paid work in small ones. But the main instrument for absorbing workers displaced by new technology is transfer within the firm, from one production process to another, or often to white-collar jobs like administration and marketing. The question of what to do with older workers comes second only to the capacity to develop and retrain workers with the necessary new skills (small businesses are particularly concerned about this) in the list of problems companies foresee. Japan has a sophisticated structure of job transfer, and most workers transferred receive on-the-job training for their new position. In almost all cases, they also have their former wages guaranteed.

Western Europe, technologically slow-moving, has been unable to create enough jobs for its younger generation. Fast-moving Japan was faced with a similar crisis in dealing with its older generation, which could have obstructed the shift in the work-force towards younger men, given the right of those employed to insist on employment security. Transfer and retraining have enabled Japan to avoid that trap. Admirers of the Japanese system will note that transfer with guaranteed wages involves heavy costs. It is in effect a subsidy to enable workers to adjust, and a major departure from the normal working of a free labour market. Relatively early retirement, however, helps to keep costs down. Many who retire move on to second, post-retirement jobs, usually at much lower levels of pay.

One final point. Japan's technological mastery does not extend to services; only 1 per cent of all industrial robots went to non-manufacturing industries in 1982. Some services, like the railways, are heavily overmanned, as are agriculture and many small firms. Others, like retail distribution, are inefficient. The glittering achievements of manufacturing industry blind observers to underemployment and low productivity in Japan's other sectors, which have absorbed those unable to maintain the pace and the high quality of work required in manufacturing. The new technologies do not respect administrative frontiers any more than they respect national ones. When they have an impact on Japan's growing but inefficient services sector, as they are beginning to do in fields like finance, the consequences for employment could be much more serious than they have so far been in manufacturing. Japan's mastery in manufacturing does not extend to its whole economy.

7 Great Britain:
Irreversible Decline?

'Far back, through creeks and inlets making
Comes silent, flooding in, the main.'

Arthur Hugh Clough,

The rate of technological development in Europe is slower and more patchy than in Japan. Some firms have introduced robots and microelectronic systems; a few have installed complete flexible manufacturing systems. But many firms are as yet untouched by the new technologies. Because the rate of unemployment is so high and provision for dealing with displaced workers so much more primitive, there has been resistance to technological changes that could threaten jobs.

The emphasis in the 1970s in Europe was on labour-saving investment rather than on investment to increase capacity. Now that there are large amounts of unused plant and equipment, owing to a deficiency of demand for products, the incentive to invest in manufacturing industry is low. A recovery of private investment in the last two years has benefited the services and private house-building, but has not been evident in manufacturing industry. Yet it is urgently needed, because much of the capital stock has become obsolete as it does not embody microelectronics. The labour force in Europe, with the exception of West Germany, is less highly trained than that of Japan; with less provision for on-the-job training and retraining, it lacks the skills required for the new technologies. Europe is trying to compete with the wrong plant and the wrong skills.

As the old industries run down, and the new ones find themselves handicapped by problems of raising venture capital and recruiting people with some experience of microelectronics, job losses in manufacturing outrun job gains. The institutional obstacles to the new technologies, ranging from old-fashioned management and suspicious trade unions to inadequate education and training, also slow down their diffusion. But in a world of international trade and exchange of information neither the knowledge nor the equipment can be excluded indefinitely.

Microelectronics in Britain

The impact of microelectronics on British industry has been charted in a detailed survey of 1,200 firms conducted by Jim Northcott and Petra Rogers for the Policy Studies Institute.[1] This study showed that 47 per cent of all British firms were using microelectronics in their processes or products. The sample, taken in 1983, indicated a big leap forward in the proportion of British firms using microelectronics, it having risen from 30 per cent in 1981. Given that the Japanese survey (cited above) showed a 59 per cent penetration of microelectronics into Japanese firms in 1982, it might be concluded that Britain is still a long way behind. But this leaves out of account the size of the firms. The Japanese Ministry of Labour survey only covered firms with more than a hundred employees, while the PSI sample extended to firms with over twenty employees, and was weighted to allow for even smaller firms in which the use of microelectronics was assumed to be low. In firms with between 100 and 200 employees, three fifths used microelectronics (more than in Japan), the proportion rising to 96 per cent in firms with over 1,000 employees (the same as in Japan). The gap between large and small firms in Britain is narrowing as small firms become more aware of the potential gains microelectronics offers, especially in production processes. In 1981, just over one sixth as many small firms used microelectronics in their processes as did large ones; two years later, the proportion was nearly one third.

Further evidence that new technology has reached small firms in Britain as well as large ones comes from an article in the *Economist* of December 1983. It reported that, in 1982, 6,723 numerically controlled machine tools were installed in firms with under fifty employees, over a quarter of the country's total of 25,802 such machines. That was a major improvement over 1976, when only 1,990 such machines, one fifth of the total, were installed in small firms. So small firms may be picking up the main lesson of microelectronics faster than expected, namely that it is as effective in small-scale production as in large.[2]

Significant differences between Japan and Britain are nevertheless indicated by these surveys. First, the proportion of products and processes in which microelectronics is used, in those British firms that have adopted new technology, is low. The PSI study showed that only 7 per cent of all manufactured products and 18 per cent of all production processes incorporated microelectronics. In other words, many firms used computers for one or two operations, or possessed a few computer-controlled machines, but they are only beginning to realize the potential for integrated systems.

Second, a much larger proportion of multinational companies with plants in Britain – firms like I B M, Ford and Toshiba – used microelectronics than British-owned companies, and that is true of every size of factory, large and small. It shows that British managers are slower to grasp the significance of new technologies than their overseas colleagues.

Third, jobs lost in processes using microelectronics are not balanced by job gains in making microelectronic equipment itself, as in Japan. Employment among British suppliers of information technology hardware actually declined from 150,000 in 1975 to 120,000 in 1983. The industry's output has grown rapidly, by some 12 per cent a year, but that has not been enough either to offset productivity gains or to keep up with competition. By contrast, Japan's rate of growth has been 23 per cent a year, the United States' 19 per cent. Japan is the major beneficiary of the automation of Britain, not Britain itself. What is true of Britain is true of Western Europe generally, though France has managed an annual growth rate in information technology of 19 per cent. The European Community's information technology trade deficit was two billion pounds in 1983, of which Britain's share was £800 million.

Differences between British industries in the rate of introduction of microelectronics resemble those in Japan. As might be expected, industries in which Britain is strong are in the vanguard of the new developments, industries in which it is weak are lagging behind. As in Japan, use is concentrated in particular industries, notably electrical engineering and paper, printing and publishing. However, in the vehicles industry – cars, ships and aircraft – use is far below that of Japan, though car manufacturing is catching up. In chemicals and metal fabrication it is similar, while in food, drink and tobacco (the province of large firms in the U K) microelectronics is more widely used in Britain than in Japan.

Recession Discourages Change

The main factors slowing down the introduction of microelectronics in Britain have been the recession, lack of awareness of what microelectronics can do and a shortage of people with the right skills and experience.

The PSI survey identified the lead-time between work starting on a microelectronic processor product to it being in use as between fifteen and twenty-five months. The largest number of new starts was in 1979, the figure falling off in 1980, and not recovering fully in 1981 or 1982. Recession, in other words, discouraged the very kind of investment most likely to improve Britain's competitivity and the productivity of its resources. Far more respondents named the economic situation above any other factor as the main brake on their introduction of microelectronics.

There are firms which are unaware of the benefits microelectronics can bring them. There are others that do not want to replace machines with many years' use ahead of them, because of the capital write-off involved. Responses showed that many small firms do not appreciate that microelectronics can be used in small-batch production or in the output of varied products. About one third of the firms questioned saw no scope for microelectronic applications at all.

Shortages of skilled and experienced people and lack of finance were the other significant factors mentioned, the former being mentioned by 42 per cent of firms in the survey, the latter by 32 per cent. Very few firms encountered opposition from their unions or employees – only 7 per cent. Skill shortages, on the other hand, have been extreme: over 50 per cent of firms starting work on microelectronics had no one on their staff with relevant experience, and over a third of these still had no one in 1981. As late as 1983, 27 per cent of users employed no such person. Engineers with experience of microelectronics are concentrated heavily in large firms and in certain industries, such as defence, aerospace and electronics. Any extensive British involvement in the huge £21 billion research programme into strategic defence (the 'Star Wars' project) proposed by President Reagan would attract even more engineers into defence and away from civil research. Furthermore, much of the work would be classified, and therefore not open to exploitation by British firms for commercial purposes.

The Threat to Jobs

British experience of job loss as a consequence of the introduction of microelectronics is very similar to that of Japan. Firms losing workers exceeded those where jobs were gained by 25·5 per cent; among process users in Britain the figure was 27 per cent. Of firms making extensive use of computer-controlled techniques – for instance, for inspection, design and handling – 60 per cent had reduced employment, and none had increased it. Where British experience differed completely from that of Japan was in the area of new products embodying microelectronics. In Japan, these new products have conquered markets abroad and at home, leading to increased employment which has offset the job losses in processes automated by microelectronics. British firms expected no net job gain in making new products, the number predicting an increase being balanced by those predicting a decline. This is a very different assumption from the one made in Japan, but then Japan is a highly competitive fast-growing manufacturer of microelectronic products, Britain a slow-growing one. The PSI study estimated that in the period 1981–3 there was a loss of about 6,000 jobs owing to product applications, and of about 28,000 owing to process applications – 34,000 overall. This is less than 5 per cent of the national job loss in the same two years. But the real impact of new technology on employment is yet to come.

Britain's share of the world market for information technology equipment is now less than 4 per cent, and the industry is close to the point where it may not survive. In a recent report, the Information Technology Economic Development Committee put its fears starkly: 'We believe that the UK IT industry now has such a small share of the world market that it can no longer continue to invest adequately in product development, in marketing, or in production facilities.'[3]

Without the offsetting bonus of new jobs generated in information technology products, the net loss of employment from information technology processes could be severe. Paradoxically, the consumer market in Britain is among the most IT-conscious in the world. Many homes possess microcomputers. Teletext is available at low cost to anyone who has access to a television set. Children are becoming familiar with microcomputers in primary schools, and with computer games in clubs and leisure centres. This market awareness is coupled with a domestic manufacturing industry which seems incapable of matching the competition from abroad. Imports will therefore continue to grow rapidly. It is a combination with disturbing implications for employment.

The Comparison

What emerges from this necessarily crude comparison between Britain and Japan is that Britain is not offsetting job losses from new technology with job gains, and is unlikely to do so, in view of the failure of those making microelectronic products to expand fast enough to maintain employment. Jobs in traditional industries have declined rapidly. Given the slowness to adopt new technology of firms in clothing, textiles, furniture and metal fabrication, there seems to be little chance that they will be able to compete with low-wage countries overseas. But there is no inevitability about that decline. Firms that have seized upon the new technologies, like those described in Chapter Twelve in Italy's knitwear industry, have proved able to compete with newly industrialized countries because of the savings of materials, energy, capital and labour made possible by microelectronics. But decline begets a mood of caution and pessimism alien to innovation and risk-taking. It is difficult to rescue those determined to drown.

Britain had one great boon in the decade of the 1980s, North Sea oil. It will be a short-lived blessing. Tax revenues from oil will peak in 1985, at an estimated £12,000–£13,000 million, a geometric rate of increase over the £1,000 million earned in 1978. By 1990, even if new fields are brought into production, tax revenues will be down to £8,000 million,

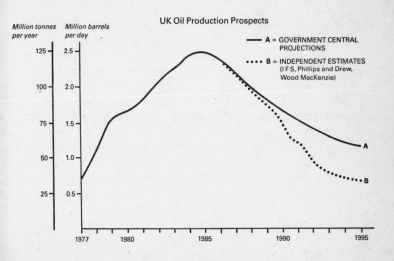

and by 1995 to under £3,000 million. The great oil bonanza will be fizzling out. Britain will have little new investment in manufacturing or in the basic structures of its economy to show for its sudden wealth, no upsurge of education, no marked improvement in the skills of its workforce. In the tradition of the imperial power it once was, Britain has invested its oil revenues abroad. Dividends from those investments will enrich the City of London and help to finance a rapidly worsening balance of trade. They will not be providing jobs for unemployed Britons, nor re-equipping manufacturers to export, nor upgrading men and women with outdated skills or no skills at all. The oil revenues have been squandered on tax-cuts for the well-off and on investments overseas, neither of which are likely to assure the country's future.

8 Jobs for the Future

'The new work is more than traditional clerical work; it involves manipulating and transmitting data via computers, actually displacing various forms of physical production activity.'

Anthony Smith, 'Telecommunications and the Fading of the Industrial Age', *Political Quarterly*, 1983

The most widely held view about the future of employment is that the new jobs will be in the services. The experience of the United States has been that millions of new service jobs have been created. Further, although the impact to date of microelectronics on service employment in Japan has been minimal, this is not because microelectronics cannot be used in services, but because services have been the least-developed sector of the Japanese economy, allowed to bumble on quietly without interference from MITI or ambitious plans for transformation by the great corporations. The evidence from the United States seems strong enough to suggest that the popular view may well be justified. But it is worth analysing the Americans' experience in more detail. It is not quite what it seems.

Between 1972 and 1982 the United States lost a million production jobs in manufacturing, in a decade during which 23 million men and women joined the labour force. But American unemployment did not rocket upwards, because over seventeen million new jobs were created in the same decade, most of them in the white-collar service area. In Europe, it is widely believed that these new jobs were mainly low-skill, low-paid jobs in distribution and fast-food restaurants. That view is distorted. The majority were professional and technical jobs requiring advanced qualifications, in many cases university degrees. It is not the expansion of services, as normally understood, but of the professional and executive section of employment that typifies the American success in creating new jobs. Before I consider this phenomenon more closely, one other qualification needs to be made.

Manufacturing employment is rather volatile in the United States, responding quickly to economic conditions. For instance, if a comparison is made not between 1972 and 1982 (a year of recession), but between

1972 and 1984 (a year of rapid recovery), then the loss of manufacturing jobs is not a million but only 240,000. Manufacturing has declined as a share of the labour force from 26 per cent in 1972 to 20·4 per cent in 1984, but it is still vigorous, and thousands of new jobs have been created in microelectronics, biotechnology and other high-tech areas. Demand for professional engineers, whose numbers have risen by half a million in the last ten years, far exceeds the supply.

The great success story of 1972 to 1982 lies in the 5·4 million new jobs, nearly a third of the total, in professional and technical occupations, and in the 3·5 million new jobs in management and executive posts. What sort of jobs were these? They included 200,000 more physicians, 300,000 more computer specialists, a quarter of a million more lawyers, half a million more technicians, even 150,000 more social scientists, and a similar number of systems analysts. Not all the new jobs were at this level, of course. A million more people worked in restaurants and fast-food shops, matched by 1·3 million more in the medical services, 600,000 of them nurses and dieticians – a rather ironic correlation. There were a million extra jobs in retail distribution, and, surprisingly, four million more clerical jobs, though numbers employed in the latter area have levelled out in the last year or two. Financial services and insurance have been another large growth area.

Many of the new jobs were information-related. In these jobs, productivity has increased little, if at all, over the last ten years, so that higher demand has fed through into higher employment. Services to business, embracing both professional jobs like accounting and relatively low-level clerical jobs in word-processing, have grown apace, nearly doubling in a decade. One reason for this increase is that work has been moved out of the manufacturing firms into specialized separate agencies of accountants, software writers and designers, and these new firms are defined as part of the service sector rather than as part of manufacturing.

One lesson emerges loud and clear from the American experience: the information society demands highly qualified people.

In the year October 1983 to October 1984, 1·3 million more new jobs were created for professionally qualified people and for executives; therefore there is no deceleration in the shift of the American economy towards high qualification and high skills. Graduate unemployment is less than half that of the general labour force, less than a third that of all 20–24 year olds. The ability of the education system to match the needs of the information society for highly educated people has now become the main determinant of a country's employment prospects.

The Service Sector

Can the Western world look to services to absorb the unemployed, including those likely to lose jobs in manufacturing in the future? Not entirely, for a retreat into services could entail a rapid collapse of manufacturing jobs, and the services depend on the manufacturing industry as the main customer for services to business. Without an efficient competitive manufacturing industry, the demand for these services would dwindle. The share of employment in manufacturing is likely to go on declining, but if manufacturing output declines too, many manufacturing-related services will go down with it.

This is why the acceleration of job losses in British manufacturing is so disturbing: the rise from 1·33 per cent a year in 1973–9 to 4·6 per cent a year in 1979–83 far outstripped the American rate of decline. In construction, annual job losses rose from 1·1 to 5·6 per cent over the same period. Producers of microelectronic processes, computer-aided designers and makers of new materials need a market for their products. The depth of Britain's recession in the years 1979–83 was so severe that even jobs in services dropped by 90,000 or 0·17 per cent. The only industries and services that produced any substantial increases in these four years were computers and electronics (but only 37,000 additional jobs), health (291,000), education (120,000), business services (106,000), banking and finance (150,000), and catering (55,000). The pattern is similar to that in the United States except that information jobs have grown less vigorously in Britain, for the more acute recession and much slower recovery have reduced job creation in all parts of the economy.

Three lessons about jobs for the future stand out. First, failure to exploit the new technologies means failure to gain new jobs in manufacturing to offset the disappearance of old jobs. Second, new jobs, whether in manufacturing or in services, are likely to demand higher qualifications than old jobs. Finally, contractionary macroeconomic policies cripple job creation in all areas of employment, including the services.

A study of employment prospects in Italy, *Jobs of the Future*, undertaken by Umberto Colombo, President of Italy's Committee for Nuclear Energy and Alternatives (ENEA), suggests that many jobs will be associated with emerging technologies, not only in manufacturing but in services too. Creating such jobs will depend on the attitude of governments and of people. Colombo, acknowledging the theoretical contributions of economists such as Joseph Schumpeter and Christopher Freeman, writes:

> If we fail to face the problem of technical innovation and its consequences to the economic and social fabric swiftly and courageously we risk losing important opportunities and experiencing only the tail-end effects of the new technologies; in other words the most destructive and alienating effects in terms of employment, of the non-rejuvenation of traditional sectors, and of a loss of competitivity of the entire economic productive system.[1]

Colombo's classification of the potential for future jobs falls into three broad areas:

1. new technologies and their applications.
2. improvement of the environment and the infrastructure.
3. human services.

Table 2

New Technologies and Their Applications	000's	The Environment and the Infrastructure	000's	Human Services	000's
Robot technicians	200	Energy technicians	2–300	Medical technicians	150
New materials	200	Housing		Geriatric social	
Biotechnologists	200	rehabilitation	150	workers	100
CAD/CAG*	100	Hazardous waste	100	Childcare	150
CAM**	100	Industrial		Leisure	50
Computer tech.	450	conservation	150		
Testing techniques	100	Land rehabilitation	40		
New manufacturing	300				
Office automation	300				
Total	1,950	Total	640–740	Total	450

* Computer-aided design/computer-aided graphics.
** Computer-aided manufacturing.

The actual realization of such employment opportunities, Colombo believes, is dependent upon the adoption of *ad hoc* policies, which need to be defined and then implemented by governments.

A similar but much more detailed study for the United States by Wassily Leontief and Faye Duchin considers three scenarios for the future. The first indicates what would happen if the dissemination and application of new technology did not increase beyond its present level; the third assumes a rapid growth in the use of technology unhampered by shortages of skill or capital; the second adopts an intermediate position. The study, which used an elaborate input–output model, is the most sophisticated set of predictions of the patterns of future employment undertaken in the United States. The third scenario, the one that assumes a rapid adoption of new technology, shows big increases in the demand for professional and scientific workers (up by as much as fourteen million by the year 2000), a modest increase in maintenance workers and a dramatic fall among clerical workers. Managers will constitute a smaller share of the labour force. Like Colombo, Leontief and Duchin expect to see very large increases in the demand for computer technicians and microelectronic engineers; they also believe that the introduction of more robots, computers, automated offices and numeri- cally controlled machine tools, while replacing the jobs of semi-skilled operators and labourers, will lead to an increased output of capital goods which will in turn create jobs producing computer-based equipment. Some displaced workers will be re-employed in maintaining and pro- gramming the equipment. Because Leontief and Duchin assume a large increase in the production of capital goods to serve the needs of the information economy, they do not expect to see any dramatic decrease in the manufacturing sector; after 1985, its share of employment levels out at around 22 per cent in their model, and that of services at about 65 per cent.[2]

The tremendous growth of jobs for professionally qualified people projected in this scenario, especially in engineering and electronics, assumes that education and training will expand at a fast enough rate to match the new needs. If they do not, the mismatch could lead to much higher unemployment and to people being employed in jobs for which their skills are inappropriate. The study suggests that as many as five million additional clerical workers and 744,000 more managers could find themselves jobless in 1990, while there would be equivalent num- bers of vacancies in other occupational categories, if office work in the 1980s is carried out by the same methods as those used in the 1970s – in other words, if the transition to new skills and qualifications is postponed.

Other evidence supports this expectation of a strong demand for highly qualified people in electronics, computer services and related engineering jobs. The *Wall Street Journal* quoted an American Electronics survey of 815 companies which showed a shortfall of 113,000 qualified electrical and electronic engineers in the United States by 1988.[3] The United States Bureau of Labour projects a continuing increase in demand for professionals and managers, though, if Leontief and Duchin are right, the demand for managers will fall off in the 1990s, perhaps because of more intelligent machines. In the blue-collar area there will be a great demand for people able to maintain sophisticated microelectronic systems. Delicate and complex systems demand a high and consistent quality of care.

The Gradual Transformation

Some of the more sensational forecasts of the effects of new technology on unemployment have already proved false. Work has not collapsed, and the United States' experience has shown that unemployment can come down as a result of macroeconomic policies despite the rapid adoption of new technology. Japan and the United States have proved that there are a lot of jobs in the new technologies, provided people are trained to fill them. Furthermore, new technologies do not replace old ones overnight. Millions of girls are still taking shorthand and typing out letters. Millions of men are turning lathes and milling bits of metal, as if computer-controlled machine tools and lasers did not exist. The diffusion of technology, despite the best efforts of government and the media, is slow. There are some firms and some individuals who will never be reached. In that sense, the effects on employment will only occur gradually.

Negative factors in other areas are more likely to have an immediate adverse effect on employment figures. For instance, in the past ten years, the largest growth of employment in Britain has been in medical services; the education profession has seen significant expansion too. Both these public services are now under pressure, as a result of expenditure cuts, to reduce, or at least not to increase, employment in the future. Fewer teachers will be needed because of low birth rates. Although the rising proportion of elderly people in society should lead to an increased need for doctors, nurses, medical technologists and social workers in geriatrics, how far and how fast this demand for public social services or their private surrogates grows will depend on the overall growth of economies and the share of the gross national product allocated to social services expenditure.

'Information Jobs'

The new technologies have been extensively studied in terms of their influence on employment and productivity in manufacturing industries; the improvements in productivity are potentially very great indeed. But the new technologies may have equally dramatic effects on jobs in the service sector, including those described as 'information jobs'.

The phrase 'information jobs', like the term 'information society', owes more to a redefinition of occupations than to the invention of microelectronics. An information job is a job in which information is communicated, processed or stored. The description therefore encompasses teachers, librarians, word processor operators, computer programmers, television producers, journalists, business executives and many, many more occupations which handle information. An information society is one in which the organization, communication and use of information is the single most important economic factor, more important than investment in capital plant and equipment or the availability of low-cost labour and raw materials. The terms are not, and cannot be, exact. Their increasing use reveals the significance of information as a factor of production, and they signal the growth of a society in which the handling of information and even of knowledge is for the first time being subjected to automation.

A major growth area for information jobs has been the servicing of industry. Many information workers are employed in serving the productive economy, as clerical workers, salespeople, managers, designers, accountants and advertisers. The complexity of modern industrial plants, many of them part of national or multinational groups, and the specialization of labour have led to more and more people being employed in coordinating all sorts of activities. Many services have been separated from manufacturing processes or have been hived off, including professional functions like accounting and legal advice, and clerical functions like word-processing and photocopying. The value of information going to the productive sector grew vastly long before microelectronics was introduced. A study undertaken at the Massachusetts Institute of Technology estimated that the value of the input of information increased four times over in real terms between 1947 and

1972, from $132 billion to $506 billion.[4] The information sector input into the consumer market grew much more slowly in these years.

Employment in the information sector (which cuts across the traditional divisions between manufacturing and services) rose in these years side by side with its value. Between 1940 and 1965, information jobs rose from 30 to nearly 50 per cent of the American work-force, and so did the value of information as a proportion of the final output of production goods.

Information jobs can be categorized according to the skills required or the kind of information produced. Broadly, 17–20 per cent of the information work-force is employed in the information investment area, actually adding to the stock of knowledge. The people in this area, about 10 per cent of the total work-force, are teachers, research scientists, designers and software engineers. A larger group, nearly a quarter of all information employees, are in clerical and office work; a similar number work as managers, supervisors and foremen. Finance and accounting, marketing and selling account for about 14 per cent each.[5]

Clerical Work

It is generally recognized that microelectronics will significantly affect the employment of clerical workers. Just as an industrial robot can replace two or three human operatives and pay for itself within two years, so a word-processor can replace four typists; in both instances, the quality of the work produced should be higher. Storage and memory systems are becoming cheaper every year, as the capacity of each semiconductor chip multiplies. Transmission systems using fibre optics or satellite links are becoming much more reliable, and here too costs are falling. Much of the communication within and between firms is already conducted by electronic mail, by-passing many current clerical processes altogether. The capacity of machines to 'read' characters or symbols, extensively used in codes in the retail trade and in the sorting of cheques, have already made many routine clerical and distribution jobs redundant.

It was developments in information-processing itself that made so many doom-laden prophets in the 1970s predict the collapse of work. Clive Jenkins and Barry Sherman, in *The Collapse of Work*, predicted that 2·6 million office jobs would disappear by 1985, and 350,000 in banking, insurance and commodity trading.[6] At the same time, the West

German electronics company Siemens estimated that 40 per cent of office jobs would have gone by 1990 in West Germany, about two million in all. Neither of these prophecies is so far being fulfilled. In both the United States and the United Kingdom employment in banking, insurance and finance increased between 1979 and 1983, mainly through the offering of new services to customers. Clerical jobs in both countries continued to grow, in Britain by 11·3 per cent between 1971 and 1980, in the United States by 38 per cent between 1973 and 1982. The number of personal secretaries, whose jobs might be thought especially vulnerable, rose in the same period in America by 25 per cent. The speed at which new equipment has been introduced has, as I have said, been slower than expected. But the main reason for this is paradoxical: the recession itself slowed down investment in services including microelectronics, just as it slowed down investment in manufacturing.

Productivity in Services

Until the last decade, the information sector had not been greatly altered by new plant and equipment. In comparison with manufacturing, the information sector and the services generally were under-capitalized. There has been far less emphasis on productivity in the services than there has been in industry, an emphasis that is characteristic of contemporary economics and that has been curiously little examined. Economists have concentrated on the productivity of labour in manufacturing to the virtual exclusion of the productivity of other factors of production like capital and energy, or of other sections of the labour force like the professions and white-collar services. Countries benefit from increases in productivity in whatever sector they appear, and whatever factor of production produces them. A greater awareness of this proposition could lead to better-balanced and sustained economic growth.

Better organization and management of information offers immense scope for higher productivity – probably more, from now on, than manufacturing.

Charles Jonscher at the Massachusetts Institute of Technology forecast that there would be a steady increase in information productivity during the 1980s, reaching 2·3 per cent a year by 1990, and 5·1 per cent a year by 2000, high enough to produce overall annual productivity figures approaching those of the golden years of the 1950s despite a very slow rate of increase in industrial productivity. What would that mean for employment? It would mean that we could not expect to see the number of information service jobs continue to increase as they have done in the last twenty years. It would mean that the service share in modern economies would be unlikely to go on growing. Jonscher himself suggested that the information workers' share in employment would level out at 50 per cent, and then fall to about 46 per cent by the end of the century.[7]

A series of case studies undertaken by British Telecom in 1982 bears out the conclusion that there is great scope for productivity increases – and for labour-saving – in white-collar jobs. Two processes already well known offer huge savings in labour: direct debiting and point-of-sale data collection. Direct debiting means that a customer's account is automatically debited with the cost of the goods sold, greatly simplifying retail transactions. Point-of-sale data collection enables retailers to keep a running register of sales so that they know what is in stock, and can arrange for automatic reordering from suppliers whenever stocks drop below a certain level, thereby saving a large part of the capital now locked up in inventories. Indeed one case study showed that savings from point-of-sale data collection in the retailing of electrical goods would amount to fourteen times the cost of installing the necessary equipment. Furthermore, shops so equipped would be able to provide faster and better service. Direct debiting of clients offered nine-fold savings, mainly on clerical staff, to an estate agency, and faster catalogue preparation gave similar cost/benefit ratios to a mail order company. Obviously, some of the benefits came from attracting business away from other companies, which would have indirect repercussions on employment elsewhere. Without taking such indirect effects into account, estimates of the consequences for employment in these eight case studies were dramatic, though the figures should be adjusted to allow for the fact that the study was published in 1982. At that time, direct debiting of clients could save 2,000 jobs for every million pounds of investment in telecommunications, point-of-sale data collection saving 1,200. Even processes with a more modest impact, such as viewdata ordering (ordering from samples and prices shown on a television screen or monitor), would have saved 500 clerical workers' jobs for every million pounds spent.

The largest benefits of all came from installing comprehensive communications systems, either within a firm or between a firm and its clients. Such improved internal communications in an engineering factory could, it was shown, save £1·45 million for a modest £50,000 investment; ordering from viewdata could reap benefits for one particular manufacturer 130 times greater than the cost of installing the necessary system.

If all the examples of job savings in these British Telecom studies were added together, 4,275 clerical and retail jobs would disappear as a result of £18 million (at 1982 prices) invested in telecommunications and electronic equipment.[8]

Blue Collar and White Collar

Clerical and retail workers will not be the only casualties of greater investment in modern communication technologies. Managerial and professional jobs will also be lost, and in some cases the losses will be very great indeed. The introduction of comprehensive electronic communications into a large architects' office, for instance, could destroy many professional jobs as well as clerical jobs, according to the British Telecom studies. Both draughtsmen's and designers' jobs would be affected. Drawing to scale can be done by computer-aided graphics; designs can be stored in component parts and then be reassembled to meet customers' requirements. Introducing microelectronics into the office reduces management jobs as well as clerical jobs. Point-of-sale data collection would cut the number of supervisors in shops and warehouses, in the ratio of one to every twelve retail salespeople who lost their jobs. Overall, the British Telecom studies showed a net saving of 932 professional and management jobs for an £18 million investment (at 1982 prices) – but of 940 for £3 million if only the most labour-saving investments were selected. Increases in jobs were indicated in only two areas, telephone ordering (presumably entirely from winning customers away from mail order companies) and energy control. The latter, estimated to produce 278 jobs for each million pounds invested, is the only case in which there was a net gain of jobs without repercussions on other companies; labour and capital replaced energy, rather than each other.

The studies did show job gains in the design, production, installation and maintenance of the telecommunications and electronic equipment itself. Just as in Japan, makers of microelectronic equipment and integrated circuits were expected to register large job gains. British Telecom assumed that businesses might make savings and improve services by the equivalent of £1,000 million in 1985, rising to £23,000 million in the year 2000. Sales of communication equipment would go up to £1,350 million in 2000, but a large proportion would be imported. The net number of new jobs projected by the studies in telecommunication services and equipment was 39,000 in 1990 and 115,000 in 2000. Against these gains must be set potential losses elsewhere that would be nine or ten times as great.

Making and servicing equipment is only one area of job gains from new technology. New services offered in finance and banking have contributed to job creation. Customers have been attracted by 24-hour autobank cash dispensers, internationally valid cheque guarantee cards and immediate access to information about individual accounts. Direct debit ticket booking has encouraged trade. As the market has grown, stimulated by new services, productivity has also improved because of better capital equipment and the automation of processes, such as cheque-sorting, which were previously done manually. The sophisticated customer can already transact much of his or her business by telex and telephone, using television advertising and teletext as shop windows. It is unlikely that the rate of increase in demand will be so fast that it will outstrip improved productivity.

The Computer in the Home

The British Telecom study looked at the business applications of telecommunication and related microelectronic equipment, not at home systems, although it made an overall estimate of the value of the household market. That estimate left out the employment effects of maintaining and servicing home information systems. Research undertaken by American computer companies suggests that home information systems could be a significant source of new jobs. The United States market for home systems is expected to increase two and a half times over in this decade, from $130 billion in 1981 to $327 billion in 1990, though sales in 1983 and 1984 proved disappointing. Penetration of personal microcomputers is proportionately higher in Britain than in the United States, suggesting a broadly equivalent rate of growth in the British home information systems too. The French have been encouraged by their government to move in the same direction: 3,000 electronic telephone directories have been distributed to French households free of charge to stimulate awareness of microelectronics in the home.

The important point about this market is that the hardware element, supplied by a small number of large companies, now makes up only one fifth or one quarter of the total value of the systems. The scope for small firms to provide information and software for personal users is considerable. The mushrooming of computer magazines and video shops is only the tip of this iceberg. There will be many jobs in the servicing and maintaining of home computer systems, and this will be a new market opportunity for small firms. The work will demand people with multiple skills in the IT field, not simply limited skills such as those of the television repairman.

Craftsmen/women

Some computer systems already complement, and in part replace, professional work. Computer-aided design, graphics and inspection operate in what were once highly skilled areas, and operate to a greater degree of accuracy than most human beings can ever achieve. Some companies integrate computer-aided designs into products which are electronically inspected. In the aerospace industry computer-aided design is already extensively used. Computers redesign products to reduce the number of parts and make them easier to assemble. Components can also be assembled in different sequences, so that different products can be produced from the same parts. Computers can work out the best routes for vehicles to deliver goods, or where parts should be stored in warehouses. They can be used to program the assembly of components, to change toolheads in sequence or to position work-processes so that the operator does not have to use any judgement at all.

Yet sophisticated as computer-based systems are, most of them leave room for craftsmen and craftswomen. Projections of future jobs do not predict that these highly skilled people will disappear. Over three quarters of machined parts for engineering products are made in small batches, of fifty or less. Modern computer-controlled machines can be programmed to use different toolheads, each performing a different function, from milling to inspection. They can therefore readily be used in batch production. The people who use them will be highly skilled people, capable of programming and adjusting the machine to meet each order. Computer-controlled machines can make individual, customized products, like shoes and furniture. A design can be drawn with the help of computer graphics and then shown in varying scales and from different angles. Once chosen, the coordinates can be fed into a computer, which automatically cuts and shapes the material and then assembles it according to the customers' wishes. Craftsmen/women, able to compete at last with standardized, mass production goods, will come back into their own. This is one area of employment that is likely to flourish.

9 The Intelligent Computer: A Threat to the Professions?

'The erosion of the power of the established professions will be a striking feature of the second phase of the Computer Revolution.'

Christopher Evans, *The Mighty Micro*, (1979)

Professional and managerial jobs have been less affected by microelectronics than manufacturing and clerical jobs because professionals and managers are in a position to make decisions: they are unlikely to decide to destroy their own jobs. But the relative security of their jobs from technological change may be threatened as the trend towards the development of artificial intelligence becomes more pronounced. The basic concept of these computers, known as fifth-generation systems, say their Japanese designers, 'will be knowledge information processing systems having problem-solving functions of a very high level. In these systems intelligence will be greatly improved to approach that of a human being...'[1]

Knowledge-based information-processing systems will be different in kind from all existing systems. They are not calculators, crunching numbers faster and faster, with expanding memory capacities and more and more information crammed on to each chip. The first four generations of computers have essentially been calculators, which work deductively and sequentially. Such machines are amazing, but they are not intelligent.

The fifth-generation computer, now under development in Japan, the United States and Britain, breaks with these sequential calculations. It will simulate human intelligence by making inferences and by pursuing lines of thought in parallel, as the human mind does. It will embody programming languages, so that users can interact with it directly, using normal speech. People will be able to instruct, talk to and argue with these computers. Most important of all, they will be able to ask the machines to explain themselves.

Fifth-generation computers will use three kinds of knowledge-based systems: knowledge of natural languages, knowledge of their own operation and knowledge appropriate to the applications for which they are being used. These applications – which can cover an almost infinite range – will depend upon expert systems. In other words, the knowledge of human experts translated by a new breed of 'knowledge engineers' into a set of rules. Such rules are not the rigid sequential mathematical rules followed by the older generations of computers. They are 'If …, then …' rules responding to information supplied by the user. Furthermore, the computer will be able to record the assumptions on which the expert's advice is based, and the logical steps used to get from assumptions to conclusions. Expert systems embody the 'rules of thumb' or inferences which allow real human experts to short-circuit the tedious business of accumulating data and then having to process all the data whether it is relevant or irrelevant to their purposes.

Doctors, engineers, farmers, prospectors – all develop a 'feel' for their professional fields, or what in computer parlance is called a domain. Experienced doctors do not apply a whole set of rules to the patient before them. They look for certain symptoms and draw inferences from other cases they have seen. Their advice is based on skill, knowledge and experience. The engineer can see how to go about building a bridge once the relevant parameters are known: the stresses involved, the design requirements demanded by the materials being used, the span to be crossed and the weight to be carried. Computers can be used to simulate bridge designs, and the choice will be narrowed by the engineer's expert knowledge. The farmer does not need a computer to know whether a cereal crop is growing well, or what the quality of a dairy herd is. But, if the right questions are put to it, a computer can refine this knowledge and make it more precise.

Expert Systems

Expert systems operate like human consultants but the potential returns from large sales of outstanding expert software mean that the quality of advice sought is likely to be high. There are all sorts of problems about expert systems, especially in domains like economics or history, where value judgements are embedded in the experts' assessments, and the same applies more subtly to medicine or architecture. What they do offer, however, is not only access to the best experts in the field, but the possibility of questioning them, a privilege not granted to those who read books or watch television programmes. Much will depend upon the abilities of knowledge engineers to transform the experience of experts into knowledge-based software systems. If they are successful, it seems highly probable that many professional people and many managers will find themselves replaced by intelligent computer systems.

Expert systems can of course improve the quality of services without replacing human beings. Inexperienced doctors might benefit from computer assistance in diagnosing patients' symptoms. Preventative medicine can benefit from using computerized information about sections of the population at risk; for instance, a computer could be programmed to notify all girls in the population between the ages of nine and twelve of the need for injections against German measles if they are to avoid complications from the disease affecting their future unborn children. Side-effects of new drugs could be rapidly identified and held on a data-base accessible to doctors throughout the country. Hospital administration could be improved and simplified. The possibilities are endless.

Expert systems can give better and quicker service. An experiment conducted in eight centres by Britain's Department of Health and Social Security to provide claimants with information from a computer about their entitlements proved tremendously popular. The 398 claimants, mostly unemployed and almost all unfamiliar with computers, much preferred them to human sources, 85 per cent saying they had learned more than they ever learned from those who staff the offices. The claimants enjoyed their own interaction with the computer, and half of them discovered they were entitled to additional benefits. Most important of all, claimants did not have to wait to learn of their entitlements. The computer provided an immediate and comprehensive print-out. The advantages for claimants in complex rule-ridden systems are clear; for the Exchequer, however, there are both costs and savings. The costs will be incurred as claimants get all the benefits they are entitled to. The savings may be made by reducing the staffing of social security offices.[2]

Personal Care

Personal services – nursing and teaching, caring for children and the elderly – have been among the most important sources of new jobs in the last decade. They too will be transformed by the advent of intelligent computers. Japanese laboratories have already designed 'intelligent' robots to assist in hospital care. In the United States, robots able to respond to simple voice commands are being used in day-centres for the elderly. Within fifteen years they will be widely available to do routine domestic work like vacuuming, cleaning and carrying utensils.

Care of the elderly and disabled will be transformed in other ways too. Microelectronics offers liberation to the disabled and housebound. Sufferers from cerebral palsy, for instance, prevented by their disability from communicating through speech or the written word, can use microcomputers with specially designed aids for the handicapped to re-establish contact with the world around them. Computers have been adapted for use with either hand- or foot-switches, while some are even operated with mouthsticks or by the user's breathing. In Britain, for people with more severe disabilities, Government-funded research into switches using the electrical charge generated by the eyeball when it moves, seems to offer further possibilities in work as well as leisure for the disabled in the future.[3]

Research is also being carried out on sensing devices that will provide a stream of signals for blind people similar to radar, allowing them to move about freely. Alarm systems are already in use that give immediate warning to a central emergency station if an old person falls. Other devices supplement failing strength; artificial muscles are being developed which will virtually replace a damaged or withered limb. The housebound and disabled will be able to retain their independence by the use of teleshopping, telebanking and occasional teleconferences with others about their problems and how to solve them. In these and other ways the burden of an ageing society should be eased.

It is too soon to say whether that burden will be replaced by the burden of an unemployed or bored society. For the next ten years, probably until the end of the century, the major issue will be changing the composition of the work-force so that the proportion of highly skilled technicians, technologists and engineers increases while that of clerical workers and traditional single-skill workers declines. Schemes for the redundant and displaced workers who cannot easily adapt to new technologies will have to be devised.

Such policies are possible. But by the end of the century, we are beyond the scope of predictions. 'We are moving', to quote Gar Alperowitz, 'into an era of extraordinary and unprecedented instability of future expectations.' Intelligent computers; robots capable of sight and touch; expert systems advising humans on political, economic, social and medical problems – such inventions will transform society so that forecasting manpower requirements becomes a gamble. As the former Chairman of Shell (U K), Mr Raisman, told me, 'forecasts give a false sense of certainty, because they are based on projecting the past. Scenarios are more useful.' The scenario for the year 2000 is a world in which human intelligence and technical ability will still be at a premium, but only intelligence and ability of the highest quality. The meritocracy is already very powerful in modern democracies. In the age of artificial intelligence its power will increase.

10 Can Small Business Create Jobs?

'The value of the small firms' sector revolves around the fact that they provide the competitive spirit that a market economy needs for efficiency. They provide an outlet for entrepreneurial talents, a wider range of goods and services to the consumer, a check to monopoly inefficiency, a source of innovation, and a seedbed for new industries.'

Alan Bollard, *Small Beginnings*, (1983)

The evidence shows that new technologies will cut into employment. They will destroy many clerical jobs, and many jobs in distribution. The professions themselves will not be entirely safe, as new generations of 'intelligent' computers are developed which can base their expert advice on memories capable of retaining millions of bits of information. One sector of the economy, however, has consistently generated jobs in spite of the shock of new technology, or perhaps partly because of it. That sector is small business.

One of the most remarkable claims made about the generation of new jobs appeared in a now famous paper by David Birch of the Massachusetts Institute of Technology in 1979.[1] He claimed that 66 per cent of all new jobs created between 1960 and 1976 in the United States were in firms with under twenty employees, and that 82 per cent were created in firms employing fewer than a hundred people. In the old industrial areas of the North-east, Birch wrote, small firms were not merely the sole job creators; they also offset a large decline in employment in every category of medium and large-sized firm those employing fifty to a hundred people and upwards.

David Birch's findings were hard to believe. They contradicted the assumptions of most businessmen and most governments in the 1960s and early 1970s; that large firms were efficient, that economies of scale kept down costs and that healthy big business meant a healthy economy. They raised doubts about the policy of encouraging firms to merge to form larger corporations, a policy much favoured in Britain in the 1960s and early 1970s under both Labour and Conservative governments. They implied that government policies devoted to keeping afloat giant firms in trouble and attracting large firms to deprived areas might be expensive and inefficient ways of saving or creating jobs.

So Birch's paper was subjected to intensive examination. Admittedly it was based on data that had serious gaps, inaccuracies and misleading definitions, but these computerized data, collected by the Dun and Bradstreet Corporation for the credit rating of firms, are the most comprehensive record of United States' companies, classified by size, date of birth and area of operation. In 1976, the files contained brief biographies of twelve million American companies.

But the files concealed many traps for the unwary. For example, a firm (or, more often, a branch) might be discovered in one year and listed for the first time, but its birth might actually have occurred several years before. Some firms moved, and could not be traced. They were removed from the files, but might still be flourishing in new locations. A successful firm would grow rapidly into another category – say, from under twenty employees to over fifty – which meant that researchers unfamiliar with its history would attribute any subsequent expansion to a medium-sized firm when in fact it should be attributed to a small one. Similarly, if a small firm merged with a large one, the small firm might be listed as a business 'death', while the additional jobs it brought to the big firm might be shown as new jobs generated there.

The most weighty criticism of Birch's research came from the Brookings Institutions, the prestigious economic research centre in Washington DC.[2] The Brookings authors agreed with some of Birch's conclusions. Between 1970 and 1980, the period covered by their study, they found that employment grew more than twice as fast in firms with under twenty employees as their share of the labour force would imply – 55 per cent compared to 23 per cent. They agreed that small firms registered a greater share of net employment gains in the slow-growing regions like the North-east and mid-Atlantic regions. But the Brookings study's conclusions differed fundamentally on the central issue. The share in employment growth of small firms, defined as those with under a hundred employees, the authors declared, was about 39 per cent, equivalent to the small firm share in total employment. The reason why Birch's figures were so much higher and the reason for the apparent rapid growth of employment in small firms between 1978 and 1980 were identical: both included branches of large firms which cannot properly be described as small businesses.

The Brookings challenge led to a detailed and painstaking analysis of the original Dun and Bradstreet data by Birch and his associates. They found that the file had gaps which the Brookings researchers had filled by extrapolations which Birch and his colleagues could not accept as soundly based. They also discovered that Dun and Bradstreet had done a 'catch-up' operation on new branches created by large firms, which led to several years' worth of new branches being attributed to a single year, 1980. These fluctuations in the raw data affected the Brookings figures. Birch and MacCracken concluded at the end of this second operation that small enterprises with under a hundred employees (not including branches of larger ones) generated 3·4 million of the 4·85 million jobs created in the United States in 1979 and 1980, 70 per cent of the total.[3] This figure is lower than Birch's estimate of 82 per cent for the earlier period which he studied, 1969–76. Birch himself believes that this can be explained by the phenomenal growth of small firms in the first three years of that period, 1969–72, and the fact that a number of large firms found themselves in difficulties at that same time. Averages for the later period, 1972–6, are closer to his revised findings. But what now seems indubitably clear is this: small firms in all sectors are generating net new jobs almost twice as fast as their share of employment would imply.

Other research undertaken in the United States confirmed Birch's conclusions. A study of small businesses in California, carried out at the Institute of Urban and Regional Development in 1981, found that over half the net new jobs were created by small, young companies in sectors other than manufacturing.[4] This study, like Birch's, showed that job losses due to contraction and firm deaths remained astonishingly constant at about 8 per cent a year. Neither the region nor the stage of the business cycle seemed to affect the figures by more than 1 per cent or so either way. What decided the net balance of employment was job gain – which varies greatly from region to region, from industry to industry and according to the stage reached in the business cycle. Of the net additional employment in California in 1976–9, 56 per cent came from firms with fewer than twenty employees, exactly twice their share of total employment.

Young Firms Grow

The California researchers discovered another fact which is bad news for policy-makers, because it demonstrates that supporting small firms is very much a gamble. Over half the new jobs in small firms were created in their first four years of existence, and most of them were concentrated in a small proportion of successful fast-growing firms. In other words, the entrepreneurs who succeeded did so convincingly. The risks were high too; half of the small firms which set up in business had disappeared four years later. But the survivors were tough. Of the firms that had been in existence for over four years prior to 1976 – in other words, those in the category of continuing firms – the very small accounted for 68 per cent of the job gains.

The picture in the manufacturing sector of California's economy was rather different. Over half the new manufacturing jobs were in firms of 250 employees or more, and less than a fifth were in very small firms. Indeed, looking at all sectors, almost all the additional jobs in large firms were in manufacturing.

This pattern of a rapid growth of jobs among small-firm survivors is repeated in a Minnesota study. In 1977, 7,105 new businesses were started in Minnesota, 98 per cent of them with under fifty employees.[5] Three years later, a third had perished, but employment among the survivors had grown by 33 per cent, three times faster than employment overall.

These American studies show a country bubbling with risk-taking entrepreneurs ready to set up new companies, and experiencing a highly volatile existence in which for many their fate will be decided within a few years. American small business is like the natural world, one of abundance and destruction.

Birch found that the fastest-growing regions were also those with the highest rate of failure: 'Just as failure appears essential to our system, so does instability.'[6] Instability characterized many of the new jobs too. In stark contrast to Japan, with its large core of life-long employees, American jobs come and go like spring snowflakes. 'The half-life of most new jobs,' says Teitz, 'is probably under four years.'[7]

The Blooming of the South-west

In the United States, jobs are growing fastest in small businesses, and most strikingly in areas where there were few jobs before. Two out of three new jobs are in the South and West. In 1978, Brookings research showed that the three old industrial regions (New England, East North Central and Mid-Atlantic) accounted for 43 per cent of salaried employment but only 21 per cent of the growth in jobs. The Pacific region, on the other hand, with 13 per cent of salaried employment, had over 20 per cent of employment growth.[8] The factors that have attracted American firms away from the great industrial cities to the South and West include the low level of unionization in these relatively undeveloped regions. A generation ago, much of the clothing industry moved from the North-east, especially New York and Massachusetts, to the South, where it could pay lower wages and operate with few restrictions. The clothing industry has been followed by the defence industries and by electronic and electrical engineering. Firms have also been lured by unspoiled environments, which enable them to attract qualified people and to choose a location without planning and land-use constraints, and with lower property taxes. Such mobility is much harder to achieve in Europe, where there are fewer undeveloped areas, the contrast between highly organized labour in the old industrial regions and low unionization in rural areas is not so marked, and variations between states and regions are not so great.

The advantages of small business do not lie only in its record of generating new jobs; it has social and human advantages too. Small business is relatively strike-free. Communications are easy, and communication lines are short. Small businesses are flexible, and not vulnerable to disruption or system malfunctioning in the way large businesses are. They play no part in causing inflationary pressures, since their wage settlements have little influence, and they are not in a position to fix prices.

Governments are beginning to ask how to establish the economic climate in which small businesses can flourish. Gone is the enthusiasm for mergers and conglomerates. Given that job losses vary little between regions and stages of the business cycle, net employment creation depends upon job gains, which in turn depend upon the formation of new companies and the runaway success of a minority of them. So the preoccupation of central and state governments and of local communities alike is how to encourage venture capital, how to bring about technology transfer and how to find market niches to enable these elusive new entrepreneurs to take root and flourish.

Europe: Small is Hopeful

Is there any reason to believe that the observations of American researchers about their own economy might also be applicable to the economy of Western Europe? And if not, if the phenomenon of vigorous small firms is absent, does that explain Europe's poor record of job creation compared to the United States? Those who advance macroeconomic explanations for Europe's stagnation, such as inadequate demand, will notice that small firms grow more rapidly than large ones in the United States of America even in an unfavourable business environment, and offset some of the large firms' job loss during the recession.

Small firms are outside the great corporate organizations which have produced price and wage structures that move readily upwards, but stickily downwards. To quote Birch one last time, 'our inability to understand the gap between the "micro" economy and "macro" economy is now seriously hampering efforts to develop policies that will generate jobs for the people and the places that need them without causing inflation at the same time.'[9] What we need, he argues, are policies that focus on those firms that will create jobs, not on the whole economy.

Western European governments have largely supported general rather than specific policies for job creation, favouring maximum impact over accuracy. Regional policies have been directed towards attracting large firms to slow-growing or declining parts of the country, or to shoring up those already there. The government of the Federal Republic of Germany spent $4·5 billion in 1984 alone on sick and declining industries. Job creation and job saving have been very expensive in terms of public capital invested per job. A recent estimate for Britain by the Comptroller and Auditor-General put the per capita cost of a new job in the less prosperous regions at as much as £40,000 of taxpayers' money at 1983 prices.[10] Now European governments are asking themselves whether these expensive policies are sensible.

For even in Europe, it is the small-business sector that is showing convincing evidence of vigour. Even in Europe, initiatives at local level suggest that the grassroots are flourishing, despite the harshness of the business climate. The American researchers point out that high interest rates make life especially difficult for small firms; in Europe, the highest real interest rates for fifty years combined with the traditional wariness of the banks towards venture capital make life very hard indeed for such firms.

As there is no European study as detailed as Dun and Bradstreet's, the evidence of employment growth in small firms is patchy. European countries do not attempt to collect statistics on small firms outside the manufacturing sector. Even within it, the definition of a small firm varies, 200 workers usually being regarded as the upper limit. Most countries use establishments as the unit for statistical purposes; but others, including France and Holland, use enterprises. The difference can be very great, because branches and subsidiaries are included in the latter definition. Statistics are not regularly up-dated, and there are no longitudinal studies to measure how rapidly small firms grow. Thus, a successful European small firm that expands into the medium-sized category will be shown as having ceased to operate. It would be present in the 1979 statistics, for example, but by 1983 would have vanished from the small-business category. Europe's 'snapshot' statistics do not give enough information; the best one can do, therefore, is to make broad comparisons and provide fragmented information.

Such comparisons as there are suggest that Italy, Norway and Spain have a much higher proportion of small companies than the rest of Western Europe.[11] Norway's experience can be explained by its geography and the absence of large cities, Italy's by its history and laws actively discriminating in favour of small companies. The Federal Republic of Germany and Great Britain have the fewest; small firms in both account for about a third of employment in manufacturing. However, the British Chancellor of the Exchequer's memorandum to the National Economic Development Council[12] showed that employment in small manufacturing establishments of under 200 employees in Britain had grown from 27 per cent of the manufacturing work-force in 1973 to 34 per cent in 1981; this is all the more encouraging since, on the basis of the American studies, manufacturing is the least likely sector for small business to flourish in. Furthermore, the number of self-employed people in Great Britain increased by nearly a quarter between 1979 and 1983 to an estimated 2¼ million, though some of them would be self-employed only because the alternative is to be unemployed; they may have very little to do.

A Hostile Climate

The evidence suggests that in the last fifteen years Western Europe has seen a similar development to the older regions of the United States with a net addition to jobs in firms employing fewer than a hundred people, and a net decline in those employing over that number. Unlike the United States, however, Europe has few regions where job growth in small firms exceeds job loss in large firms.

One reason, Keynesians will argue, is inadequate demand: in recovering from the recession, Europe has grown more slowly than the United States. But it is not the only reason. The climate for small firms has been much less friendly in Europe than in the United States. The major banks have only recently become interested in venture capital. So much of their business lies in international transactions and with multinational companies that small firms appear as risky customers, demanding disproportionate time and effort. European entrepreneurs can rarely raise credit for new businesses on the strength of their personal reputation or local standing. Often small entrepreneurs have to stake their houses or savings as collateral. Furthermore, most banks refuse to finance secondhand or leased machinery, although small businesses can rarely afford to start up with expensive new equipment. Failure – and the American statistics show that between a quarter and a third of new small-business ventures perish within four years – is much more heavily penalized in Europe than in the United States. Bankruptcy still carries a social stigma.

Until recently governments have been little more helpful than the banks. Schemes to support the introduction of microelectronics or other new technologies have often laid down a minimum eligible size far above the scale of the smaller firms. Public purchasing is heavily biased towards large suppliers who can offer discounts on big orders. But in some areas attitudes towards smaller firms have at last begun to improve.

Community and Neighbourhood: Focuses for Change

Despite the harshness of the economic climate for small business, something very significant is happening through a combination of small business, the self-employed and, at the local level, a partnership between the public and private sectors. The phenomenon is too recent to be easily recognized, and there is no adequate economic description of it. Springing up in the interstices of the mixed economy, partly official, partly unofficial, neither corporate nor statist, a third sector is growing.

It is spreading fast at the grassroots. It represents not just a response to unemployment but a rejection of the large hierarchical and bureaucratic structures that characterized the later stages of the industrial age. It also reflects two other related social phenomena: decentralization and the new awareness of neighbourhood and community as sources of an individual's sense of belonging somewhere, of having roots and identity in a fast-changing, sometimes frightening time. Opportunities have widened tremendously in the years since the Second World War: for travel, education and communication. Many people who were confined by the narrow horizons of villages or small towns longed to escape from them, and to create materially richer and fuller lives. Yet in the 1970s and 1980s a new mood developed, a desire to conserve the environment and the best of the past, to cherish local bonds and friendships.

Evidence of this new mood can be seen everywhere. City centres are no longer being razed and rebuilt, as they were in the 1960s; now they are being refurbished and saved. Old houses are being carefully renovated; old markets and shopping streets are restricted to pedestrians; river walks and paths restored to their old uses. City after city in Europe, from Edinburgh to Prague, demonstrates this desire to save and restore the past. There has been a revolt against bigness too, because it is seen as impersonal and remote. People want the place in which they live and work to be on a human scale. Tower blocks and huge housing estates are rejected by tenants and house-buyers alike; some modern tower blocks have even been razed because no one wants to live in them. Parents do not want their children to go to huge high schools. They do not want to work in giant plants or vast offices, where industrial relations are often sour. And at the political level, people want more power devolved to states and regions, or even to the town and neighbourhood level.

Rediscovering the Individual

The desire to recover individuality (for that, I believe, is what it is) also manifests itself in a growing rejection of mass production. As people get used to a higher standard of living, and as they benefit from better education, they want to be able to express personal choices in their own lives, not to be driven into uniformity. Consumers in the industrialized world have become more demanding and more precise about what they want. They want high quality, not just quantity. Look at the growth of specialized restaurants and food shops, of crafts and ethnic goods, of individualized products. Mass production and mass services fail to satisfy this discriminating new generation, the children of those for whom having enough was itself the fulfilment of a dream. The demand for tailor-made 'personalized' goods and services creates a host of opportunities for the third sector, and one that will offer many jobs.

The third sector benefits immensely from the way microelectronics and communications are developing. Those developments themselves favour decentralized, small-scale, responsive production of goods and services. A generation ago, the main advances being made in computers were in huge mainframes holding large data-bases, to which one gained access by dependent terminals. Computers seemed likely to reinforce the tendency to centralization which had emerged in big business and in big government, and to strengthen powerful hierarchical systems of control. It looked as if individual choices and preferences would be submerged in an undifferentiated drive to satisfy the lowest common denominator.

What has transformed that prospect is the advent of the microcomputer, together with the dramatic decline in the cost of hardware by 30 per cent a year or more. The microcomputer gives both small firms and individuals the computing capacity only large mainframes possessed thirty years ago, and at about a hundredth of the cost. The microcomputer network and the flexible computer-controlled machine tool make new technology 'user-friendly' for the small firm. New technology in communication favours the small and local against the large: cable television as compared to national networks, local newspapers as compared to national ones, district heating schemes as compared to national electricity energy grids, and conservation rather than great power stations. Many strands have come together to make this new third sector not a temporary phenomenon, but a paradigm shift; its potential is only just beginning to be realized.

11 New Patterns, New Possibilities

'The third sector borrows some of its characteristics from the private sector: autonomy, private initiative, drive for efficiency and competitiveness, decisions based on cost-benefit considerations.... But its aims are collective in nature and similar to those of the public services.'

Statement by the OECD Secretariat, 1984

The third sector in the economy is characteristically made up of small enterprises, but ownership and management can take many forms. At one end of the spectrum there are traditional small businesses, the self-employed and family groups in the private sector. At the other, there are manufacturing cooperatives and voluntary agencies in the public sector, managing local employment and training schemes, or social enterprises holding a contract from government departments. In between there is a host of projects combining the private and public sectors, particularly at local level: the *boutiques de gestion* in France, local enterprise trusts in Britain, joint development teams in areas damaged by the collapse of a traditional industry, private industry councils training unemployed youngsters, and many more. In some countries, notably Italy, a considerable part of the third sector is in the unofficial or 'black' economy, often driven there by high social insurance charges, or to avoid tax. A third sector may be a response to excessive regulation, some of it determined by government, some by trade unions. Many of these regulations are necessary for health or safety or decent working conditions, but they have become so elaborate and expensive that many enterprises try to avoid them.

The third sector will go on growing for a variety of reasons. The OECD's Business and Industrialists' Advisory Committee (BIAC) put it this way at a recent conference: 'One can assume that modern technology favours decentralization, furthers small and medium-sized enterprises and tends to encourage people towards more self-employment.'[1] BIAC might have added that periods in which a new technology develops fast, putting a premium on product innovation, are good for small enterprises. Booze Allen and Hamilton, a leading

American information industry company, distinguishes between three categories of manufacturing unit (the same applies to services):

1. Standard products, relatively stable design, mass production. The critical factor is *price*.

2. Variable products, batch or low-volume production. The critical factor is *flexibility*.

3. Customized or one-off products meeting varied and specific market demands. The critical factor is *innovation*.

The latter two types of manufacturing unit are the growing ones, and they suit small firms very well. The first type is inflexible. That is why more and more market niches are revealed that mass products cannot fill. Mass products meet the first phase of the 'revolution of rising expectations' but they disappoint more mature expectations of what constitutes the good life.

Consumer choice, contemporary attitudes and new technology may all favour the third sector, but the truth is that it has a very high death rate, as the American studies show. What can be done to encourage births and reduce deaths, so that the net addition to employment and growth will be greater?

Small enterprises, whether private or public, need midwives and guardians: midwives to assist at the birth, guardians to advise and help them. The midwives are the banks and venture capital companies and government departments that put up money, the guardians the organizations that have grown up in recent years bringing together government, private industry, the trade unions and the professions at the local level, to offer advice and help.

Midwives and Guardians

As mentioned above, finance has not been easily raised for new small businesses in Western Europe, partly because banks are reluctant to lend to firms without a track record. Where small businesses want to move into the high-technology field, they will find few banks or credit companies with the technological expertise to understand their proposals, although knowledge is said to be growing among bank managers in areas where high-tech firms have established themselves, in the silicon valleys and silicon glens. It is precisely new firms without a track record, but with a good marketable idea, that are most likely to multiply jobs.

There has been a marked change for the better recently. Both private firms and banks have set up venture capital finance companies, sometimes in conjunction with one another. The London Stock Exchange now has a lively and growing section for unlisted securities. Governments have encouraged venture capital through tax concessions, such as tax holidays or permitting investors to write off venture capital ploughed into small companies against tax. In the Netherlands and in Britain, the national governments provide loan guarantees, covering up to 80 per cent of risk capital. In Britain, the maximum cover is £75,000, and in return the investor pays a 3 per cent risk premium on normal interest rates. The French Government offers low-interest loans to small businesses, though loans from government sources need to conform to regional or sectoral policies, unlike private funds. A new and promising source of capital is the finance company jointly supported by public and private bodies, as in the case of the one supported by the Scottish Development Agency, a public authority, and the privately owned Bank of Scotland.

Over-the-counter markets, not launched in Europe until the London Stock Exchange opened its unlisted securities market in 1980, are still very small. Britain's had about 150 companies in 1983, France's Deuxième Marché hors Côte, thirty-five, Sweden's, fifteen. In West Germany, such a market does not really exist. Indeed, the Federal Republic, perhaps because its traditional industry has not been so hard hit, is a bad place to raise venture capital. Wagnisfinanzierung, founded in 1975 by twenty-nine West German banks to help small businesses, is a very staid organization. A German banker told John Dizard of *Fortune*, 'You will see what is the past, not the future of German venture capital.'[2] German managers and engineers, securely employed in high-status jobs, are much less likely than their American counterparts to break away to form a new company. Even if they do, raising venture capital without surrendering most of the equity in a new company is not yet feasible in Germany.

Gaps remain in the venture capital scene. Many venture capital companies will still not look at a business which wants to borrow £10,000 or less. They will not lend for working capital, such as materials or parts. Some loans are limited to manufacturing only – as indeed are many government-financed loans and grants such as regional funds. There remains a need for small loans to start up companies. One particularly adventurous agency, the Greater London Enterprise Board, arranges regular meetings at which would-be entrepreneurs outline their proposals to potential investors. Afterwards, proposers and investors meet informally. About half the proposers have succeeded in raising the money they need.

The European venture capital scene is none the less far better than it was, and small enterprises are responding to it. A recent Welsh development agency report referred to some examples of small firms setting themselves up in Wales: one farming and freezing trout, one building sand yachts, one making advanced robots – a varied and exciting industrial world.

Ideas and Markets

Besides finance, small firms need markets. I have referred already to the market opportunities that are emerging, particularly for the automated production of customized products. Such products were once the province of the rich, the fussy and the determinedly homespun. Now they are attracting a far wider clientele. Suits, dresses, furniture, shoes and many other personal or household products can be made to order; even individually designed houses can become possible for people with limited incomes. In Liverpool, houses designed to meet the personal needs of individual families in the Hesketh Street housing cooperative were built within the cost limits that apply to standard municipal housing.

Marketing, however, can be difficult for new small firms. The market for most products is dominated by long-established firms, and heavy advertising of consumer products puts a premium on well-known brand names. To get into the market, small firms may supply local traders or they may supply large companies. Large companies can improve the quality and reliability of small firms' output, and provide a stable market in return, as has happened in Japan and with several leading companies in Western Europe, such as retailers marketing own-brand products. In Sweden, development contracts are placed with small firms so that their initial market is assured. More than 70 per cent of the small firms started in the past ten years there have collaborated with customers, and over half had a development contract.

Governments can help too. Mention has already been made of the Small Business Administration in the United States, which ensures that some part of Federal Government contracts goes to small firms, including those placed by the Department of Defense. That practice should be copied by nationalized industries and public purchasers in Europe. The Irish Government's development agencies have tried to match the needs of new multinationals coming into the country with indigenous suppliers, thus saving imports and providing jobs. Sometimes a marketing expert is employed by a group of small companies, or a person with marketing experience is seconded for a while to a small company. By using local advertising outlets not only to advertise their own products, but to make their purchasing requirements known as well, small businesses provide markets for one another. British Steel Corporation Industries, a subsidiary of the British Steel Corporation and a pioneer of the third sector, set up to create jobs for redundant steelworkers, found that a large part of the orders generated by the small businesses in its workshop complexes went to other firms using the complexes.

Guardians: Advice and Help

BSC Industries found out that ready advice and help can be as important as finance. In a world of taxes, planning requirements, statutory standards, health and safety regulations, social security and much else, many small businesses are simply unable to cope. Nor can they afford to employ a panel of professionals to advise them. It was recognition of this that led to the enterprise trust movement, and its sister, the *boutique de gestion* in France.

The first local enterprise trust in Britain was established in 1978 at St Helen's in Merseyside by Pilkington's, a famous glass-making company, when it became clear that the new float glass technology would destroy many of its employees' jobs. The firm set up a trust including representatives from the local authority, the banks and other firms in an effort to create alternative jobs. It proved remarkably successful, though it could not offset the drop in glass-manufacturing employment completely. Soon after other English towns began to emulate St Helen's; by 1981 twenty had done so. After that, the movement burgeoned. By the end of 1984, over 200 local enterprise trusts were in existence, and another fifty were being mooted.

The help offered to new businesses is comprehensive and is provided by experts in each area. Seconded bank managers and accountants offer advice on accounts, tax liabilities and how to raise finance; local authority officials help to speed planning permission and to provide basic utilities and road access. Some local councils convert unwanted factories or industrial sites to create small workshops and offices, or make premises initially available at a nominal rent. Local enterprise agencies, like the Greater London Enterprise Board, are forging links with institutions of higher education, using them as sources of new products and processes. The GLEB is gradually building up a bank of new product ideas, and these can be offered to would-be entrepreneurs. Science parks, often associated with famous universities like Louvain in Belgium or Cambridge in Britain, are intended to demonstrate their scientists' discoveries to the business community. Sometimes, as in Cambridge, a business park is built alongside the science park.

Many small business people are too preoccupied with survival to take advantage of the innovative treasures on offer to them. For these men and women, outreach programmes are needed. At Limerick, in Eire, the Institute of Higher Education places its engineering students in local firms to help them solve technical difficulties, and gets the students of marketing to assess and develop their market prospects. In Scotland, the University of Stirling offers its graduates support in establishing new companies around their own inventions or innovations. Everywhere in Western Europe, efforts are being made to bridge the gap between old educational institutions and new businesses, and some of the efforts are bearing fruit.

12 Information Networks for Small Business

'Networks exist to foster self-help, to exchange information, to change society, to improve productivity and work life, and to share resources. They are structured to transmit information in a way that is quicker, more high touch, and more energy-efficient than any other process we know.'

John Naisbitt, *Megatrends*, (1982)

Information is the raw material of the new technologies. According to the quality of their information, firms will live or die. Small firms have limited access to information. Microcomputers can only use the data to which they are allowed access, and some of that data will be jealously preserved by large firms and by governments. Major companies like Citibank and I B M have access to massive amounts of data. They already have their own international information communications networks. Others have entered into exclusive deals to buy a particular data-base; names and addresses for direct mail selling are a commonplace example. Unless they protect their own interests, small businesses could find themselves left with crumbs of information from the data-banks of the large and powerful.

Local area networks are therefore beginning to be established to satisfy the needs of small companies for information. Communications networks linking a number of small firms can become the extended nervous systems of small businesses, enabling them to keep pace with bigger competitors. Such networks are among the most promising developments in the third sector of local enterprise and employment creation, because they make possible the advantages of scale while retaining the flexibility of small entities.

A local area network can carry out a large number of functions. It can make possible the combined purchasing of expensive equipment. Firms can share a business computer, expensive peripheral equipment and software programmes for such routine requirements as drawing up accounts or paying wages. They can offer each other spare capacity or raw materials, or seek help to fulfil an urgent contract. A network of firms can match short-time in one firm with overtime in another, to enable their employees to have a steady work-load. Information about technological developments and market opportunities can be diffused very quickly. The PSI study quoted earlier showed that the time between a new process becoming available and its adoption is normally fifteen to eighteen months.[1] Local area networks can make companies aware of new processes rapidly and should reduce this lead-time. The networks can also carry information from government agencies, for instance matching the requirements of public purchasing agencies with the productive capacity of small companies. Local area networks can be excellent matchmakers, bringing unsatisfied needs together with the entrepreneurs willing to satisfy them and the financiers willing to finance them.

How do local area networks function? The most advanced system ('state of the art') is one in which each firm or member of the network has its own microcomputer linked by interactive systems to all the other members. Teletext carries the information about, for example, a market opportunity or an offer of raw materials, and any firm in the system can respond instantaneously and directly to the source of that information. The network carries electronic mail, and can serve other purposes too; it can carry group training courses using graphics or videos, design sketches of new fashions or newsflashes of specific interest to the network's members. Local area networks are not limited to industry. They may in future link local constituency associations to a political party headquarters, providing instant two-way communication during an election. They may bring together social workers and the people they look after, students at separate study stations, even bishops and the clergy in their diocese.

Fully interactive cable or optic fibre systems are expensive, so some networks will rely on cheaper methods of communication. These include earth satellite systems, developing rapidly in the United States, twisted wires systems with limited feedback, and teletext systems relying on a telephoned response.

Old Areas Revive

Three illustrations will give some indication of the immense potential of networks. The first comes from the famous complex of cooperatives in Mondragon, Spain, which has revitalized the whole area. Mondragon's hundred cooperatives benefit from a shared research and development institute, Ikerlan, which works on prototypes of new machinery and new products incorporating the latest technology. Information about new processes and products is made known quickly through Mondragon's network of cooperatives. If any member cooperative is interested in exploiting a new product, the Empresarial division of the cooperative complex will undertake a brief pre-feasibility study. If this is positive, a detailed study follows, which may last as long as eighteen months. A new cooperative may be established to exploit a new product if none of the existing ones is suitable. The key factor is the speed with which innovations are made known, and the ready access of all the Mondragon cooperatives to that knowledge.

The second example comes from Italy, where the traditional knitwear industry around Prato, based on 12,000 tiny firms, was being killed by competition from Third World countries paying low wages. For centuries, these tiny firms had clubbed together to support the *Impannatore*, a high-powered person or team of people who arranged contracts throughout the world for fabrics and textiles. Italian law lays much less stringent conditions on firms employing under fifteen people than on larger firms in matters like hours and security of employment. So the Prato firms stayed small, employing 47,000 people between them. The *Impannatore* shared out contracts among this host of small suppliers.

The problems of coordinating the supplies of raw materials and designs for such a galaxy of little firms, and then organizing deliveries, are acute. The danger is that the ancient system will not be able to respond quickly enough to sudden changes of fashion, nor be able to match prices elsewhere. So the Prato textile industry has become the scene of an experiment in creating a local area network. The employers, the two craft unions, the local authority, the banks and the telecommunications company have been brought together and between them have raised some £400,000 to support a pilot scheme for 300 small firms. Each will receive a television monitor, and the monitors will carry local teletext rather like Prestel, the BBC system. The material carried will not be national news, however, but information specific to the industry, about market opportunities, available labour and raw materials, prices and designs. The scheme can be developed to get bids from firms seeking a share in the *Impannatore*'s contracts, and to work out delivery dates and pick-up routes for lorries. The network should be able to share a computer-aided design system to speed up the preparation of samples of textiles to catch the fashion market, for the Prato industry has moved up-market to compete in high-quality textiles. Automation of looms is being brought in, and the network should be useful in spreading knowledge of new technology.

Italy has no interactive systems, for it boasts neither cable systems nor fibre optic communications. The Prato pilot scheme depends upon linking teletext with conventional telephone lines. Despite the technical difficulties, the potential is enormous, and could be reproduced in other countries.

The third example is the Greater London Enterprise Board, which has established five networks in London, two based on geographical areas and three on product categories – energy, transport and new technologies. The networks bring local people and local organizations together with one or more of London's larger higher-education institutions. Each has its own workshop centre where work can be done on new product designs and prototypes. There is a strong ideological commitment in the Greater London Enterprise Board. New products must be socially useful, conserving energy and raw materials, and human-centred. Cooperatives are preferred to conventional private firms, and the latter will only be supported by the Board if they submit an enterprise plan for approval which must satisfy pretty tough conditions on industrial participation, trade unions, wages and conditions, and non-discrimination on grounds of race or sex.

Private industry in London has reacted coolly to the GLEB. The Board has had some widely publicized failures and embarrassments, but it has proved that creativity and inventiveness do spring up even in unpromising inner-city neighbourhoods, and that academic institutions and local communities can stimulate one another. The Board now claims that the five networks' product banks contain 1,500 new product ideas, including such winners as a scientific computer work-station at an eighth of the cost of competitive products and an expert system for the care of diabetics in the community. Some 3,500 jobs have been created at a cost of £4,700 a job, which is comparable to the cost of new jobs in small high-technology firms in Scotland. The GLEB has the advantage of access to funds from the Greater London Council, which has provided help to start up companies. The interest of the GLEB network lies in the liaison between the local communities and polytechnics or universities, and in the brave attempt to foster human-centred technology. The networks themselves are primarily based on human links, not computerized ones. The GLEB is probably trying to do too many things at once, and some of its goals conflict: for instance, creating jobs while insisting that new firms conform to enterprise plans decreed by the GLEB. Although it may not be altogether clear what its priorities are, the GLEB does demonstrate that there is the potential in institutions of higher education and in local communities for producing socially and commercially useful new products, and hence jobs, provided some catalyst brings them together.

Company Networks

Networks between company headquarters and their branches or subsidiaries are well known, and networks linking firms with each other, or subcontractors with their customers, are developing quickly. Less familiar, however, is the practice of turning a conventional company into a network, as Rank-Xerox has done.

Faced with the prospect of considerable redundancies among staff familiar with information technology, Rank-Xerox hit upon the idea of creating a network of subcontractors. Ex-members of staff could set themselves up as individual companies, working from home with microcomputers and terminals supplied by the company. The company would offer them a contract for up to half their time, the rest depending on their own initiative. Work would be paid for on the basis of a fee for work done, not by a salary or a wage which would endanger the self-employed status of the subcontractors, who became known as intrapreneurs. Rank-Xerox also established a support association, Xanadu, which offered information on business possibilities and counselled its members on the skills they required. It also arranged bulk purchasing of equipment and stationery, and has established neighbourhood offices able to double as social centres where intrapreneurs could meet.

Being an intrapreneur can be a lonely business. Another firm involved with new technology, the Control Data Corporation, established a system under which people worked from home rather than in a central office. Their homes, equipped with data terminals and linked to the company, became known as 'electronic cottages'. It was soon discovered that the workers disliked their isolation. Work after all is not just a way of making a living. It is an important social activity which enables people to meet one another and for many is an essential element in a full and satisfying life.

On the other hand, intrapreneurship, also known as networking, can give ordinary individuals an unusual degree of control over their own lives. Intrapreneurs can decide when they work during the day or the week, to suit their own personal and family requirements. They can decide how hard they work – intensively for short periods or in a more relaxed way for longer. They can combine earning with caring for children or elderly relatives, which may prove a boon to married women, though it could lead to them overworking just because the problems of fitting work into formal patterns of office hours and a particular place have been overcome. The hassle and expense of commuting can be avoided, and intrapreneurs can travel at less congested times of day. Those who are disabled or housebound can also work if they are able and want to. The decline in the cost of microcomputers and terminals linked to mainframes now makes networking relatively inexpensive.

Rank-Xerox argues that because it makes substantial savings on office costs it can afford to employ more intrapreneurs than it could traditional office workers. The salary of an office worker might average £10,000 a year, but the actual cost to the firm would be almost three times as much. Nearly a third of this would be the cost of office space in a central location, and 15–20 per cent would be non-wage costs like national insurance and pension contributions.

There, of course, is the rub. Intrapreneurs do not enjoy the security of occupational pensions and unemployment benefit. In law, they are self-employed workers. Provision for their old age, sickness or other hazards of life has to come from their own pockets. Intrapreneurs will be attractive to many firms because of the large savings on overheads, but it is a system that could undermine the present structure of the welfare state.

However, being an intrapreneur suits a lot of people, especially those who like to control their own time. As many as 29 per cent of all workers may be working from home by the end of the century, although if they do houses are likely to have to be altered or redesigned. Because of the desire for social intercourse, more people are likely to work from neighbourhood offices linked to a small headquarters by fast interactive systems than from home. Only staff whose physical presence is essential, like those dealing directly with the public, will remain in the head office, if there is a head office at all. The great office blocks still being built in our cities may prove to be dinosaurs, doomed to early obsolescence in an age of networks.

Networking, intrapreneurship and working from home will change the distribution of population and bring about new patterns of living.

People living in rural areas will be able to keep in touch with their firms through interactive communication networks. Distance from work will no longer determine local labour markets.

Flexible Working

The wide acceptance of the flexible day, known as flexitime, in which people work four or five core hours but are then free to determine when they work, has already brought about an improvement in the quality of life for many people, enabling them to avoid travelling in rush hours or having to shop at the most crowded times of day. It has also led to experiments in flexible working weeks and flexible working years. The concept is the same: the employee contracts to undertake a certain number of hours of work, but the exact way in which that contract is discharged can be negotiated to suit the mutual requirements of employer and employee. In certain industries and services for which there is a seasonal pattern of demand, the flexible year can offer an elegant solution, a positive sum game from which everyone benefits.

Less Work, More Jobs

Shorter hours or shorter working lives are often believed to be panaceas for unemployment. If there is not enough work to go round, sharing it out by shorter hours appears to be the answer. In Chapter Three I described some work-sharing schemes, though they were intended only to tide firms and their workers over temporary difficulties. If unemployment is long term, why not share work out by reducing working hours drastically?

There has been a steady decline in weekly, annual and lifetime hours of work over the last century, partly offset by a longer life expectation and a greater involvement of women in formal paid work. This gradual decline is continuing; for instance, cuts in the basic working week below forty hours have been made law in France. In the Federal Republic of Germany reductions in hours were brought about by an arbitration agreement in 1984 which ended the prolonged metal workers' strike. A reduction more drastic than an hour or so a week is necessary if extra jobs are to be created. The one hour a week reduction in France in 1982 produced only a few thousand additional jobs. An Austrian plan which aimed to maintain full employment while encouraging the use of new technologies proposed a reduction of one sixth in weekly hours worked, from forty-two to thirty-five.[2]

The snag is, of course, that wages can decline. Trade unions will insist that there is no loss of pay when hours are reduced. In that case, unit costs of production will increase, making many products uncompetitive with those of their overseas competitors. Employees are unlikely to accept large reductions in income. Even if they do, the point of the whole exercise – to reduce unemployment – may be gainsaid by those who are already employed taking second jobs to maintain their incomes. Laws to stop moonlighting or the taking of second jobs are notoriously difficult to enforce.

There are opportunities for beneficial trade-offs all the same. Let me take seasonal industries. The car industry has a highly seasonal pattern of demand: people like to buy the new designs early, and trade then falls off over the year. Fashion is another highly seasonal industry, with heavy demand in the spring and autumn and low demand between those peak periods. Retailing peaks at Christmas-time and during the summer, but is low in between. Flexible contracts that allow longer hours during peak periods and shorter hours when demand is low enable employees to have more leisure, and employers to keep costs of overtime down. In a large work-force, it becomes possible to fit in periods of education leave or retraining courses. There are also prospects for additional jobs, since some employees will be hoping to trade more time off for less pay. Flexible hours and flexible working lives mean that employees are no longer faced with a choice between a full-time, forty hours a week job or nothing. There are many people who want to work a twenty- or thirty-hour week.

One central obstacle has to be faced: the rigid structure of social security systems. Pension and insurance rights are tied to a statutory minimum of hours, weeks and years of work because they are paid on the basis of contributions made by employees. This is not the place to embark on a discussion of how the welfare state should be reformed. But a more flexible system based on partial contributions, or financed by taxes, is an essential prerequisite of creating jobs through shorter hours and shorter working lives.

Pessimists and Optimists

Sharing out limited work is the pessimist's answer to structural unemployment. Creating new jobs through small business and publicly financed economic reconstruction, while encouraging new products and services, is the optimist's answer. Both depend upon changes in the institutions of Western societies, because those institutions are not responding adequately to the needs of the new technological revolution. The new technologies need adaptable people with multiple skills. The training and education systems and the trade unions have been slow to respond. To be used for the benefit of human beings, the new technological epoch will require men and women who have an understanding of the humanities and social sciences as well as numeracy and a grasp of scientific method. The education systems of most Western countries still divide culture between the arts and humanities on one side, science and engineering on the other. To flourish, the new technologies need to be nourished by a free and abundant flow of information. Indeed, the freedom of information flow may be the single greatest asset of the democracies in the new epoch; the command economies of the Soviet bloc will face a painful dilemma between loosening the governments' iron grip on information or falling badly behind in the new information-based industries. The Soviet Union does not permit its citizens to buy personal microcomputers for private use, and keeps tight control over computers, printers and even photocopying machines in schools, colleges and other public places. The dilemma, however, does not confront the Soviet bloc alone. It also faces some Western European countries which have long histories of controlling official information.

Political institutions are closely involved in the control of information, so they too are bound to be affected by technologies for handling and processing it. The reactions and attitudes of politicians and officials will help to determine the speed of adoption of the new technologies. But the flow of ideas and decisions will not be one-way. Technological developments will have profound consequences for the future of politics, in the democracies as well as in the dictatorships and monolithic states. The last section of this book is concerned with these institutional changes, which will be decisive for the health and happiness of our societies, and for the prospects of those who want jobs.

13 The Bootstrap Economy

'Local enterprise trusts are a means of achieving business development and job creation within a local area by drawing together the resources of the business community and the public authorities.'

The Scottish Development Agency, 1983

The exponential rate of growth of local enterprise trusts and other local employment initiatives creates its own problems. The greatest difficulty is to get sustained and continuing financial support for trusts already in being, as distinct from getting help to start a new trust, which often attracts local publicity and much goodwill. The limited number of companies which initiated the local enterprise movement face increasing demands both for finance and for the secondment of able people, and these demands are outstripping their capacity. The body that represents them, Business in the Community, tries to broaden the range of established firms willing to offer support.

In France, where locally based *boutiques de gestion* are also spreading fast (there were sixty-four of these in mid-1985), financing is arranged differently. Local agencies pay 1 per cent of their turnover each year to the national liaison committee, and can only receive public money if they belong to it. Contracts are then concluded between the government or regional public authorities on the one side, and the agencies on the other. Each agency has a board of directors drawn from elected officials, local business people and professional men and women; initial advice is free, but subsequent advice is charged for. The system is more formal than in Britain, perhaps necessarily so since it receives much more public finance.

Small Business and High Technology

In the United States, state governments have come to play an increasingly important role in employment creation and job-saving. Typically, the American states have accepted a responsibility for economic development, which takes the form of trying to attract industries by publicity and a variety of other incentives. In the last five years, high-technology industries have become magnets for states concerned about job losses or about low levels of income. Both non-industrialized states and old industrial states have pursued high-technology companies with a range of incentives, including seed money for new ventures and collaboration on research and development with local universities and colleges. The United States Office of Technology Assessment (OTA) identified thirty-eight separate programmes in twenty-two states specifically dedicated to creating, attracting or retaining high-technology companies, many of them programmes launched within the three years preceding publication of its report in 1984.

As in the case of the British and French local employment initiatives, the states made public money available to businesses that had newly been attracted to them or were just starting up. Financial assistance was available in half the programmes studied by the OTA, mainly taking the form of loan guarantees or help in raising venture capital, sometimes by providing a first initial launching fund. Training programmes, organized in partnership with the private sector, or by the making of grants to training agencies, were another favoured form of state assistance, applying to about a third of the schemes surveyed. In a number of cases, state universities were involved in fostering new high-technology businesses, often but not always by their own graduates or faculty.

Two states, California and Massachusetts, have been the bell-wethers of high technology. In neither state is a high proportion of the work-force employed in manufacturing. In 1980 just under a fifth of California's work-force was so employed; in Massachusetts, 26 per cent. Yet both states were far ahead of all the others in respect of the proportion of manufacturing workers employed in high technology – 30 per cent in California, an amazing 34.8 per cent in Massachusetts. The magic of Silicon Valley and of Route 128, those eldorados of high tech, continued to excite a generation or more after they became well known.

These states and others mainly on the eastern seaboard have been joined by states faced with problems of serious job loss, in particular the old industrial states of the Midwest, like Indiana, Michigan and Ohio, which are now looking hopefully to the new technologies. These old industrial states have much lower proportions of their work-forces involved in high-tech industries. The old industries and the new do not coexist happily.

However, the decision of the old industrial states to shift towards new-technology industries is certainly the correct one. During the 1978–80 recession, the states which had supported programmes for high technology established over several years suffered considerably less from loss of jobs than those without such programmes. Indeed their gains in high-technology jobs, 9·5 per cent over the two years, more than exceeded the loss in ordinary manufacturing jobs. The traditional industrial states were less fortunate, losing 7·6 per cent of their manufacturing jobs and then seeing a decline in high-technology jobs of over 4 per cent. Some of the high-tech firms had moved to states where the administrations were more friendly.

The United States, supposedly the great example of the free market, is more of a mixed economy than some suppose. The Federal Government has had little to do with promoting employment, but the states have been very active. According to the 1983 report of the National Governors' Association, 'the real and effective initiative for economic development and for the provision of jobs is shifting from the federal government to the states'. At the state level, the partnership between the private and public sectors is alive and well in the United States too. The retreat of the Federal Government does not mark any real fading away of the public sector's influence, but rather a shift in the level at which it operates.

In another respect, American state governments and European governments share a common attitude, indeed in this instance a common prejudice. Both believe that there is something special about manufacturing industry. High tech is an acceptable industry for job creation because it has glamour, yet is about wealth creation and making things. European governments usually limit their capital allowances and other assistance schemes only to manufacturing industry, or occasionally to industry-related services as well. The American states behave in exactly the same way. Of the sixteen states with dedicated high-tech programmes that were studied in depth by the OTA, ten specifically targeted manufacturing industry, eight research and development, and only three were prepared to consider service industries at all.[1]

Local Politics

Local authorities are of course political entities, and this may colour their approach. In American states an initiative started by a governor of one party (and many of the high-technology initiatives are started by governors) may be unacceptable to a successor of another party who may feel obliged to start all over again. In Britain the Greater London Enterprise Board, sponsored by the ideologically active Labour authority, the Greater London Council, gave priority to workers' cooperatives, specifically those started by women or members of ethnic minorities. In some local enterprise trusts, elected councillors have sought a majority of the seats, against resistance from representatives of the private sector. In the United States, city administrations, which play a useful subsidiary role in local employment initiatives, sometimes look more favourably on proposals from community-based organizations that are friendly towards the ruling party. Development agencies may have to walk a delicate line between national government and state or local government where their political views collide. But on the whole local employment initiatives have not been shaped or scarred by politics. Partnership between the public and private sectors has been their salient characteristic, and they have worked well. The movement, however, is still in its infancy; it is too soon to predict how it may develop.

The lesson that local initiatives are beneficial is being learned by central government agencies as well as by the private sector. Development agencies now spend their public money much more thoughtfully than they once did, working closely with local communities and often with private enterprise as well. One example is the venture capital finance company jointly established by the privately owned Bank of Scotland and the Scottish Development Agency (SDA). A good rural example is that of the Highlands and Islands Development Board, which used counterpart funds, a pound of local money being matched by a pound of public money, to establish new industries and cooperatives in the north of Scotland, including knitwear, fish-farming and other productive small-scale activities. Cooperatives established in this way have not only kept many remote villages and crofts alive, but have also reversed the population drift into the cities and south of the border.

Inner cities are not physically remote, but they are often isolated from the mainstream of society. Private sector businesses are reluctant to establish themselves in areas with run-down housing or high crime rates. But one very successful American project was the Bedford/Stuyvesant scheme in Brooklyn, New York, intended to show how a depressed inner city neighbourhood can be economically rejuvenated. The scheme was run by a community-based organization headed by Frank Thomas, now head of the Ford Foundation, and was financed partly by Federal funds and partly by private sector finance as a result of participation by the Wall Street financial community. IBM established an assembly plant in the locality, which is still flourishing.

The success of the Bedford/Stuyvesant scheme, originally proposed in 1965 by Senator Robert Kennedy as a model, led to community development programmes being established in some seventy cities, backed by federal finance for administration and launch capital.

In Watts, California, another community organization succeeded in getting development going, creating some 500 permanent jobs in the inner city, and twice as many training places. Experience showed that the commitment of private sector finance was crucial. Without such a commitment the results were patchy. The Federal legislation, Title VII of the Economic Opportunity Act, has now been repealed, and the local community action programmes that replaced it are threatened with the loss of the block grants on which they depend.

In some big West German cities, like Berlin, groups committed to alternative life-styles and to conserving the environment have set up self-managed enterprises which carry out social welfare work, or recycle waste, or clean up the neighbourhood. Often they receive some funding from city or *Land* authorities. Partnership between voluntary agencies and the local community is becoming a reality, just like the partnership with private companies.

Private Industry Councils

Private Industry Councils, which resemble Britain's Business in the Community, were started in 1978 with encouragement from the United States Federal Government specifically to address the persistent sore of black youth unemployment in the United States. They were designed to organize private sector participation in training, federally funded at that time through the CETA programme. Unemployment among young black men and women has been for many years two or three times higher than white youth unemployment, and that has itself been twice or more that of adults. Figures of 60 or even 70 per cent unemployment among 16–21-year-olds are not unknown in the black ghettoes of big American cities. Clearly, in an economy dominated by the private sector, that sector has to help find solutions. Private industry councils usually work closely with the city and state authorities; under the Job Training Partnership Act of 1982 their status is equal to that of city and state officials in the design and implementation of training programmes for disadvantaged young people and adults. One of their main objectives is to encourage black youngsters to graduate from high school and not to drop out before graduation as many do. So they pledge themselves to provide summer jobs and sometimes part-time work all through the year. In cities like Boston and Baltimore, firms commit themselves to employing a certain number of youngsters each year who must attend school regularly until they graduate, and who must also complete their work and training programmes.

Private Industry Councils, one Baltimore businesswoman told me, were the alternative to having one's business burned down. Whatever her motivation may have been, Private Industry Councils have committed themselves to the health and prosperity of their own communities. They are another sign of the third sector's vigour.

Decentralizing Power

Central governments have in the past regarded economic development as being one of their primary responsibilities. Large sums of money have been spent on regional policies or to prop up ailing industries. There is still a place for such policies, especially in the poorest areas, provided they are carefully devised and targeted towards the creation of jobs, and are more than prestige projects intended to confer political benefits on the government that authorizes them.

The dilemma for central governments is how they deal with the new bootstrap economy of local employment initiatives. Public money is an important factor in getting new local enterprises off the ground, but it is public money in small amounts to launch and sustain them rather than long-term subsidies. Interference by central government is damaging, whether it takes the form of regulation or restriction. The political complement of the third sector in the economy is the decentralization of decision-making. Regional and local agencies must have a degree of autonomy to enable them to address themselves to local problems and to work together with the private sector. The power to raise funds locally, through local income taxes as well as property taxes or rates, is an important element of local autonomy. Property taxes are a heavy burden on local enterprises, especially on those that are growing fast. Local income taxes do not have the same disincentive effect.

More important even than the ways of raising local finance is the principle of decentralization itself. Central governments fail to learn the lesson that they can destroy initiative and innovation by their own heavy-handedness. The United States Federal Government has retreated, and the states have stepped into the gap. In Britain, on the other hand, central government has become highly interventionist, restricting what local governments are permitted to do and imposing heavy penalties on those which fail to conform. It is a policy of central control that flies in the face of the new trends in advanced economies. Yet the record of regional policies conducted by central government does not bear out the belief that central government knows best.

14 Regional Policy

'The traditional response of regions and localities suffering from a lack of job opportunities has been to try to create employment by offering incentives to private enterprise or to seek to influence the location of public sector employment. This approach has had to be modified because of the dearth of new private investment projects and the freezing of public sector expansion in most countries.'

Sir Douglas Wass, *Report of OECD Conference on Employment Growth in the Context of Structural Change*, February 1984

Regional policies have been pursued by governments since the war to attract firms to poor or backward regions. The instruments are many: automatic grants, selective grants, training courses tailored to the needs of an incoming firm and loans at subsidized interest rates. Recently, governments wedded to free market philosophies have produced new incentives, described in earlier chapters. Freeports and free enterprise zones have been created to attract new firms or those engaged in entrepôt trade or in assembling components for export.

These incentives have had considerable success in attracting footloose firms. Eire's Industrial Development Agency, for instance, with its generous capital allowances, attracted scores of multinational companies, some in electronics and electrical engineering. Sfadco, the development agency operating in the remote and poor counties in the west of Ireland near Shannon, built on Shannon's initial advantage – that until the 1960s aircraft had to stop there because they could not cross the Atlantic direct – by exploiting the creation in 1959 of a freeport, a customs-free zone.

The United Kingdom similarly offered capital allowances: an automatic 22 per cent grant on buildings, plant and machinery for industrial use in the development areas, to which selective help could be added. It is estimated that over the last twenty years, about 500,000 jobs were created in the poorer regions and countries of the United Kingdom. But even these new jobs failed to offset the decline in employment, both absolute and relative, in these poorer regions. Old industries shrank faster than new ones could be attracted.

There are some curious features about regional policy, if job creation is its main objective. As in most American states, grants have until recently only been made to manufacturing industry. They are not usually made to industry-related services, like software production, and certainly not to other services. Grants have been automatic, unrelated to the number of jobs created, so that capital-intensive firms like chemicals or petroleum have benefited most. There has been a strong emphasis on attracting big companies, especially prestigious multi-nationals; home-grown firms, particularly small ones, have been relatively neglected. And there has been little emphasis until recently on the regional environment – its natural attractions, its leisure facilities, its schools and services – because industry was not supposed to weigh such frivolous considerations in the balance.

Regional policy got what it bargained for: big, traditional, capital-intensive plants. In some regions, like North-east England, three quarters of the total public funds available went to firms of that kind. Financial incentives were dangled before the big fish, such as car companies like Ford or Nissan. Countries outbid one another to attract them, as Belgium and Britain did in an attempt to land a new car engines plant in the late 1970s. The major beneficiaries were not the unemployed, but the shareholders of big companies. Over the last twenty years, an estimated twenty billion pounds has been spent by Britain alone in regional grants and assistance, creating at current prices half a million jobs at a staggering £30,000 to £40,000 per job. The figure in other countries, like Eire, was somewhat lower, but not much. Regional policy created jobs expensively.

Small firm developments have proved that jobs can be created for much less. In the 1960s and 1970s British Steel Industries created permanent jobs for as little as £1,000 a job, and many local enterprise trusts show similar figures. Even industries using quite sophisticated plant and machinery, like civil engineering, can create some new jobs for less than £10,000, and the figure for house repair or renovations, because the work is so labour-intensive, is considerably lower.

It can be argued that the regions should not be expected to create badly paid low-level jobs, but no conditions have been laid down in regional policies about the kinds of jobs to be created. It might be sensible to pay grants related not only to the number of jobs, but also to their quality and level of skill, in order to attract and keep highly skilled people. Poor regions will not break out of their relative poverty unless they move towards industries with high added value which can offer good jobs to qualified people.

Japanese Industry Moves Out

In Japan, the upsurge of modern industry in the last twenty-five years has occurred in the big cities. Rural areas, with land that is difficult to cultivate and few natural resources, have fallen behind. Educated young people, unable to find jobs in which they could use their new qualifications, moved to the cities. But the pressure of population and the speed of industrial development have destroyed the urban environment; Tokyo is a city deprived of open space, parks and places for children to play. Streets became congested with traffic and the air polluted by fumes. So those who could afford to do so began to move back to the countryside. So did new and mobile industries; in 1977, the trend for industry to move into the major cities reversed itself, and firms increasingly established plants in the regions. The number rose from 1,278 in 1977 to 2,088 in 1981. More important, the trend was particularly marked among high-technology industries like pharmaceuticals, telecommunications and electronics. From a low point of only sixty-eight such plants established in the regions in 1977, the number jumped to 249 in 1981.

MITI was not slow to perceive this trend, nor the desire of many Japanese to move into – or back to – more attractive environments. But if they were to do so, the regions needed to be able to offer a wide range of jobs. The movement of high-technology and high-added-value establishments should be sustained and encouraged.

In 1980, MITI, together with leading firms and representatives of local government, came up with a plan for creating 'Technopolises' in the regions, built around high-technology industries together with research and development in the regions' own universities and research institutes. Such schemes are not new in the domain of regional policy. Most industrial countries with any kind of regional policy are trying to build links between educational institutions and industry, and to attract high-technology firms. The difference, as so often with Japan, lay in the shared commitment of government, local government and private industry to the achievement of the Technopolis concept. The heart of that concept was a new industrial structure, embodying high-technology industries, the development of human resources and the preservation of the natural environment.

By 1983, nineteen sites had been identified as potential Technopolises, chosen because they had the essential requirements of access to rapid transport, a qualified labour force, proximity to related industries, a good basic infrastructure, and access to scientific and technical knowledge. The Government in the same year enacted legislation to provide tax incentives and subsidies for relocating firms and for the areas themselves.

The plans are ambitious. In a case study of three proposed Technopolises for the OECD, Yasuo Kuwahara, of the Japan Institute of Labour, estimated the potential for job creation. The first proposed Technopolis he describes is Sasebo in Nagasaki prefecture, a port previously heavily dependent on shipbuilding and coal-mining. At the centre of Sasebo's redevelopment will be the production of integrated circuits, already well established on the island of Kyushu. While the high-technology firms are expected to create only 4,620 new jobs by 1990 and 8,640 by 2000, local firms will be encouraged to supply intermediate goods, thus magnifying the multiplier effects of the new firms.

Throughout the development of Technopolises, local related industries are expected to supply parts and materials to the core high technology sector, as well as selling their own products in external markets. This pattern of development, if successfully achieved, will contribute to the independence of the local economy.[1]

In addition, construction of the Technopolis is expected to create directly and indirectly 33,200 jobs in 1983–90, and a further 36,800 in 1990–2000.

Kuwahara's second example, Nishi-Harima, near Osaka, is being built close to established heavy industries and will concentrate on advanced engineering including machine tools, and medical equipment including test facilities. Construction of the Technopolis will create 66,000 jobs and the high-technology industries themselves about 6,700. The indirect effect of the latter on local industries is expected to more than double the additional jobs once the Technopolis is completed, to a total of some 15,800 jobs. As with the other Technopolises, 'the local industrial structure will be transformed into one characterised by a higher value-added margin.'[2]

The Technopolis concept is not limited to Japan. In Scotland, the Scottish Development Agency has identified Dundee as a city ideally placed to be the centre of high-technology development. It has a complex of education institutions, including a university which produces nearly a quarter of Scotland's output of technologists and technicians. It has the necessary rapid transport links and is situated in beautiful countryside. It has already attracted several companies engaged in the manufacture of computers and electronic equipment. Public sector investment in Dundee between 1982 and 1986 will amount to £24 million, pledged from three sources: the Scottish Development Agency, Tayside Region and the district council. Private investment is estimated to be £16 million over the three years. As an additional incentive, parts of Dundee have been included in an enterprise zone.

Everywhere the lesson is the same. Regeneration of the regions will only happen if the industrial structure embraces new technologies with an emphasis on high value-added output. Given an objective shared by public agencies and private companies, it can be accomplished.

There is nothing new under the sun. Japan's Technopolises resemble in many ways Britain's New Towns, built on greenfield sites in the 1950s and 1960s, and attracting the advanced industries of those decades – engineering, printing, aerospace, scientific instruments and electronics. The New Towns proved to be centres of growth in their own regions, though most of the first group was built around London to relieve population pressures there. The New Towns in the North-east, the North-west and Scotland have more modern industrial patterns than old towns, and have indeed created jobs, many of them higher value-added jobs than those in traditional smokestack industries. Like Japan's Technopolises, the New Towns were born of a partnership between the public and private sectors. No more New Towns are being built, because of the demands they make on public expenditure; this indicates the difference between British and Japanese attitudes towards funding.

The Poorest Areas

It is difficult to see how the poorest and most remote areas can be revived without substantial public investment. In some localities the collapse of traditional industry and the associated deterioration of the infrastructure have gone so far that the local market is deeply depressed and there is little potential for private enterprise. Often it is the people with initiative or marketable skills that have moved out, and service firms associated with traditional industry have contracted or closed. Merseyside is such a region, a branch economy in which branches are still being closed, and net job loss has continued over many years. The environment has deteriorated, and is unattractive to firms looking for places to start up. Key workers are unlikely to want to move there.

Merseyside compares unfavourably with Scotland, which has succeeded in attracting high-technology plants by changing from its old image, that of 'Red Clydeside', a region of heavy industry and embittered industrial relations, to one of lovely countryside, plenty of leisure facilities and go-ahead modern industry. The Scottish Development Agency has concentrated on four new industrial areas: electronics, health care, energy-related technology and advanced engineering. It has also put a lot of effort into improving the local environment, the most impressive single project being the rehabilitation of the East End of Glasgow, the GEAR project.

Glasgow was notorious for having the worst slums in the whole of Britain, overcrowded stone tenements five and six storeys high. But the old tenements are solidly constructed in heavy stone blocks, and demolishing them would be very expensive. So, instead, much of the East End has been rehabilitated. The old stone tenements have been gutted and rebuilt inside; derelict sites have been turned into parks and gardens, or used for low-rise pleasantly designed houses and bungalows; an old factory building, the Templeton carpet factory, has been converted into a business centre containing workshops and offices. Throughout the East End the best has been saved and reused, the worst pulled down and replaced with human-scale buildings. People now want to live and work there. Private house-building is going on apace, with hundreds of houses completed and nearly two thousand planned. The East End, once Britain's worst slum, is now becoming increasingly fashionable.

It has been an expensive operation, costing nearly £200 million over six years; some £60 million have come from private companies (mainly house-builders and commercial property developers), the rest from central and local government. Private capital has been increasingly willing to move in as public investment has transformed the city's prospects; it is inconceivable that private capital would have gone to the East End before. As the environment changed, the East End became a neighbourhood capable of revival and growth.

Scotland has been Britain's regional success story. Even in the Highlands, strong on beauty but weak on employment opportunities, the outflow of population has been reversed. Indeed, the population of the Highlands has increased by nearly a fifth in the last twenty years. The

Highlands and Islands Development Board has created 16,000 jobs at an average cost of £10,000 per job, a remarkable achievement in a far-flung and thinly populated area. The efficiency and flair of the SDA and the Highlands and Islands Development Board have been an important factor in this success. But it is also the case that per capita public investment in Scotland has been the highest of all the regions of the UK, apart from Northern Ireland: over £1,100 per capita between 1971 and 1980, while the average for the whole UK during this period was £785.[3]

The revival of the poorest regions has to start with the infrastructure, and first of all with the rehabilitation of the local environment. Planners now realize that new roads built through spoilheaps and new factories in derelict industrial sites will not attract industry; nor will managers and technologists want to work in polluted air and grimy buildings. Next come communications – roads, ports, railways, telecommunications – then housing and industrial buildings. Some of these can be rehabilitated and refurbished, keeping the local characteristics of the region; others must be replaced, but in harmony with what is already there. Educational institutions are an essential part of the redevelopment of the infrastructure – to provide ideas for industry, to train workers and to develop new products.

Real Jobs at Low Cost

The construction and civil engineering industries – those most involved in infrastructure developments – are labour-intensive. A study by Cambridge Econometrics in 1981 estimated the capital investment per permanent job at £2,300 for civil engineering work and £3,400 for house-building at 1981 prices.[4] At 1985 values, the cost per job is less than a fifth of the estimated average cost of a job produced by regional policy incentives. That average is distorted by the requirement that grants must be made to manufacturing industry. Infrastructure development in the regions would create far more jobs for the same amount of public money.

Obviously no region can live on infrastructure alone, but once that has been improved, private sector companies are ready to move in. This is the lesson the Scottish Development Agency learned from GEAR; spend public money where only public money is available, and use it as a bait to draw private money in afterwards. The Scottish Development

Agency has successfully used the partnership between private and public sectors to reconstruct the Scottish economy and to transform it from one dependent on heavy, smokestack industries to one associated with electronics, biotechnology and an unspoiled natural environment.

The transformation is far from complete. Scotland's central belt still has areas of industrial blight, derelict mills and worn housing. Unemployment is above – though only just above – the national average. Nevertheless, the Scottish economy is clearly on the move; per capita GNP is now second only to that of the prosperous South-east of England. Such an achievement would have been unimaginable a generation ago. It testifies to what can be done when economic ideology is subordinated to a practical partnership between the private and public sectors.

The Scottish achievement owes a lot to the adaptability of the Scottish Development Agency, which has learned to live with governments of different political complexions by emphasizing and encouraging either its private or its public sector partners. England has no agency capable of bringing together vertically divided government departments into regional development teams. The poorer regions have suffered seriously in consequence, for national expenditure on regional development and on public investment in the infrastructure have been drastically reduced.

In the five years from 1976 to 1983, public investment fell both absolutely and proportionately in the seven largest OECD countries. This is surprising, for public works have traditionally been, since the days of Franklin Roosevelt, a favoured way of dealing with mass unemployment. In the United Kingdom, the drop was dramatic, from 5 per cent of gross national product in 1974 to 1·9 per cent in 1982. Employment in civil engineering alone fell by 60 per cent; home-building and house improvement, road-building and sewage system replacement were all cut back. The consequence is a large back-log of work to be done, and an increasing incidence of breakdown – crumbling drains, potholed roads, deteriorating houses. The fabric of the English regions is getting thin.

Conservation Makes Jobs

The present position is absurd. Work is not being done even where it would cost little more to employ people than to keep them unemployed, quite apart from the benefit to the community. Energy and water provide excellent examples. OECD calculations show that the ratio of energy costs to labour costs is now almost twice what it was before the oil price shocks of 1973 and 1979. In other words, it makes economic sense to substitute labour for energy. Conservation of energy by better control systems in homes and industry, and by insulating existing houses, uses a lot of labour, and saves energy. A well-insulated house can save more than a third of the energy a house with more limited insulation needs. If the house is specially designed to conserve energy and has a heat pump, the figure can rise to two thirds. The return on energy-conserving investment is well above that on industrial investment, and has the advantage not only of being labour-intensive but also of being import-saving.

In March 1985, a two-year public inquiry into the construction in Suffolk of the Sizewell B PWR (pressurized water reactor) came to an end. The reactor is intended to be the first of a new generation of nuclear power stations in Britain, each one costing over a billion pounds. While undoubtedly the construction of a nuclear power station would provide several thousand jobs during the construction period, the operation of such a station creates very few jobs indeed. Investment in conserving elsewhere the energy that the new power station is designed to provide would have created far more permanent jobs and would avoid adding to nuclear wastes. However, energy conservation is still not treated as a serious alternative to energy supply. It is one more example of a blinkered attitude inherited from the age of the Industrial Revolution.

Water, looked upon as a free gift, is becoming more expensive and scarce. In Britain a considerable price is paid for the leaks in the system, which account for between 25 and 30 per cent of main water supplies. While reservoir construction continues, often against fierce opposition from environmental lobbies, water conservation is not taken seriously. Reconstruction of parts of the water and sewage system is now becoming urgent. Apart from leaks, the cost of sewage system collapses in traffic disruption and disturbance to business can be very substantial indeed, four or five times the expense involved in repairing the broken pipes. New water mains and sewage systems can be built to incorporate new technologies, such as closed-circuit television inspection systems, which give advance notice of potential collapses. Sophisticated waste treatment systems can be introduced as well. As for water use, the House of Lords Select Committee on Employment in its 1982 report proposed that lavatory cisterns be converted to a dual flush system, which would save water and employ much more labour than building a new reservoir to meet the demands of wasteful water use.

Unfortunately, neither energy nor water conservation rate as prestige projects. Governments are much more willing to spend money on attracting automobile companies by investment allowances, or on subsidizing aluminium refineries and petrochemical complexes, than on such humble activities as conservation. The irony is that these expensive projects, which are launched in the name of creating jobs, often create little work, but a great deal of scepticism about the price of job creation schemes.

Public investment in the infrastructure, however, can create jobs at low cost. If the projects are carefully chosen, employment can be maximized for any given investment. House improvement and modernization is particularly labour-intensive. Neighbourhood plans to improve whole areas at a time minimize the cost, and can be combined with insulation and water conservation in a single renovation programme. The local environment and the employment prospects of poor localities would be transformed and so would the potential for attracting new firms, some of them finding a market by supplying the builders and conservers.

What has happened instead has been the use of the construction industry as an economic regulator. Carrots and sticks replace one another with bewildering speed. In Britain, for instance, home improvement grants were raised in 1983, an election year, and reduced in 1984, with an estimated loss of 10,000 jobs. The cost of unemployment benefit for the redundant workers was broadly the same as the savings from the reduction in house improvement grants.

Counter-cyclical public investment is one proven way of offsetting the consequences of a recession. Western European governments now reduce public investment during a recession, thereby aggravating its effects. But the passage of time cannot be stopped. The economic fabric becomes older and weaker; it tears and then disintegrates. Eventually it has to be replaced.

The Lessons

There is no simple single solution to the persistent problem of unemployment in Western Europe. No wand can be waved to provide jobs for everyone. But that does not mean nothing can be done. In the first part of this book, I have tried to show that a great deal can be accomplished to create permanent jobs which will enhance and enrich the community.

Dependence on large firms, made even larger by mergers and take-overs, and prestige projects partly financed by public money character-ized the approach of governments in the 1960s and early 1970s. The waste of public money and the failure to make a major impact on regional unemployment gave these policies a bad name, and went a long way to sour attitudes towards any use of public expenditure to stimulate growth or create jobs. The reaction, however, was as unreasonable as the policies were misjudged. Public investment is essential to regenerate old industrial areas or inner-city slums, for private capital cannot get an adequate return. As Scotland has shown, private capital will come in once the local environment has been improved, and its contribution should be welcomed. At the other end of the spectrum, small businesses in the private sector offer promising opportunities for job generation, but again much depends on the support available from local authorities, educational institutions and the banks. Seed-money for innovations from public sources, loan guarantees and subsidized interest rates for the initial start-up period create a climate in which new businesses can establish themselves. In the United States, many new companies start as spin-offs from existing large companies; this occurs only rarely in Europe, and the ethos of large companies does not favour it. Therefore other ways to stimulate the formation of new companies must be found. The experience of Inmos and Celltech in the United Kingdom, and of new product development in Japan, indicates that the public sector can play a crucial role in providing risk capital, or guaranteeing private sector sources against loss. The image of a vigorous risk-taking private sector is at odds with the reality of cautious institutionalized finance markets, in which young firms find it difficult to raise capital.

The economy is not a homogeneous market, but consists of a number of sectors in which different factors operate. As the Japanese have discovered, that part of the economy which is involved in international trade must be highly competitive, and cannot afford to carry unnecessary manpower or to use obsolete equipment. Some industries, however, operate in local markets, like many house-builders and providers of small-scale services. Service industries can operate on a large scale, like transport or health services, but they do not compete, except at the margin, with similar industries in other countries. To apply the same policies to all sectors indiscriminately means either an inefficient internationally traded sector, or much higher unemployment in locally traded sectors than would otherwise occur. It is foolish to protect or featherbed internationally traded manufacturing or service companies; they become uncompetitive and lose markets. However, public investment in locally traded industries and services in decaying regions is a very different proposition. Such regions have no chance to compete until they have been brought up to the starting line. The legacy of the industrial past has to be borne by the whole national community, and not by the regions on their own.

I have tried to show in the preceding chapters some of the ways in which unemployment can be tackled:

1. At the macroeconomic level, by fiscal policies that stimulate those European economies or sectors within them where unused capacity and unemployment are high. That means ceasing to reduce public borrowing as a proportion of gross national product.

2. By greater public investment in the infrastructure, particularly in regions where environmental rehabilitation and house-building and repair provide opportunities for low-cost jobs.

3. By giving a much higher priority to the conservation of energy, land and water, where savings on resources meet the cost of job creation over a relatively short period.

4. By encouraging the formation of new small companies and the expansion of existing small and medium-sized companies through changes in public purchasing; matchmaking to meet the requirements of large private companies; advice and support through local enterprise trusts; and packages combining public and private sources of finance.

5. By responsive education and training to meet the great and growing demand for advanced and flexible skills.

6. By evolving a cooperative basis for industrial relations based on participation and profit-sharing, instead of the adversarial attitudes of the first industrial revolution from which demarcation disputes, resistance to skill-training for adults, control over entry, inflexibility on wages and autocratic managements have derived.

7. By using employment insurance and other forms of income maintenance to put people back to work; guaranteeing jobs in community schemes; combining shared starter-jobs with training; using funds to retrain redundant workers in new skills; and setting unemployed people up in their own businesses.

None of these approaches to job generation is precluded by the coming of the new technologies, but all have to take them into account. The new technologies will not only change the pattern of employment in the services and professions as well as in manufacturing; they will also alter existing institutions, from work-places to schools, from the family to government, indeed the democratic system itself. It is to those changes that I now turn.

PART II

A NEW EPOCH

'The open society, the unrestricted access to knowledge, the unplanned and uninhibited association of men for its furtherance – these are what may make a vast, complex, ever growing, ever changing, ever more specialized and expert technological world, nevertheless a world of human community.'

J. Robert Oppenheimer, *Science and the Common Understanding*, (1953)

15 The Skills Crisis

'Our principal concern is that we are aware from our experience that there are very serious shortages of certain high technology skills. These shortages are getting worse. Unless the problem is solved, new technology developments in the UK will be very seriously impaired.'

Submission by fourteen manufacturing companies to the UK Government, June 1984

Everywhere countries are clamouring for new-technology skills. The United States has estimated that it will need 132,000 more graduates in electronics in 1990, whilst Britain was reckoned to be short of 25,000 people with information technology (IT) skills as long ago as 1978.[1] There is fierce competition in Japan for every graduate in engineering from a good university. Internationally as well as nationally, the shortage of high-technology skills is acute. The demand is not only for the highest skills, the systems and knowledge engineers working at the frontiers of innovation; there is also a strong market for technicians and for people with the capacity to undertake high-quality, sophisticated maintenance, to program robots and keep them running, to service the multiplying number of home information systems.

The British skills shortage is particularly severe. In June 1984, fourteen leading manufacturing companies sent a memorandum to the Government drawing attention to the 'very serious shortages of certain high technology skills'. The fourteen firms, all of them anxious to maintain their positions in highly competitive international markets, were right to be worried. The number of home students taking first degrees in engineering and technology in British universities has actually declined since 1982, and the number of postgraduates has fallen steeply, though there has been a very small increase in students seeking first degrees in these subjects at the polytechnics. The same depressing trend holds for less elevated qualifications too. There has been a decline in the number of technicians qualifying in subjects bearing upon information technology. As for engineering apprentices, the drop in their numbers has been spectacular.

The shortages, detailed below, are serious and almost certainly understated in the statistics. What is even more disturbing is the complacent unawareness in Britain of how much relevant skills matter. British management has notoriously neglected the development of its human capital. Managers have been bent on getting rid of labour rather than on getting full value from their employees. Trade unions have defended time-served apprenticeships as a way of limiting entry to skilled trades, as if the balance between the market for skilled and unskilled people was established for all time many decades ago. These attitudes stand in the way of a modern Britain that can exploit the high quality of its science and the originality of its inventors by moving technologically up-market. The high-technology industries and services are the very ones that need flexible up-to-date skills. For lack of such skills, and given the prevailing apathy towards training, Britain is sadly likely to settle instead for lower real wages and low-tech jobs in a declining economy.

For once, government does not deserve the lion's share of the blame. Industrial training boards were established for the major industries in 1964. They had the power to levy firms for training costs, and to repay with grants those firms that undertook training of a satisfactory standard. There was grumbling in industry about the levy, and the costs of administering the levy/grant system. Firms with good training records demanded exemption, on the grounds that an unnecessary administrative expense was incurred if they were included. As the recession deepened, the pressure to relieve industry of optional economic burdens grew. In 1982, the Government acceded to that pressure, and abolished all but six of the Industrial Training Boards, together with the compulsory grant/levy system. Since then, training in industry, especially of apprentices, has deteriorated further. The Youth Training Scheme, while it meets the need of school-leavers for basic training in life and work skills, is no substitute for the on-the-job skill-training of young people that has now largely disappeared.

The shortage of people with appropriate skills is the most significant obstacle to the adoption and progress of information technologies, as a recent comparative study of manufacturing in the United Kingdom, West Germany and France has shown. In all three countries, a large number of the establishments surveyed gave lack of specialist technical expertise as their main difficulty – 55 per cent of the respondents in West Germany, 51 per cent in France and 45 per cent in Britain.[2] The reason the proportion of British firms so responding was lower than in the other countries was not because skills in Britain are in readier supply. On the contrary, Britain has fewer professional engineers with microelectronics experience than West Germany. The reason was the presence of another factor vying for first place: lack of demand. Inadequate demand for their firms' products counted for much less in France and West Germany.

The Department of Trade and Industry's committee on skills shortages, the Butcher Committee, whose first report was published in 1984, quoted an estimate by the official body responsible for advancing information technology, the Alvey Directorate, that the shortage of professional engineers in information technology was 1,500 in 1984, and would rise to 5,000 by 1987–8. If information technology is defined as those firms manufacturing microelectronic hardware and software, the figure may be correct, but as a guide to the current shortage of skills it is highly misleading.

The PSI Survey of microelectronics in European industry quoted above asked sample firms how many qualified engineers with microelectronics expertise they now employed, and how many they would like to employ. British product-users employed 2,866 engineers and wanted 3,870; British process-users had 2,051 and wanted 2,827. Grossed up from the sample to an estimate for the whole of British manufacturing industry, the figures were calculated as 22,000 engineers currently employed by product users and 24,000 by process users, compared to 31,000 needed for the former and 36,000 for the latter, a current shortfall of 21,000.

Even this figure seriously underestimates the need for qualified people with IT skills, for it includes no figure for the services. As the services too adopt information technology, industries like transport, retail distribution and banking will need highly skilled maintenance staff, system designers, software writers and knowledge engineers. Given that manufacturing accounts for only one fifth and services for three fifths of employment, the shortfall of people with information technology and engineering skills is probably between 60,000 and 80,000.

Lack of highly skilled people means fewer jobs for those with lesser skills. An unpublished survey from Imperial College of software firms describes this ricochet effect: 'It was several times remarked that although shortages of the relatively simple skills were not at present acute, this was partly due to the lack of more skilled people to provide the work. Each highly skilled engineer would be expected to generate several jobs at lower skill levels to support him.'[3] There is an indirect negative effect on employment as well as a direct one.

Countries that fall behind in the competition for IT hardware and software are driven to import them. Europe has become a significant importer of IT products. For Britain alone, the balance of trade deficit in information technology was £2 billion in 1983, exceeding the surplus earned by the rest of the engineering industry. As Table 3 shows, Britain has been successfully exporting engineering products that do not require high-technology skills. It has been lagging behind in the new, high value-added area, and particularly in electronic equipment. The table clearly charts the decline of a great manufacturing country.

Table 3: The UK Engineering Industry: Balance of Trade, 1984 (whole year)

	Exports minus imports (£ million)
Metal goods	−153
Mechanical engineering	+1,965
Electronics	−2,238
Electrical engineering (less electronics)	−210
Vehicles	−2,092
Aerospace	+869
Instruments	−272
Total engineering	−2,131

Source: Department of Trade and Industry, April 1985

We can precisely gauge the correlated decline in the supply of skills. In 1982, 2,955 young people graduated in electrical engineering (which includes electronics) with a first degree, 322 with a higher degree. There were 4,395 first degrees in mathematics or computer science, and 2,266 graduates qualified in physics. The numbers graduating in all these subjects decline from 1984 on. This is because the swingeing cuts in university funding made in 1981, in real terms amounting to 15 per cent, did not spare engineering and technology. Indeed, Britain's newly established technological universities were hit hardest, two of them, Aston and Salford, sustaining cuts of over 30 per cent. Faced with Government insistence that the cuts be made over a period of only three years, the universities had to move fast. So they cut both student numbers and faculty, and could not exempt the more expensive departments of science and technology.

The number of university students studying for first degrees in engineering and technology were fewer in 1982–3 than the year before by 1·2 per cent, with a corresponding figure for the arts of 2·8 per cent. That may seem a modest decline but the trend is unmistakable and is continuing. For postgraduates, those capable of the kind of advanced research that Japan is doing on the fifth-generation computer and in biotechnology, the decline has been much faster and more pronounced, and has gone on longer. There were fewer postgraduate students of engineering and technology in Britain in 1982–3 than there had been in 1972–3, and 10 per cent fewer than in 1977–8. Of this small number, over half the technology and engineering postgraduates came from overseas. In mathematics and physics, numbers were also down.

This disturbing story of an education and training system producing fewer skilled people, not more, as Britain is swept into an age of information technology, is repeated at every level.

Technicians are the field officers of the new technology, vital to its programming, maintenance and effective operation. Table 4 shows what happened to them in the five years 1979/80 to 1983/4.

The leaps and bounds of the late 1970s and early 1980s petered out in the recession. The paradox is that any sustained recovery now would be choked off by skill shortages. Firms accounting for 21 per cent of the jobs in Britain's office machinery and data processing equipment industries recently gave skill shortages as a 'major factor' limiting output.[4] Since the number of technicians in office equipment had fallen by half since 1978, and had even fallen slightly in electronic data processing equipment, the phrase 'a major factor' was a truly British piece of understatement. Scientists and technologists in the electronics industry, whose numbers increased by 45 per cent between 1978 and 1983, cannot be efficiently used if there are not enough technicians to go round. Yet the number employed hardly changed in those five years.

Apprenticeship

The traditional skilled man in engineering, and it is almost always a man, not a woman, is the craftsman. He is usually, though not always, trained through a long and thorough apprenticeship. The apprenticeship system has prevailed in Britain ever since the Statute of Artificers of 1593, and traditionally apprentices have to 'serve their time', that is, complete a certain number of years of training rather than achieve a set standard of performance. The number of years required for an apprenticeship has been reduced over the centuries in most trades from

Table 4:   *Registrations for Technician Training in Engineering*

	1979/80	1980/81	1981/2	1982/3	1983/4
NC	33,992	33,808	28,836	25,620	22,980
ND	4,854	8,418	9,490	10,800	10,008
HNC	6,271	14,070	18,052	17,555	15,915
HND	498	1,006	1,964	3,347	3,620
Total	45,615	57,302	58,342	57,332	52,603

Awards for Technician Training in Engineering

	1979/80	1980/81	1981/2	1982/3	1983/4
NC	10,840	16,798	19,360	16,406	14,151
ND	1,080	2,207	3,003	4,571	4,101
HNC	203	2,476	6,680	8,738	9,426
HND	45	183	474	943	1,176
Total	12,168	21,664	29,517	30,658	28,854

(Key: NC = National Certificate; ND = National Diploma; HNC = Higher National Certificate; HND = Higher National Diploma

Source: Business and Technician Education Council (BTEC)*

* The Business Education Council (BEC) was formed in 1977, the Technician Education Council in 1978. On 1 October 1983, BTEC took over the registration of students and the validation of courses from both of them.

seven to four. But repeated efforts to replace time-served apprenticeships with achievement-related ones, in which the apprentice would qualify when he attained a certain level of skill, have been rebuffed.

In 1984, the national committee of the engineers' union, the AUEW, rejected its President's recommendation in favour of standards-based training. The union feared a diminished status for craftsmen, and a dilution of apprenticeship by youth training courses and short retraining courses for adults. It sought to protect existing craftsmen's jobs. But the consequence will be to cut further the number of apprentices and worsen skill shortages which in turn inhibit the growth of employment. In 1983, 10,500 young people started as engineering apprentices, two fifths of the average annual intake into the industry between 1973 and 1978, and the lowest figure on record. Some argue that craftsmen, particularly single-skill craftsmen, are no longer needed by the engineering industry. Certainly multi-skill apprenticeships are better suited to the new epoch. What is incontrovertible, however, is that the British engineering industry cannot compete, and may not even survive, on the basis of a rapid decline in skills.

Drawing attention to the catastrophic drop, the Engineering Industry Training Board commented in its Annual Report for 1983/4:

Decline in recruitment of young people for basic craft and technician training continued in 1983, the total number falling to 8911 ... The total is over 1600 below the number recruited in 1982, more than 50 per cent lower than in 1981 and some 1600 below intake levels in the 1970s. This decline combined with high redundancy levels amongst trainees means that by 1986/1987 the supply of newly trained craftsmen and technicians will have fallen to 50 per cent of its 1979 level. Unless the engineering industry declines further, this can only mean skill shortages in the medium term, some signs of which are already beginning to emerge particularly in the electronics sector.

The decline in traditional apprenticeships would not be of such consequence if a similar number of boys and girls were being trained in more modern multi-skill technician courses. The disturbing truth is that technician training in engineering is itself falling, as indicated above. Unable to compete in a high-technology, high-skill market, Britain will become dependent on low-technology products, and will only be able to compete against low-wage countries by cutting its own wage levels.

The Scores Fall

The United States is short of skills too. There are thirty-four vacancies waiting for every American Ph.D. in computer science. Taking population size into account, Japan has nearly twice as many graduate engineers as the United States per million of its population.[5] Although the number of students majoring in computer science in the United States is rising fast, the quality of departments is very mixed. As in Britain, there has been a marked drop in the number of postgraduate students in the natural sciences and engineering. Their numbers fell by a quarter in the 1970s as students became disillusioned with technology and doubtful about science.

The United States and Europe share the problems of falling school rolls and pressure to cut education budgets. In some American states and cities, schools have closed down early in the academic year to save money; in others teachers cannot be paid. Universities, particularly private universities, have felt the cold winds of recession and fees have risen dramatically. But the central issue of United States education, in so far as it affects skills, is the prolonged decline in standards and the consequent loss of confidence in the high school.

To enter university, an American high-school graduate must take and pass a series of tests known as scholastic aptitude tests (SAT). Though set in the form of simple questions or multiple choices, the tests are intended to establish a student's proficiency in verbal and non-verbal reasoning. There are no written essays and no specialized subject examinations in the SAT. What increasingly worries Americans is that standards in English and mathematics have fallen year after year for the past twenty years. Half of all American schoolchildren study no mathematics after the age of sixteen; history (other than American history) and modern languages are disappearing from the curriculum. Over a quarter drop out of school before graduating, a figure that it has proved extremely difficult to reduce.

There are explanations for the fall in standards. A growing Hispanic population for whom English is not the mother tongue and the dominance of television over the written word are often cited as causes. The effect of women's liberation has been to open up new opportunities for able women, so that they are no longer restricted to teaching and a few professions. The quality of schoolteachers has therefore fallen. None of these factors is likely to change, so there is little likelihood of a sudden recovery in academic standards, though the long decline does at last appear to be levelling out.

For the Europeans, the issue is not so much falling standards as the suitability of educational systems inherited from the past. The French have a magnificent education system for a meritocracy, but the gap in opportunities between children born in Paris or Lyon and those in rural areas remains great. French universities take in large numbers of students, but wastage rates are very high and academic teaching is formal.

The Meisters Sing

The Federal Republic of Germany has, in common with the other German-speaking countries, Austria and Switzerland, an impressive apprenticeship system, which 60 per cent of German school-leavers enter. Virtually every occupation is included, and apprenticeships last for three or three and a half years. The quality of the training is closely monitored by Chambers of Commerce and Trade, sustained by a strong and traditional public regard for apprenticeship as an institution. The standing of a company in its local community depends on the excellence of its training, and companies with a good reputation can select their apprentices from the most capable school-leavers.

Apprenticeships take most young West Germans out of the labour market until the age of eighteen or nineteen. When, in the mid 1970s, the Federal Republic confronted the consequences of the high birth rates of the late 1950s and 1960s, the policy adopted embraced a marked expansion of apprenticeships. Spurred on by legislation passed in 1976, the Training Places Promotion Act, West German companies created 145,000 additional training places, making a total of 625,000. So positive was the response that the legislation never had to be activated.

The training content of apprenticeship courses is regularly revised and up-dated by joint committees of employers and trade unions advised by the Federal Institute of Vocational Education. Adapting to the latest technologies has brought two major innovations: the cooperative year, and the combining of separate skills into clusters of skills, broadening the range of competence. The cooperative year is split between blocks of full-time vocational and general education and full-time on-the-job training. It has been widely adopted in the metal trades, West Germany's core manufacturing sector, to ensure high initial standards, and has been recently extended to eighteen months. Two years of more specialized training follow. But the second stage is itself much broader than in the past. Six skill-clusters have replaced forty-two separate skills in mechanical engineering; four in electrical engineering now embody the twelve separate skills previously taught.

Training in clerical work is also undergoing a transformation, and one with greater social implications. The Federal Republic, like most of its neighbours, used to divide office work into shorthand typists, copy typists, filing clerks, office administrators, telephone operators and receptionists, and that is not a complete list. Boys used to be trained for three years in supervisory white-collar jobs, girls for two. Now a general apprenticeship in office skills, with the emphasis on microelectronic equipment and data processing, is replacing the traditional clerical apprenticeship. It will last three to three and a half years for boys and girls alike.

The development of apprenticeship syllabuses in these important fields of employment bears witness to the adaptability of the German system. The fact that a growing number of young people holding the *Abitur*, the qualification for entry to higher education, prefer to go into good apprenticeships is evidence of the job prospects they offer; by contrast, a completed apprenticeship is not recognized as any kind of qualification for entry to higher education.

The system does have its faults. Training for some is still narrowly defined in terms of a single skill or a few closely related skills. Many apprentices are in occupations like carpentry or butchery, where demand is insufficient to absorb them. Some of them end up in semi-skilled or unskilled jobs, and it is fair to ask whether their training has any relevance to their work or to their lives. Three years' initial training may be too long in a fast-moving world, especially for apprentices contracted to technologically backward firms. All are obliged to attend vocational college two days a week, but there is little cooperation between the colleges and the employers, and the quality of the general education offered is frequently poor. Vocational teachers are not highly regarded in Germany: their salaries and their conditions of work reflect their second-class status.

Whatever the criticisms that may be made, however, the commitment of West Germany and two other German-speaking countries, Austria and Switzerland, to the quality of their work-forces has repaid them handsomely. No other countries so effectively prepare all their young people for work.

The skills of the existing work-force are not neglected either. In 1980, the Federal Government created a DM 500 million fund to retrain workers in the new technologies. Although private firms had to match government finance with an equal contribution, within forty-eight hours bids from them had exhausted all the money available. On-the-job retraining is a recognized part of a system that has provided two thirds of the employed population with vocational skills.

Japanese Training

The Japanese, like the West Germans, have a well-recognized pecking order in education. West German parents know which firms offer the most prestigious apprenticeships in their region. Japanese parents know which universities guarantee lifetime employment with the most renowned firms in Japan. For the Japanese child, school is an ordeal punctuated by examinations, and those examinations determine his or her future career. Almost all Japanese children are educated to the age of eighteen, when the individual pupils' academic records decide which university they attend, or whether they attend university at all. Two fifths of Japanese children go to technical high schools at the age of fifteen, and from there enter manufacturing industries, mainly in blue-collar jobs. Three fifths of all high-school graduates going into manufacturing industries come from these technical high schools. Of the general high-school graduates, 60 per cent go into employment, many into the services. The other 40 per cent go on to higher education.

Japan has to cope with the same social attitudes as Western Europe. Vocational education is looked down upon by parents. It is very difficult to get into a university from a technical high school. Teachers resist the introduction of vocational preparation in general high schools, though they reluctantly accept it in the final year for the school-leavers: there is a legacy from centuries of history elevating thinkers over makers. But Japan has three great strengths:

1. Its children are highly motivated: they know there are jobs for all at the conclusion of their education, and that their educational achievement will decide what their status and pay will be.

2. Teaching is an honoured profession. Salaries are fairly good. The profession attracts men as well as women. In the high schools male teachers predominate.

3. The curriculum is broad. All Japanese children learn mathematics and science until they graduate from high school. Standards of teaching in these subjects are high.

Japan does not have an elaborate national system of apprenticeship for school-leavers like West Germany. But it does have extensive schemes of on-the-job training by private companies. Most of the big companies prefer to undertake their own training, stressing diversified skills. Nor is training concentrated only on young recruits. Because of the Japanese tradition of seniority, greater skill often goes with age. Training occurs throughout the working life, and is a factor in redeploying workers from old jobs to new ones for which new skills are required.

A Patchwork of Responses

Youth unemployment, long-term unemployment and redundancies among established workers caused by overseas competition or inadequate demand have compelled countries to look for answers to the despair of those without work, or at least for schemes to assuage it. Public works and employment subsidies do not commend themselves to conservative governments because they increase public expenditure, and that has to be paid for by higher taxes or by borrowing. But training is regarded as being in a different category. It adds value to human capital. It serves the needs of private industry. And it keeps unemployed and potentially disruptive young people off the streets.

The Youth Training Scheme

One of the most ambitious of such schemes is Britain's Youth Training Scheme (YTS). It was originally intended to offer every sixteen-year-old school-leaver a year of work experience and training, and it now extends to seventeen-year-old youngsters as well. In 1984-5, 400,000 training places were on offer. Much of the training is conducted by private employers on their own premises: these are called Mode A schemes. Others are run by voluntary agencies or by further-education colleges and have a larger element of public funding. These Mode B schemes have been valuable for disadvantaged youngsters, particularly for those from ethnic minorities and deprived backgrounds. As they are more expensive, places have been limited to 70,000; that means that some good courses have been closed reduced in size and may soon be phased out completely. Tight constraints on spending hamper training in skills that require modern equipment. There is a strong case for differential funding of courses. It is unusual for YTS schemes to reach a standard that will be recognized as equivalent to a first-year apprenticeship.

The main reason why the YTS is not yet a satisfactory bridge from school to work is that employers do not see it as an essential preparation for all young workers. Their attitude towards it remains ambivalent, balanced between viewing the scheme as essential basic training like the first year of the West German apprenticeship system, and as a lifeboat for the young unemployed which incidentally provides employers with cheap labour. The schemes themselves reflect this difference, some having a weighty training element, others little more than the further education component of thirteen weeks or its equivalent required to satisfy course requirements. Achieving recognition for courses of such a variable standard is problematic. In practice, some courses lead to exemption from training requirements, like the 1,300 training places recognized by the Engineering Industry Training Board in 1984 as equivalent to a first foundation year of an engineering craftsman's apprenticeship. Most, however, do not. Maintaining a high and consistent quality of training is essential if a YTS course is not to be a dead end, leading nowhere except to another YTS course. That requires monitoring and inspection by inspectors like those employed by the Department of Education and Science for further education. Even given inspection of the quality of schemes, it is difficult to achieve adequate skill-training in one year. A two-year scheme should lead on to a further, more specialized year for skilled technicians, craftsmen and craftswomen, in which the necessary qualifications can be acquired.

Tutors and Counsellors

Fullemploy is a voluntary agency in Britain. It trains unemployed youngsters, many of them from deprived black inner-city ghettoes, in computer skills, using funds provided by the Manpower Services Commission. Once trained, over 80 per cent of Fullemploy's young people get jobs, mainly in computer-related fields. The success stories of Fullemploy prove that high drop-out rates and high failure rates are not endemic in the young black community. Why has it succeeded?

The key lies in pastoral care. For centuries, undergraduates in Britain's ancient universities have had tutors, not only to teach them, but also to counsel and befriend them. Wastage rates in these universities are among the lowest in the world. Even when the student has graduated, the tutors take an interest in his or her career, and are usually willing to continue to offer advice.

What works so well for privileged young people works well for underprivileged young people too. Fullemploy's students are assigned their own tutor, who may be consulted, in an informal setting, at any time, Fullemploy's alumni can continue to consult their tutors for up to eighteen months after placement in a job. They are encouraged to use the social facilities and to discuss their difficulties. This continuing support helps young people to regain the habit of work and to feel someone is concerned that they succeed. But it is expensive, costing as much as £10,000 a year for each trainee.

The information technology centres (ITECs), the first of which was established in 1981, also have a good placement record, though per capita costs are high. The centres offer a year's training in information technology to school-leavers, and many have been located in inner cities. Government funding has been limited to a grant of £55,000 and a subsequent supplement of £20,000, plus the normal managing agency fee and trainee allowances under the Youth Training Scheme. The grants are spent on equipping the centres, and help to meet trainers' salaries. A number of early information technology centres now face a crisis, since they have exhausted the initial grant, and cannot yet finance themselves out of revenue from consultancy and contract work for local firms. In some hard-pressed inner-city areas, and in some depressed industrial towns, it is not reasonable to expect them to do so. Information technology centres have been successful in placing young people from disadvantaged backgrounds in permanent jobs, and have eased skill shortages in industry. Continuing public assistance, covering a declining proportion of their expenditure, would be an excellent investment.

US Training: A Private Sector Responsibility

The Federal Government of the United States has devolved responsibility for training upon the individual states, but in practice the private sector on its own undertakes most of the training done. It is an impressive effort. A recent Carnegie Foundation study estimated the cost of training in the private sector at $40 billion, two thirds as much as the total expenditure on all higher and further education beyond the age of eighteen.[6] Much of the training is directed at managers, executives and engineers, and much is carried out on the job.

Initial training of young people, on the other hand, has been neglected. Vocational schools are not highly regarded, and apprenticeships are in practice only to be found in the construction industry. Even those are not intended for school-leavers but for adults. The most neglected person in the American labour market is the inner-city black or Hispanic youngster. There are few opportunities offered to him or her aside from high school, and many inner-city schools have appallingly low standards and cope with terrible social problems.

Alarmed by the riots in Watts and elsewhere in the 1960s, private industry councils decided to tackle the problems presented by unemployed young people. Private industry is seen by the United States administration as the powerhouse behind training. Private industry councils must by law have a majority from the private sector. They are responsible for drawing up training programmes.

One of the most impressive American schemes operates in Boston's inner-city schools, an education system that in 1982 was approaching breakdown. In that year, the Superintendent of Boston's schools signed a compact with Boston's Private Industry Council. The businesses in that council pledged themselves to provide a thousand summer jobs and to hire 400 high-school graduates in return for a consistent improvement in the partnership schools, both in standards and in attendance. Boston schools had enormous problems; drop-out rates in some inner-city schools reached 45 per cent. A third of high-school students could not read well enough to follow the work set for them. Many had no motivation to improve. Society offered them no future other than dead-end jobs or scavenging in the unofficial economy of drugs and prostitution.

Two years after its establishment, and despite the absence of Federal funds, the Boston Compact had met and surpassed all its goals. The Compact had been signed by 316 firms. Six hundred high-school graduates had been hired for permanent jobs, three quarters of them from the black and Hispanic communities. Furthermore, of those placed in 1983, 80 per cent were still working nearly a year later. All the students had been enrolled in a Job Collaboration programme in which they were encouraged to attend school regularly and to work hard to improve their grades, and were offered counselling in job preparation. The personal commitment of each student was matched by the commitment of the firm to provide employment after graduation. The Compact's goals are a 5 per cent increase each year in the proportion of students graduating, and minimum competence in reading and mathematics to be achieved by all high-school graduates by 1986.

The Boston Compact is an uncommon success story in the United States, for youth training is a serious lacuna in that country, even though Congress voted over $3 billion in 1984 to help private industry councils and the states produce training programmes for young people, especially Hispanics and blacks. Summer jobs are part of the tradition of an American childhood, and the United States does not suffer from the academic snobbery of Europe and Japan. The United States does, however, rely too exclusively on high-school graduation as the gateway to professional and educational qualifications. School-sick students, whose high schools are parodies of what an educational institution should be, cannot be cajoled or threatened into staying on until graduation. The United States should produce alternative routes through technician training and on-the-job apprenticeships for young people, reviving the depressed image of vocational education, and coupling it with a general academic education and education in life skills. The lack of motivation which casts a pall over the black inner cities might then disappear.

The Learning Adult

If the United States has little to teach Europe about youth training, it has much to offer in the field of retraining. The main responsibility lies with employers, though the United States Congress has voted relatively small sums of Federal money, for example $223 million in 1984-5, specifically for the retraining of workers who lose their jobs through plant closures. These 'displaced workers' are concentrated in the old industrial areas of the Middle West and parts of the East coast, where unemployment is far above the national average, and long-term unemployment approaches a quarter of the total.[7] Unfortunately Federal funds are distributed between states on a mathematical formula which does not take into account the existence of localities with severe unemployment.

Nevertheless, some excellent retraining programmes have surfaced, not least in the car industry, which has been hit hard by competition from imports. Several years ago in Southgate, a suburb of Detroit, nearly 8,500 people, many of them skilled blue-collar workers, lost their jobs when two large car plants, a chemical factory and a tyre factory all shut down. The sixteen towns and neighbourhoods formed a consortium, the Downriver Community Conference, to seek new jobs, and to retrain workers and help them through the trauma of job loss. Individual redundant workers are given a series of tests to find out what their interests are, where their abilities lie and their general educational level. He or she can discuss whether to look for a job immediately, or to retrain. Short-term training and long-term courses are both available. The Community Conference runs workshops on interview skills and job search, and employs several people whose task is to identify actual vacancies and potential openings for those with appropriate training.

Some redundant workers have retrained in new technologies. Others have gone into small businesses locally. By the end of 1983, two thirds of the workers who had sought help had been placed in jobs. Six schemes based on the Downriver model are now being financed by the US Department of Labor in other parts of the country.

It is not only local councils and local businesses that are learning about training for new jobs. In 1982, the United Auto-Workers (UAW), negotiating its usual wage contract, agreed with the major employers, General Motors and Ford, that 5 cents an hour should be set aside for each union member, to be used for the training and resettlement of dis-placed car-workers. A National Development and Training Center for Ford workers was established at Dearborn, Michigan, which uses many of the diagnostic and interviewing techniques pioneered at Downriver.

The United Auto Workers has played a crucial role in this programme, which altogether covers some 53,000 employees. The union has not stood out against change, nor tried to stop its members moving to other jobs. Rather it has fought to provide them with a future, even if it is in another industry or service or as a self-employed person. It is an extension of the bargaining aims of trade unionism that deserves to be followed in other industries and in other countries where unions are sometimes criticized as conservative and unimaginative.

Several states have embarked on similar adult training initiatives. California levies a small tax for training, equivalent to one tenth of 1 per cent of unemployment benefit, which yields about $50 million a year. Agencies are invited to apply for training contracts, the costs of which are met from the training fund, based on the individual agency's performance in placing successful trainees. The choice of contractors is made by a panel of employers, state legislators and unions. The scheme suffers from the drawback that agencies will obviously choose the most trainable workers, so it does not meet the need to train the most disadvantaged, but it is a constructive response to the needs of redundant workers.

Investing state benefits in making people employable rather than in keeping them unemployed is made peculiarly difficult in the United States by Federal laws which decree that unemployment insurance can only be used to pay cash benefits to the unemployed. Every retraining scheme therefore requires another source of funding. The state of Delaware, like California, imposes its own tax on employers, amounting to 1 per cent of unemployment insurance payments. This fund is used to provide career counselling, not only for high-school graduates, but for anyone unemployed for six weeks or more. Training courses are offered as well as career advice, with costs paid for up to six months. About a quarter of those receiving counselling opt for a training course.

The United States enjoys a substantial commitment from many firms to on-the-job training. Firms like IBM, Xerox and AT&T up-grade the skills of their staff on a regular basis. Modern-minded unions, like the International Union of Electricians and the United Auto Workers, regard the right to training and retraining as being as important to their members' welfare as wages themselves.

This attitude is shared by many European trade unions too. The Italian metal workers' union has won the right to regular sabbaticals for training and education. Paid education leave is a feature of collective bargains in some French industries. In-service training, once restricted to the medical profession and to teachers, is seen now as the key to a modern, highly skilled work-force.

In some companies, employees' skills are regularly up-graded. Their managements appreciate the importance of human capital. But the mismatch between vacancies for people skilled in new technologies and those with old skills no one wants remains disturbing. There used to be a correlation between unemployment and vacancies in the same industry, according to Professor James Medoff of Harvard, as one would indeed expect. When vacancies rose, unemployment fell, and vice versa. But that correlation has not worked well since 1969, presumably because the vacancies are for people with very different skills than those possessed by the redundant workers in the industry. This finding is paralleled by evidence from Britain's Professional and Executive Register, which shows that the largest increases in unemployment are among people with skills now superseded by the computer, particularly draughtsmen.

The education and training systems are not meeting the requirements of the new epoch rapidly enough. The challenge to them, however, is much greater than simply filling the unfilled vacancies for engineers and technicians. It is to construct a system capable of educating men and women well beyond the elementary level that sufficed for earlier stages of the industrial revolution. It is to recognize that these men and women must be able to comprehend technology and to use it to make a better world, and that, if they are to do so, they must understand not only computers, but the human beings and the human societies those computers are meant to serve.

16 Education: The Determinant of Tomorrow's Success

'Many persons will learn two, three or four careers in a lifetime as telecommunications, automation and later, machine intelligence will cause entirely different work patterns. Electronics will create both the need and the tools for lifelong learning.'

James Martin, *The Wired Society*, (1978)

Educational Programmes

What kind of future can we in the West look forward to? Living as we do in a period of instability, moving from the era of the first Industrial Revolution, of mass production and mass consumption, to a new era of information-based societies, prediction becomes risky. But three elements are likely to appear in all the scenarios for the next ten years:

1. The infusion of every area of human life by microelectronics and other new technologies.
2. The disappearance of national frontiers as significant barriers to the movement of goods, services, currencies and, above all, information.
3. Uncertainty about what work means since it can no longer be defined in the traditional terms of a lifetime's career of paid employment for eight hours a day, forty hours a week, over forty or fifty years. The shakiness of the traditional idea of work obliges us to reconstruct the base on which our insurance systems, our welfare state, and not least our formal education system have heretofore been built.

These three characteristics of future industrial societies demand a major transformation of our educational systems.

The information society is not about a new set of artefacts, like video-recorders or computer games. It is about a systems revolution, for the new microelectronic technologies are reaching into every part of our lives and into every occupation. They furnish the home as well as the office. They will reshape clerical jobs as well as manufacturing jobs; they will transform professional jobs and public services, from medical diagnosis to the care of the elderly. Their use, misuse or abuse will be determined by the education and training of those who control or operate them. The quality of the education system is likely to be one of the main determinants of a society's success in adapting to the microelectronics revolution.

Will the Computer Replace the Teacher?

Educational technology, like other information technology, has its buffs and its Luddites. The buffs believe that computers teach mathematics and science better than the humans do, that computer graphics will make training much easier, and that intelligent computers will make better decisions than confused men and women. They believe local networks can replace human interaction, and they long for the day when artificial intelligence will bring an ordered and logical society.

The Luddites, on the other hand, believe computer-aided instruction will destroy jobs, especially if fostered by governments bent on cutting education budgets. Computers, they point out, cannot teach children how to interact with one another, and how to become constructive members of society. Computer-aided instruction may be stilted and conformist. After all, both programmed learning and language laboratories, those earlier milestones of educational technology, were not quite the unqualified success that some claimed they were. Furthermore, say the Luddites, computers will be the cause of new educational inequalities.

The truth lies somewhere between these extremes. Computers cannot replace teachers, but they can complement them. They are at least as good at transmitting information as teachers, and are probably more accurate. They can assist the understanding of spatial relations or principles of physics through graphics which can move or change shape. But they cannot argue what conclusions should be drawn from information where judgements are to be made or where values must be taken into account. They do not appreciate music or feel moved by poetry. Faith and friendship are not meaningful concepts to computers. So teachers will need to become tutors and counsellors rather than purveyors of information. The teacher's job should become much more exciting.

Technology is not the same as civilization. Qualitative values are rarer and harder to learn than quantitative ones. No education deserves the name that fails to arouse curiosity about ideas, awareness of beauty, concern about ethics and involvement in society. Computers cannot teach these things. We should beware of thinking that, because they cannot be taught by computers, such things are not worth learning.

The Schools Respond

Since computers and computer systems are pervasive, neither children nor their teachers can afford to be unfamiliar with them. Boys and girls should feel familiar and at ease with computers. They will then naturally employ computers as tools for learning, and later on as complements to working life or research. Already the school and college generation turns to computers as readily as it turns to books or television. Gaining familiarity with computers is more difficult for the teachers, most of them born and educated before computers became inexpensive and widely available. To keep pace with their pupils, they need in-service training as well as the opportunity to use computers outside school time, for instance in teachers' centres equipped with a wide range of hardware and software. It is encouraging to note that nearly a third of Britain's teachers have now completed courses in computer literacy (though many of those courses last only a few days).[1]

Important as the education of children in computer skills is, there is a more ambitious educational objective: to extend this familiarity and ability beyond the schools to the whole population, including those whose education was limited or who left school before microchips were invented. For in the information society the old as well as the poor are disadvantaged. This objective serves another purpose too, namely to encourage discussion in society about the uses to which our astonishing new technological capabilities are to be directed. The information revolution will change work, social institutions, human relationships, government – all of them areas shaped by social values. To date, the substantial and growing literature on the information revolution has fought shy of value judgements or of exploring its implications for society. But there is a great danger in allowing the tide of technological advance to submerge our capacity for judgement. That is why education must address itself to stimulating thought on these issues, so that the shape of the future is not designed by default.

These tasks, especially the last, entail organizational changes in education of a fundamental kind. Such changes will be difficult to make, and some existing institutions will resist them. If they are not made, education as a public service will be by-passed by packaged instruction commercially sold to private consumers, which may be excellent as a supplement to formal education, but is disturbing as a substitute.

To return to the first new task of the education system, making pupils familiar with the computer is now accepted as a useful element of schooling, even for very young children. Almost all primary schools in Britain boast at least one microcomputer; schools in better-off areas may possess several. A survey conducted by the UK Government's Microelectronics Education Programme in 1984 estimated that the average secondary school had nine microcomputers.[2] But it is nevertheless difficult to provide sufficient microcomputer time to allow every child adequate access.

This difficulty is compounded in the British educational system by financial stringency. A computer is provided free of charge to each primary school, but without the software that it requires to be of any use. Software for computers competes with textbooks for the limited sums available to schools. In poor neighbourhoods, parents cannot be looked to to make good these gaps in the provision of educational materials. So both at school and at home, the child from the prosperous area benefits from much more access to computer time than the child from the poor area.

In secondary and higher education, computers are too often seen as specialized tools for scientists and engineers, or, even more narrowly, for computer scientists. The Microelectronics Education survey found that only 6 per cent of modern language teachers, 14 per cent of craft and design teachers and a fifth of those in business and economics used microcomputers, compared to 65 per cent of science teachers and 56 per cent of mathematics teachers.[3] The survey showed that the scale and sweep of the microelectronic era had not yet been understood.

Computers are not the basis of a new discipline, computer science. They are a tool to be used in all subjects, from literature to engineering. Students of geography, history or poetry can search through the literature using key words to discover new sources and cross-references that illuminate their work. Computer simulations assist the engineer, and computer models enable economists and social scientists to test their conclusions. The universities most advanced in understanding the impact of the computer, like Brown and Carnegie-Mellon in the United States, or Strathclyde in Scotland, are planning to ensure that every student in *every* faculty has the use of a microcomputer and access to printers, local networks and ultimately to libraries of data-banks at university level – in practice a work-station or study-station for each individual, whatever the subject studied.

The potential for discrimination is apparent in the differential use of computers between various subjects. If a pupil at a secondary school specializes in arts subjects, he or she is much less likely than the pupil specializing in mathematics or science to understand the potential of computers as tools for study and decision-making. In most education systems, girls concentrate on arts and humanities, boys on mathematics and science. The computer in the schools could widen again the painfully narrowed gap between opportunities for boys and for girls.

There is another source of anxiety in the differential use of computers as between subjects. Decision-makers in politics and administration are drawn largely from the humanities and social science. Decision-making is likely to be profoundly altered by the advent of artificial intelligence, and its corollary, knowledge-based systems. Decision-makers with no more than an elementary familiarity with computers will not be well placed to incorporate these advanced systems into the structures of government and administration. Concerned to conceal their own ignorance, they may too readily accept expert advice.

The second, equally urgent objective of the education system is to meet the need for men and women with specific information technology skills. These new skills are required by those who design, control, adjust and maintain computerized systems. True, we will not need thousands of programmers trained in computer languages, as was thought likely only a few years ago. The latest microcomputers are instructed by pointing to symbols or letters on the screen with a 'mouse', or even with the human hand; soon they will accept instructions given by the human voice. To use the contemporary jargon, computers are becoming increasingly 'user-friendly'. But at the next level of sophistication, the demand for information technology skills will be enormous. And at present, as the previous chapter has explained, it is not being met.

The Fading of Frontiers

National frontiers are no longer barriers to the flow of information, for shortwave radio and now earth satellites allow both words and pictures to be plucked from the air.

The message is clear. English may be the world's most widely used language, but if Britain is to make full use of the possibilities now being offered for operating within other cultural communities, it must acquire a greater command of foreign languages. Language teaching in British schools is in a desperate plight, the most damaged victim of falling rolls and cuts in the number of teachers. If, as is possible, France chooses a French-based computer language and a French-based computer network, brilliant computer buffs with no knowledge of French will find themselves excluded from a very large market. Languages are important in crossing frontiers, and our school curricula should make time for them. In addition, the teaching of history and geography should not be based on exclusive study of a particular nation, even if it is our own. Surviving in the new world of sophisticated weaponry and 'star wars' depends on international understanding, and to that understanding education can make a critical contribution.

'Breaking the Bonds of Time and Space'

Formal education in advanced industrial countries is largely conducted in institutions called schools and colleges, by teachers or lecturers in classrooms. It is concentrated on the first ten or fifteen years of life after infancy and is supposed to prepare boys and girls for work and for life. To meet the demands that will be made upon it, education in an information society will have to escape from these formal structures, structures which make less and less sense in a world where change is so rapid that knowledge and skills learned in one decade are obsolete in the next. Within ten years of graduation, young men and women will be working with processes and buying products which had not even been invented in their schooldays. We cannot acquire in the first twenty or so years of our lives the knowledge and skills we will need to guide us through a lifetime in the modern world. The business of learning has to accompany us throughout our lives if we are to take an active part in societies that change so rapidly, and are to be able to contribute to the decisions that shape them.

Nor, in the modern world, need the process of learning be confined to schools and colleges. The personal, portable microcomputer means that information – and indeed instruction – of the highest quality will be available where and when a student wants it. For the last century education has been a service designed by those who work in it, the teachers and administrators, not greatly influenced by its consumers, the students and schoolchildren. The dictates of time and space are now becoming irrelevant. New demands are being made by consumers outside the traditional market for education, by adults who want to study in their own time and often in their own homes. There has always been a demand for adult education, though it has long been the Cinderella of the system. Microcomputers convert that demand into a market for educational software as important as the market for educational books, and one that will readily compete with the provision made by formal educational institutions, public or private. More than that, adults now able to benefit from a continuing education will demand that their learning achievements be recognized. The pressure for accreditation and mutual recognition of qualifications will become more and more powerful. Informal learning, through life experience and work experience, will be given its due place alongside formal education.

A Broad Foundation

Formal education during childhood and adolescence is itself likely to change, partly because of the emergence of a parallel informal system of education much more formidable than at present, partly because it is no longer appropriate to the needs of our society. Education in Britain, and particularly in England and Wales, is narrow and specialized, shaped by the pressures of a public examination system that expects academically inclined children to master only two or three subjects at eighteen. As for those young people who leave school at sixteen or seventeen, schools are under pressure to make education more job-oriented. This has its ironies at a time when half the school-leavers in many areas cannot get jobs anyway, and need to know how to survive long periods of unemployment and gain value from leisure and unpaid occupations. The basis of an information society cannot be a narrow job-related type of education. It must be a broad foundation embracing the humanities and the sciences as well as vocational education, for all children, independent of academic ability. Such a broad foundation is valuable whatever changes in work and skills there may be.

The experience of a country like Japan, well ahead of Europe in information technology, demonstrates the advantage of a general education based on language and culture as well as on science and technology. Japanese children study both language-based subjects and mathematics-based subjects throughout their school lives. 'The great accomplishment of Japan's primary and secondary education,' wrote Thomas Rohlen, 'lies not in its creation of a brilliant élite . . . but in its generation of such a high *average* level of capability.'[4]

That high *average* level leads to a society that is able to exploit the new technologies effectively. An educated élite combined with a low average level of education may have suited the old industrial society and have met the needs of a traditional agricultural society, but it makes no sense in an information society.

Information technology spans blue- and white-collar skills, making the old distinction unnecessary. The architect will use computer-aided graphics; so will the furniture-maker and the shoe-maker. Distinctions based on future occupations cannot be sustained either. The systems designer and the knowledge engineer need to be educated in language and logic as well as in mathematics and engineering.

An illustration of the way in which information technology is bringing science and humanities together again is the fifth-generation computer. Its languages depend on logic, its intelligent knowledge-based systems on philosophical concepts, its capacity to infer and simulate on the intuitive abilities of the human mind, its speed and efficiency on engineering. With it, C. P. Snow's two cultures come together again.[5]

Subject Disciplines Transcended

Computers enable their users to discover associations and interrelationships between as well as within subject disciplines. Subject disciplines are only artificial ways of organizing knowledge, of imposing order on a confusing plethora of facts. The memories of computers can handle the organization of data for us, widening our intellectual scope. Technology breaks down the frontiers between disciplines and confronts education with the limitations it has itself chosen to impose.

In Britain, those limitations are peculiarly constricting. Boys and girls emerge from a broad primary education, in which practical and project work is pursued alongside the basic skills of reading, writing, arithmetic and, nowadays, familiarity with calculators and simple computers as well. They then move on to a secondary stage in which their range of subjects is narrowed from a broad curriculum in the first three years to one determined for the next two years by the requirements of public examinations. Children understandably concentrate on those subjects which they are most likely to pass, though English language and mathematics are the basic requirement for so many subsequent courses that most pupils attempt them. After the 16-plus examinations, the curriculum narrows again, to two or three subjects at Advanced level. At the age of sixteen or earlier, most English and Welsh pupils, unlike Scottish pupils, abandon formal education in one culture – science or the humanities – for ever.

A broad education would mean delaying such specialization at least until the end of secondary schooling, while maintaining a core curriculum to which options could be added. At present the core curriculum consists of academic disciplines, though in some schools a vocational element is now included. An experiment in vocational education, the Technical and Vocational Education Initiative (TVEI), was recently introduced in schools in sixty-one English and Welsh education authorities, intended mainly for less academic children in the last two years of compulsory education. This experiment proved so popular that some local education authorities have introduced it in all their schools, and in some of those schools all the pupils are taking the course.

A grasp of technology and an understanding of its consequences for society are fundamental requirements for the well-educated man or woman in the last decade of this century. These men and women will have to make choices and decisions for which an understanding of technology is essential. A generation of technologically and scientifically ignorant politicians, administrators and teachers will make obtuse decisions. Equally, a generation of scientists and technologists untutored in the possible implications for human societies will make insensitive choices which could have disturbing consequences. Technology should therefore be part of a broad curriculum, for all secondary children. They should take part in the TVEI initiative, and should have to achieve a level of proficiency in it as part of the requirements for passing the public examinations taken at sixteen. Such a requirement could root out the inherent snobbery of an education system long based on the assumption that the academic is first-rate and the practical second-rate, that thinkers are more valuable than makers.

The public examinations at sixteen – the Ordinary level General Certificate of Education for more academic children, the Certificate of Secondary Education for less academic children – survive because parents want them as measures of their children's achievement, and employers use them as a sieving mechanism for selecting employees. Educationally, however, the case for retaining the 16-plus examinations, shortly to be combined into a single General Certificate of Secondary Education covering eight different grades, is weak. It fails to measure creativity, imagination or initiative. It tests factual memory, the attribute most readily replaced by the computer. A mixture of tests and assessments of work done, combined with a full profile of a child's experience, initiative and contribution to the community inside and outside school would be a much better basis for determining his or her future career.

An Advanced level examination at eighteen will still be necessary to select entrants to higher education, given the restricted number of places available, but it should be broadened to cover the core curriculum subjects with the addition of two or three options. The international baccalaureate is a useful model, with one reservation: it is itself a very academic examination. There is no reason why vocational achievement of a high order should not be recognized by the equivalent of an A-level certificate. Indeed, vocational proficiency should be a compulsory element in a broader examination whose core includes both science and arts subjects.

The Transition from School to Work

Beyond sixteen, some order needs to be brought into the chaos of new examinations and qualifications in Britain. There are now A–O levels, A levels, S levels, Certificates of Extended Education, Certificates of Pre-Vocational Education, Business and Technician Education certificates, C G L I qualifications and of course apprenticeships, ordinary and higher national certificates and diplomas, and the Youth Training Scheme. Soon, another examination, the A–S level, will be brought in to broaden the A-level curriculum. Fragmentation of a post-sixteen educational system that is already suffering the trauma of a decline in numbers is neither economic nor sensible. What is needed now is a system of mutual accreditation between academic and vocational courses, so that people can move on up the educational ladder by either route and gain exemption from part of the time requirement of higher courses if they have achieved a sufficient standard on the lower ones. So often today, young men and women climb up the ladder of vocational courses to find that the platform they reach when they qualify is a ceiling. Educational achievement should never be a dead end.

The Lindop Committee reported in April 1985 on the problem of academic validation for degrees awarded by public sector institutions, and rightly concluded that many polytechnics were capable of validating their own degrees. The most urgent problem of validation lies lower down the system, with the proliferation of sub-degree courses, both academic and vocational, whose status is unclear. To that proliferation, open learning courses add further complexities. The Council of National Academic Awards might usefully be reconstituted as the Council of National Academic and Vocational Awards, using its undoubted expertise to validate and give credit weightings to sub-degree courses, to facilitate transfer between and among them. Few actions would do more to overcome the desperate shortage of skills and qualifications in Britain today.

The Dovecot and the Campfire

The image evoted by education in Europe is that of a dovecot: the rows of little boxes in the dovecot, one above another, each box cut off from its neighbours, resemble educational institutions that are separate and not interlinked, each knowing its place in the hierarchy. A more open system, such as that in the United States, suggests instead a campfire – people may be nearer to or further from its heat and light but no one is excluded completely.

But the partitions between the dovecot's boxes are starting to be dismantled. Some European students do get into higher education by the vocational route. Others move from formal qualifications to vocational ones; it is not unknown for a West German youngster with an *Abitur* (the 18-plus academic qualification) to enter an apprenticeship. A few bold institutions, such as the Open University in Britain, now have procedures for crediting appropriate experience in place of examination passes. The CNAA now interprets its regulations to permit experiential learning as an entry qualification, and sixteen higher-education institutions are prepared to admit such students.[6]

Discretionary entry to higher education has a long and chequered history. Traditional universities and colleges have often exercised discretion in admitting underqualified candidates who perform well in an interview or who have the 'right background'. Paradoxically reliance on examination results grew out of a healthy desire to exclude personal bias, influence or privilege from determining entry to higher education. But there is much that examinations miss. Students whose life experience goes beyond school can fairly present what they have learned from that experience as grounds for accepting them for higher education. The record shows that their final academic achievements are better than those of the formally qualified.

The Challenge to Higher Education

Institutions of higher education in Europe, with a few exceptions, have been as carefully compartmentalized as the schools, colleges and apprenticeship systems for the sixteen- to nineteen-year-olds. Apart from traditional extramural departments, their work has been done inside their own walls, and mainly, though not exclusively, with full-time students entering straight from school. The polytechnics and their equivalents in other countries are similar to the universities in offering first-degree and postgraduate courses, but they have a different administrative structure and are entirely within the public sector. The two channels remain separate.

The flood of demands now being made on higher education will burst these administrative banks. If the universities keep to their ancient closeted ways, they will be by-passed within a generation. For potential students, many needing to up-grade and up-date their skills and knowledge, will provide a rich market for commercially produced educational software and distance learning courses. Major computer firms like Wang and Rank-Xerox are already gearing up to supply it. A few educational institutions have caught on to the significance of this new market, and so, in the case of Britain, have the governments.

Distance Learning

The first experiments in distance learning – educating people at a distance from the teaching institution by a combination of textbooks and written material with radio, television and now microcomputers – were pioneered by the National Extension College at Cambridge, and then attempted on a large scale by the Open University in Britain (originally called the University of the Air). It has now been complemented by an Open Tech (technical college) engaged in producing distance learning systems for technical qualifications, mainly at sub-degree level, on which it cooperates closely with the Cranfield Institute of Technology, itself strongly oriented towards industrial applications.

The Open University idea has taken root in a number of geographically dispersed countries, including Canada, Venezuela and Malaysia.

In this new kind of higher education, the university or polytechnic becomes the centre of a network, the sun of an educational solar system. Much of its work is conducted through the design of appropriate material for learning at home or in the work-place; commercially available material in the subject is assessed and rated in terms of its quality, just as consumer bodies and design institutes rate goods and services now. Since much study in future will be conducted outside the walls of institutions, using video-tapes and educational packages, lecturers will find themselves spending more of their time as tutors, counselling students, and answering their questions and commenting on their work. As interactive (two-way) systems become cheaper, universities and polytechnics will establish local networks of students using cable or fibre optics to take part in teleseminars, and to give and receive information. In a few pioneering American universities, student hostels already have cable systems that make multiple communication possible.

Senior school pupils who do not need supervision, undergraduates and older students will be able to draw up learning schedules to suit themselves, deciding on the order in which they learn and the time of study. The community of scholars will thus become a network of scholars, each determining the pattern of his or her education.

The Open University is one key to Britain's educational future. It has already proved the potential of students lacking formal qualifications. In 1983, more than 40 per cent of its undergraduate intake lacked the two A levels normally required for entry to a degree course. Yet the standards of its degrees have been rigorously maintained, examination papers and coursework being regularly assessed by examiners from outside universities. A pass degree requires six credits, each credit representing twelve to fourteen hours' study a week for thirty-two weeks – more than many internal students manage in three years at university. Up to 1984, 65,000 students had graduated, and the cost for each was about half that for a graduate at a traditional university.

The Open University also trains thousands of people at work, in updating courses and short courses, with a heavy accent on microelectronics. For example, it runs courses on the industrial applications of computers and on microelectronics for teachers. A course on microprocessors and product development conducted in conjunction with the Department of Trade and Industry reached 25,000 people. Some of its training is in-house, tailored to the needs of a particular company. All of its continuing education is self-financing.

Distance learning is most effective if it is complemented by personal contact with a tutor or counsellor. The Open University maintains 260 study centres, and has some 5,000 part-time tutors and counsellors for its 100,000 students. The support provided by this decentralized teaching and counselling together with residential summer schools has been crucial in reducing the high wastage so often associated with external degrees.

The Open Tech in conjunction with the Cranfield Institute of Technology has done valuable work in developing curricula for technical courses, where video-discs embodying demonstrations and graphics promise to be important tools for distance learning. Both the Open University and the Open Tech have the potential to make a major contribution to the future open learning system, able to match the private sector in innovation and flexibility while maintaining the standards of the public sector of higher education. They will need support and adequate resources to do so.

The combination of new educational materials with flexible, decentralized tuition and counselling may be the best answer to the need for continuing education and for the up-grading and up-dating of skills in the population as a whole. New materials with great potential are being developed. Stanford University in California, for example, has been developing instructional video-tapes. In Britain, the Open University has used them in a major in-house training programme for Marconi, the electronics company. Individual learning packages, including video recordings of lectures and demonstrations by outstanding teachers, is the next step. Video-centres will make the tapes available cheaply or even free of charge. Beyond that lie interactive systems, like those being experimented with at Brown University in the United States and at Strathclyde in Scotland, where students can record questions and comments on the tutors' monitors which can then be dealt with in the tutors' own time. The role of the teacher will change from that of an authority to that of an adviser. Many will work from home, others will be peripatetic.

The development of distance learning and individualized learning packages around existing institutions, responsible for maintaining standards and providing personal tuition and counselling, could multiply many times over the output of our best teachers, and make the vision of *éducation permanente* a reality.[7]

17 Men, Machines and Management

'So long as methods of production were primitive, the great mass of the people were necessarily tied down to dreary, exhausting manual labour.... But since the arrival of the machine the whole pattern has altered. The justification for class distinctions, if there is a justification, is no longer the same, because there is no mechanical reason why the average human being should continue to be a drudge.'

George Orwell, *James Burnham and the Managerial Revolution*, (1946)

Technology is a means, not an end in itself. It should be a means to a better, richer society in which knowledge and therefore power is widely distributed, and people live fulfilled and satisfying lives. But this is not always the way technology is used at present. Too often technology becomes its own justification and technologies are pursued regardless of the consequences for human beings. But this is not inherent in technology; it is human beings who choose how to employ the resources and the power it provides.

Investments in new capital equipment are made because they are profitable. It is often believed that wherever a capital investment enables labour to be saved, it is worth making, provided the savings on wages exceed the costs of amortizing the capital. But capital investment can also be used to make labour more productive. Computer-based industrial systems are no different from their predecessors in this respect. On the one hand, the new systems can be designed to allow workers to use their own judgement, to employ computer processes as adjuncts and aids, and to increase the skill content of jobs. On the other, they can be designed to program human beings 'out of the loop', to remove human intervention as far as possible, taking the skill content out of existing jobs. The choice is likely to be influenced by the extent to which managements consult workers, whether there is mutual trust between them, and whether the ethos of the society is one of cooperation or conflict.

In a consultative industrial relations structure, the workers who operate computer-based systems will be asked to suggest how best to use them and what adjustments need to be made. If adjustments are frequent, for instance when using a computer-controlled machine tool for a wide range of functions, the involvement of the operator is normally necessary. Computer-controlled machines can be designed to make the interface, or interchange between the human operator and the machine, simple and easy. As an illustration of this, a robot may be programmed to perform a certain operation from detailed rules, or it can simulate that operation done by a human being. The first de-skills work; the second enriches it. Computer-aided design can manipulate modules of a standard design to provide different scales or shapes. Alternatively computer graphics can enable designers to produce a variety of three-dimensional displays, allowing the customer to select exactly what he or she wants. The first constrains the designer's imagination; the second enhances it.

Where management is characterized by hierarchical structures in which workers are given orders from above rather than consulted in an attempt to reach a consensus, workers' use of their own discretion is likely to be programmed out. Managements of this kind, often matched by an equally hierarchical trade union or group of trade unions, will choose to program their computers and design their systems at the centre or in the planning office, not on the factory floor. New technologies will be a way of retrieving control over labour.

There is an analogy with the choice between centrally managed mainframe computers, allowing their owners control over access to the data stored in them, and distributed networks, from which microcomputer users can freely draw and to which they can contribute information. The former will be chosen by coercive societies frightened of permitting information to move freely among their people. The latter will be chosen by open societies which believe that the more information citizens have, the better their decisions will be – in other words, societies which trust ordinary people's judgements. A society's implicit values determine the system chosen. It is not simply a choice of technologies.

New technologies are developed by engineers and not by social scientists. It is therefore a matter of some concern that few engineering departments of universities take great interest in the human relations consequences of their work. If new technologies are developed by specialists with little sympathy for the consequences for human beings, microelectronics may compel people to act like robots instead of freeing them from dreary and repetitive jobs.

Taylorism

The dominant industrial relations philosophy in the engineering depart-ments and business schools of Western countries was for many years Taylorism. Frederick Taylor (1856–1915) was an American engineer who wrote several books at the beginning of this century, describing the techniques he adopted to increase the output of workers. He believed that work should be broken down into specialized repetitive modules which would not require skill or judgement. 'Under our system,' he wrote 'the workman is told minutely just what he is to do and how to do it; and any improvement which he makes upon the orders given to him is fatal to success.'[1] The factory system which Frederick Taylor approved of was satirized in the classic 1936 Charlie Chaplin film, *Modern Times*.

Taylor's doctrines were seized upon by the new business schools which trained the influential managers of the mass production age. What managers wanted were trouble-free manufacturing systems which put control in their hands, and that is precisely what the engineers gave them. Human beings could not be replaced. No one had then designed a robot capable of flexible operation, nor a computer. Even when computers were first developed, they were huge, clumsy and expensive calculating machines utilizing valves. So Taylorism made some kind of sense in an industrial America which achieved its apotheosis in the huge assembly line plant producing thousands of identical objects, cars or cookers or bottled soft drinks, and whose labour force had come off the cotton plantations of the South or from the sweatshops of the North-east, with at best elementary education.

What is strange is that Taylorism should have survived unchanged in an age where the mass production line is disappearing and where the level of education almost universally attained in industrialized countries is so much higher. Mentally handicapped people are adept at assembly line work; they like its imposed disciplines and regularity. People of average and above-average intelligence find it soul-destroying, though poverty or lack of opportunity may drive them to work in such jobs. Engineering designs that compel people to work far below capacity are designs for bored and frustrated workers, and bored and frustrated workers make trouble for managers. So managers then try to reduce the use of labour even further.

Such a simple lesson – but evidently one that has not been fully learned, despite some important experiments, such as that of Volvo in Sweden, which abandoned the mass production of cars twenty years ago. In 1979, a professional engineer, Howard Rosenbrock, started work on a flexible manufacturing system designed to interact with human beings rather than to subordinate them. He believed that the new technology could go in one of two directions, to humanization or to standardization and substitution. Rosenbrock also believed that social considerations – the relation of people to machines – should be taken into account in designing new systems, just as economic considerations are. He found, however, that 'in production engineering, and in the development of new technology, it [Taylorism] remains strongly dominant: a heavier burden of proof and justification is placed upon any alternative than upon Taylorism itself'.[2]

At the University of Manchester Institute of Science and Technology (U M I S T), where Howard Rosenbrock worked, a simple flexible manufacturing system had already been designed by some of his colleagues which included a robot and a numerically controlled lathe capable of being programmed by its operator, who would make the first part of a batch, recording his or her operations for a computer which could then play them back. The robot would be programmed at the same time, with final adjustments being made manually. The operator, using the computer as an interface with the machine, would be in control, able to readjust the program if circumstances changed, for instance if some of the parts were wanted immediately or some machines were not available.

No British machine tool manufacturer showed any interest in U M I S T's lathe, Rosenbrock reported four years later. Perhaps the last thing they wanted was operator control. For operator control could mean demarcation disputes and arguments about whether the operator was or was not a craftsman, and to which of the many unions he or she should belong. Operators in control would have to be involved and consulted; they could not just be told to get on with it. Human beings might gum up the works.

But someone *was* interested – the Japanese. Rosenbrock's work fitted in with their philosophy of management.

Japan: The Productivity Doctrine

If Japan ever espoused Taylorism, it decisively ceased to do so twenty-five years ago, after a period of tense and bitter industrial strife, itself the product of fierce ideological debate both within the unions and between certain unions and company managements. The Japanese came to recognize that a country largely dependent for food, energy and raw materials on the world outside had to be competitive. They concluded that higher productivity based on modern technology and on cooperation would improve their competitiveness, while bringing benefits to both management and labour.

The new consensus was not reached without strain. The trade union movement split, and a new federation, Domei (the Japanese Confederation of Labour) broke away from the parent body, Sohyo (the General Council of Trade Unions of Japan). Sohyo was at that time strongly influenced by Marxist ideology, believing in the doctrine of class war. Sohyo saw cooperation in raising productivity as a recipe for exploitation of the workers, and it was sceptical about industrial consultation. Domei took with it many of the private sector unions; Sohyo retained most of those representing public sector workers. Some unions remained independent and did not affiliate to any centre; these included the important Autoworkers' Union. Most of these unions are now loosely associated in the Federation of Independent Unions of Japan, the Churitsuroren.

The productivity movement, which started in 1955, was based on three principles: 'stable employment, labour–management cooperation and consultation, and fair distribution of the fruit generated'.[3] To the productivity movement and to its three principles, the Japanese authorities attribute their industrial success. They believe the principles are equally relevant to new technology: 'What we learned from this experience is that in order for advanced technology to result in higher productivity and bring about benefit for the people, the technology must be supported by mutual trust and understanding between labour and management.'[4]

Japan's productivity movement emphasized not only economic efficiency but also human relations within firms. 'Whether the life is rich and the work is satisfactory,' says their White Paper on industrial relations, 'is decisively important for a man's whole life.'[5] The workshop was identified as the basic unit of industrial relations, the place in which consultation on new technologies and new working methods should take place. Seizing on the American idea of 'quality circles', the Japanese developed a range of small-group activities directed towards eliminating defects in products, increasing productivity, consulting on new processes and bettering working conditions. Workers were encouraged to put forward suggestions for improving their firm's performance, suggestions that were, if useful, widely publicized and rewarded. Small-group activities were promoted strongly by management and most of the unions supported them. By the early 1970s, over 80 per cent of manufacturing firms had some form of workshop level consultation.

The reaction of Japanese industry – management and unions alike – to the first oil price shock in 1973 was to make consultation yet more intensive. A survey on trade union activities undertaken by the Japan Institute of Labour at the end of 1981 showed that in half to two thirds of the firms surveyed meetings became more frequent, more information was supplied by management and more opinions were given by trade union officials or trade union members, and that this happened at every level – workshop, plant and enterprise.[6]

The social partners in Japan value the success and harmony that the productivity movement has brought them. They are anxious that the introduction of new technology should not put these achievements at risk. The Japan Productivity Centre therefore urged that there should be consultation as microelectronics and other technologies are introduced, at the enterprise and factory level, through a joint management–labour council, and this proposal has been widely adopted.

Obviously the introduction of new technology into Japanese industries has not taken place without union concern, amounting in a few cases to active resistance. Several Japanese unions, such as the Telecommunications Workers' Union and the Nissan Automobile Workers' Union, will not agree to new technology if it leads to the dismissal or lay-off of union members. Other Japanese unions insist that union members are protected, but will agree to their transfer provided their wages are guaranteed. What is encouraging is that the emphasis on good human relations is everywhere apparent. Significantly, the chapter on new technologies in the summary of the White Paper on industrial relations is headed 'Bringing New Technologies Back to Human Hands'.[7]

It is of course possible to argue that Japan's obsession with human relations in industry will soon be outdated by technological advance. Already hundreds of flexible manufacturing systems have been installed in Japan and elsewhere where the only human workers are those controlling the computers and those monitoring operations – perhaps half a dozen people looking after a vast industrial enterprise. Unless one assumes, however, that human beings will be superseded in every part of the production function, including planning, administration, marketing and maintenance, human relations will remain of paramount importance. In the service sector, as new technologies begin to enter, the man/machine interface will determine the quality of what is offered, in education, health care, tourism or transport. Many small firms will fill market niches, even in manufacturing, their survival made easier by the adaptability of computer-controlled machine tools to batch and bespoke production. As so often in the areas surveyed in this study, it is the human institutions, in this case management–worker and management–union relations, which will determine whether new technologies add to or subtract from the sum of human happiness.

It would be wrong, however, to suggest that no thought at all has been given to the human implications of technology in the West. The research of the Tavistock Institute in Britain and others led to efforts to humanize work by job rotation, job enrichment, ergonomics and self-management. Some important firms have introduced quality circles and small-group activities. A recent comparison of West German and British firms using numerically controlled machine tools showed that West German operators were allowed a greater degree of autonomy in programming by large firms; in small firms, the position of the two countries was similar. The difference in the former case may be explained by the fact that the Federal Republic has an extensive system of industrial consultation required by law, while Britain does not.[8]

The End of Taylorism?

The deeper issue, however, is whether Taylorism is any longer a viable doctrine, given the composition of the labour force in an information-based economy. The Japanese and American findings are clear enough: microelectronic processes need new skills in addition to old ones. They are more complicated to maintain, and require highly qualified people. In Japan, firms that had introduced microelectronics wanted more science and technology graduates, fewer arts graduates and semi-skilled people. Perhaps partly as a consequence, the proportion of men, and particularly young men, employed by them rose, while that of women declined. Older men were transferred to other jobs, so the age of the work-force declined in these firms, though nationally the average age is going up.[9]

A dramatic example of the move upwards in terms of qualifications required is the Kamakura factory of Mitsubishi, which makes electronic equipment. Of the ninety technical employees recruited in 1983, seventy were university graduates and half of these held masters' degrees.

One cannot read across to Western economies without modification, as if Japan were a crystal ball in which our own futures can be seen. For one thing, Japan's large companies have a lifelong employment system. Older workers, unable to adapt to new processes, are transferred to other jobs within the firm. Most retire in their late fifties. Retired workers often move on to post-retirement jobs, but these usually pay much lower wages than were earned in the large firm. If times get really hard, subcontracted work is brought in-house, and the small suppliers take the strain of the recession. Many small firms employ temporary workers – students, or those without qualifications. Temporary workers are laid off without compunction. So are women. It is remarkable that few women in Japan enjoy any security of employment or any opportunity to work with new technologies. 'In most cases', declared a survey by the Japanese Electrical Machine Workers' Union, 'male workers in their twenties and thirties are assigned to new processes using microelectronics. Female workers and middle-aged and elderly workers are excluded from such processes.'[10] Evidence from other countries does not show – at least not yet – a marked comparative decline in the number of women workers, perhaps because microelectronics has only recently reached the services, perhaps because women in Western countries have achieved more equal status with men.

Japan will discover that it cannot afford to treat half its population as an underclass. The talents and skills of women are not being fully used, and, to put it at its most hard-headed, that will damage Japanese competitiveness. Western Europe, for its part, will have to learn the lesson, repeated in a remark made to me on my last visit to Japan, that 'there are no longer white collar and blue collar workers'.[11]

One message does hold good across all countries and all industries pervaded by microelectronics, and that is the hunger for advanced skills in science and engineering. Of the firms in Japan that had introduced microelectronics equipment, three fifths to three quarters had increased the number of engineers and technicians they employed. Less than a fifth now employed fewer, and those that did were firms which were contracting anyway.[12]

The doctrines of Frederick Taylor are inappropriate for a highly qualified, highly educated work-force. The application of his ideas to such a work-force could produce explosive consequences. Management has to meet the skill and knowledge requirements of the technologies it employs. It must then manage skilled and informed employees in the light of changing social attitudes. Men and women live up or down to the expectations others have of them. Employers who expect their workers to be uncooperative and bloody-minded will get what they expect. It is significant that Japanese firms in Britain achieve similar productivity levels to those in Japan and enjoy industrial peace. Indeed, some have no-strike agreements with their unions. The work-force and the unions are the same as in the British firm next door. But the management style is different.

The New-Style Unions

It is not only management that has to learn how to cope with a new, qualified, classless work-force – the unions have to as well. In all the industrialized countries, trade union membership is falling, absolutely and relatively. It is now below 20 per cent in the United States and under 30 per cent in Japan. The bastions of trade union organization are the great manufacturing corporations. It is already clear that jobs are declining in manufacturing, and that the employment share of large firms is falling. To survive, the trade unions have to engage the interest of a new kind of worker, whose needs are not met by bargaining aims limited to wages and hours of work.

Research in the United States has shown that wages in the new-technology industries are substantially lower than in the traditional smokestack industries. The main reason for this is that the firms in the new industries have started in, or moved to, states in the South and West where trade unions have not established themselves and wage rates are relatively low. According to the Congressional Research Service, wages in the car and metalworking industries were between $10·70 and $13·30 an hour in 1982, compared to $7·16 an hour for electronic components and $7·95 for computers and office equipment. Unions seeking to organize in these new industries, or to retain their members in traditional industries suffering from overseas competition, are responding by widening their bargaining aims to include consultation on the introduction of new technologies, provision for retraining older workers, agreement on working conditions including the degree of exposure to visual display units, the content of work, and health and safety. Some far-seeing trade union leaders want to bargain about the design of new manufacturing systems to ensure human control.

Little by little, the old pattern of industrial relations is changing. In a path-breaking new agreement signed with the Japanese car manufacturing company Nissan, in April 1985, the British Amalgamated Union of Engineering Workers has abandoned traditional job demarcations, and accepted compulsory conciliation of disputes, though the right to strike in the last resort remains. In exchange, Nissan will recognize only this trade union. Modern unions and modern management recognize that they are playing in a new game, in which innovation, creativity and judgement are the aces in the pack. None of these is fostered by Taylorism. None of them flourishes in a climate of confrontational industrial relations, a hold-over from the industrial past. To break away from that past demands a recognition – as it did in Japan in the 1950s – that there will be benefits for both labour and management in cooperation and consultation, that industrial relations are not a zero-sum game.

Given their importance for productivity and for technical change, is there a case for legally imposing consultative structures? Several continental Western European countries have adopted some kind of statutory structure of co-determination, and in Britain such a solution was advocated by the Bullock Committee in 1976. The level of consultation that really matters is the workshop or factory floor, not the board, but a change in the composition of the board may give a lead lower down the hierarchy of the enterprise.

European management is still slow to involve workers, and small-group activity is much less extensive than in Japan. A number of firms threatened with liquidation have been rescued by management or employee buy-outs. In the case of the British National Freight Corporation, the employees purchased the company when it was privatized; this has been a great success. Direct involvement of employees through share ownership can be a way of improving productivity and personal commitment, though there is a tendency for ownership to revert to large shareholders as employees sell their own shareholdings. It has often been argued that ownership matters less than management to the success and style of any firm. When involvement is the name of the game, however, the distribution of shares among employees can be a valuable complement to industrial cooperation. High tech depends on the high value of individual skills and individual creativity.

Electronic systems are sophisticated, interdependent and easily disrupted. Strikes, disputes and stoppages are therefore prohibitively expensive. So principles of good industrial practice should become the basis of legislation on industrial democracy, leaving each firm to choose its own model of participation in consultation with its work-force. The best models, I believe, will be those in which ownership itself is directly shared, leading to a common commitment to the firm's success.

Ownership apart, good industrial relations depend upon communications within the firm, as well as on information about what other firms are doing, and why. Ideally there should be a two-way flow, from management down, and from the shop floor and office up. The flow of information is itself influenced by the attitudes of those who manage not firms, but the nation itself.

18 The Information Flow: Access and Control

'The law as it now stands shows a complete failure to understand that accessibility of information about the government of the country is of vital importance in a democracy.'

From the written evidence of Professor H. W. R. Wade to the Franks Committee, 1972

Those who control information and access to it are the power-holders in society. They always have been. From the time of papyrus scrolls to Gutenberg's printing press, rulers have tried to control the flow of information to their subjects. For centuries, illiteracy, the inability to use information in written form, distanced the vast majority of the people from their rulers; access to information was barred by lack of education. But the industrial age demanded literate workers, capable at least of reading instructions and communicating in writing. Paradoxically, while specialization of labour and fragmented tasks might deskill jobs, written communications were required to put the fragments together. A basically literate society provided a market for mass circulation books and newspapers. The availability of information increased alongside the capacity to use it. Universal secondary education and the expansion of higher education after the Second World War created a market for more sophisticated information, conveyed through a wide range of different artefacts and through many different media.

The quantity of information remains important. But quality has become the critical variable. Using technical terms like 'software' does much to obscure this simple truth. Societies in the information age will flourish if their people are well educated, have access to information of all kinds, understand how to select from a confusion of abundance, and have the wisdom to use that information for human and humane ends.

In an earlier chapter I concluded that the quality of education will be one vital determinant of the success of societies in adapting to information technology; another will be the ease of access to information itself.

Access

Access to information is access to the critical raw material of the new technologies. If whole sectors of the population are not to be excluded from playing their part in a future information society, every citizen in a democracy will need access to information in the public domain through computers as well as through books and printed material. Access should not be prohibitively expensive either. It was expensive to own a private library, so expensive that few, aside from scholarly members of the aristocracy, ever achieved it before books could be printed in large numbers. Even then it was the free public libraries as much as the relative fall in book prices that opened up treasure-houses of information to ordinary men and women. Today, the microcomputer has fallen in price as printed books did, and can give users access to vast quantities of information. But if that information is stored in data-banks owned by private corporations, access is likely to be controlled and expensive. If it is in the possession of the official bureaucracy, access may be limited or even forbidden.

Access to information in the public domain is as important a civil right as the suffrage itself. Indeed, the choice made possible by the suffrage is far more effective if it is based on truthful and abundant information. What this means for the future is that information technology should be as readily available as books are today. Microcomputers linked to official data-bases should be available to the public in libraries, social security and employment offices, and post offices, either free of charge or on payment of the cost of the time used only. As expert systems explaining legislation and regulations are drawn up, they too should be made accessible. The experiments already conducted, like the one mentioned earlier for benefit claimants, show how quickly members of the public take advantage of such opportunities.

The easier the access to information, the better the use people make of it. Once they become familiar with information artefacts – typewriters, word-processors, computers – people begin to find creative ways of using them. They try out new methods by which their work may be complemented or improved. They group the artefacts together into systems and networks, learning as they go. The software they demand becomes more adventurous and more ingenious; in short, the quality of information improves.

Availability

But access alone is not enough. What matters as well is the amount of information held in public data-bases, in other words, availability as well as access. If large amounts of information relevant to individual or social choices and decisions are kept secret, or if access to them is restricted, the quality of democracy will suffer. The benefits of information technology will go to an élite of bureaucrats or meritocrats or corporations.

In most modern democracies, the institutions of government have come to recognize that a better-educated population demands more information, not least about the administration of the state itself. The role of government, even in democracies, is incomparably greater than it was before the Second World War. So the electors who fund government through taxation, and who are directly affected by it, want to know what it does and why. An educated electorate is inclined to argue with government officials about their decisions and choices and about their priorities. Official information is the ammunition which they need to conduct their campaigns.

The argument for easy and open access to information is not only that it will strengthen democracy and make for wiser political choices, though that argument is of pre-eminent importance. Access to information is the *sine qua non* of a thriving modern economy. There are many customers for high-quality software, and software is likely to constitute 90 per cent of the expenditure on information technology by the end of the decade. Those customers are much more likely to look for their software in an information-rich society than in one where, to use Daniel Bell's words, 'scarcity has been imposed'. The quality of that information will be better.

The Power of the Executive

In Europe, once a continent of monarchs, information has historically been closely controlled, the prerogative of the ruler and later of the educated élite. Access to information together with education in how to use it determined who shared in political power. The tiny minority educated through the Church and the ancient universities were permitted to join, in the management of society, those who inherited power from birth or who became wealthy. In some European countries, like

Great Britain and the Scandinavian countries, representative institutions developed which had to be consulted before the monarch could levy taxes on his or her subjects. Gradually freedom was extended to include freedom of speech. But control over public information remained with the executive, and the executive – the monarch or the government – decided how much or how little to release. Before this century, only one government, that of Sweden, recognized the right of citizens to obtain and receive information, a right granted to them as long ago as 1766.

Perhaps it is the advent of a generation of high-school and college graduates that has persuaded governments in the Western democracies to adopt freedom of information laws. The first significant move was the United States Freedom of Information Act of 1967 which reached the statute book at a time of anxious self-questioning by Americans, after Kennedy's assassination and during the worst of the Vietnam war. Shaken by the vulnerability and failures of government, the United States Congress moved the burden of proof from the individual seeking information to the authorities refusing it.

The Act, further strengthened in 1974 and 1976 after Watergate, gives any member of the public the right to request information from 'any executive department, military department, government corporation, government controlled corporation, or other establishment in the executive branch of government (including the Executive Office of President) or any independent regulatory agency'.[1] Certain kinds of information, such as sensitive financial matters and confidential personal data, are exempted. So is disclosure of data if it can be shown to be harmful to the interests of the state, but a refusal on those grounds is subject to challenge in the courts.

Many democratic governments in the West have now followed the United States' example, although few have gone as far. They recognize the public's right to see official documents. They define certain exempted areas. They establish a right of appeal against a refusal to disclose information requested, not to the government itself, but to a body or person independent of government. The roll-call includes countries with parliamentary systems on the British model (Canada, Australia and New Zealand), constitutional monarchies (Norway, Denmark and the Netherlands) and countries with a long tradition of secrecy (France).

The Crown's Secrets

One major democracy clings to a draconian regime of official secrecy – the United Kingdom. Since 1911, when the Official Secrets Act was passed in a mood of panic through an almost empty House of Commons, at the time of the Agadir crisis, the United Kingdom has had the strictest controls over official information of any European country outside the Soviet bloc. The Official Secrets Act covers all government servants, and some in public corporations as well, people in the armed forces and the police. There is no right to official information, and information classified as restricted, confidential, secret or top secret is not made publicly available. An example of the lengths to which secrecy goes is the invisibility of Cabinet committees. These committees are the real decision-makers; some of their decisions are not even presented to the Cabinet, let alone discussed there. Indeed a decision as critical as the barring of trade union membership to employees of GCHQ, Cheltenham, appears not to have been considered by the Cabinet at all. Cabinet committees do not officially exist. Among all the official bureaucracies of the West only Whitehall and Dublin refuse to name them or to say who serves on them. No press reports are given of them, and no journalist may openly ask about them and expect to receive an answer.

Officials themselves classify documents, and are criminally liable if they disclose classified information without the authority of the Minister. The natural desire of officials to play safe means that innocent documents are routinely classified, and many are over-classified. Papers bearing the classification 'secret' often disclose little more than well-informed leaders in newspapers. Those marked 'restricted' are no more sensitive than the general run of news stories. The Official Secrets Act, together with the thirty-year rule which bars publication of official records for that period, is too often used to protect ministers and civil servants from blame for their own mistakes, as the Home Secretary of the time, Merlyn Rees, pointed out to the House of Commons in November 1976, when he introduced a Green Paper intended as a first step towards legislation to reform the Official Secrets Act. The standards of public debate on the great issues of the day are therefore often reduced to little more than an exchange of epithets and slogans.

Individual liberties in Britain, which has no written constitution, no Bill of Rights, and little statute law on the subject, depends upon the integrity of ministers. Civil servants are instructed to be loyal to them even if they disagree with the policies they espouse. The Official Secrets Act provides the government of the day with penalties against aberrant officials that frighten off all but the most determined. Parliament may make trouble, but is not sufficiently well briefed or well staffed to be an effective guardian of the people's liberties. Furthermore, a Government majority can override Opposition objections, and back-bench Government MPs know that the rewards of politics are largely reserved for the loyal.

Accountability to Parliament, the theoretical safeguard against an abuse of executive power, is in practice weakened by Party discipline. The sticks of the Whips and the carrots of preferment and patronage mean that the Government of the day, given a majority in Parliament, can get whatever legislation it wants through the House of Commons, though not always through the House of Lords.

Repeated attempts have been made to reform the Official Secrets Act. In 1968, the Fulton Report on the Civil Service declared: 'The public interest would be better served if there were more openness.'[2] Four years later, the Frank Committee recommended the repeal of Section Two of the Official Secrets Act, and its replacement by an Official Information Act. But the Conservative Government of the day backed away from so radical a proposal. The Labour Opposition committed itself to legislate on freedom of information. When returned to power in 1974, the Labour Government began work on a bill, but was hampered by divided views within the Government and the Party. One section of opinion wanted to concentrate on repeal of Section Two of the Official Secrets Act 1911, the catch-all section. It felt that the legislative problems of passing a freedom of information bill would be so immense as to destroy all chance of reform, especially given the Government's minuscule majority. The other section of opinion wanted to go for the radical solution of a freedom of information bill, believing objections based on cost and administrative difficulty were deliberate efforts to obstruct reform. These divided views and the disappearance of the Government's majority destroyed whatever chance there had been of getting legislation through Parliament. By the time the Labour Government fell in June 1979, no bill had been introduced.

The Croham Directive

But something else had been accomplished. In July 1977, Sir Douglas Allen, then head of the Civil Service, issued a memorandum with the backing of the Prime Minister, James Callaghan, calling on the heads of departments to make departmental papers, such as background papers for policy studies, public wherever possible. Ministers would no longer have to authorize such publication, although they could stop it. The Croham directive, as it came to be known, was issued at a time when ministers were interested in improving public consultation. Education had been the subject of a 'great debate' begun in the autumn of 1976, and conducted in major cities up and down the country to which representatives of industry, the trade unions, teachers and parents' organizations were invited. The Energy Secretary, Anthony Benn, had organized an energy conference to which organizations interested in energy policy sent members. In 1976, the first statute allowing individuals the right to see their personal records, the Consumer Credit Act, was passed, though the records concerned only dealt with a person's credit rating.

The Croham directive led to the publication by some government departments of many previously classified documents. Rather surprisingly, the Foreign and Commonwealth Office was among the most forthcoming. But in some other departments, little or nothing was done.

Even these limited steps aroused resistance, and not only among ministers and civil servants. Lay members of official committees may dislike their proceedings being published. It diminishes their importance in their own eyes, and may subject them to criticism. Officials feel exposed to public comment and some invoke the myth of ministerial responsibility to argue that freedom of information is not compatible with British constitutional practice. Ministers may oppose reform on the same grounds. The collective responsibility of the Cabinet for Government policy teaches ministers to be tight-lipped in public, and the lobby system enables them to say privately what they think about their colleagues' policies without any risk of being identified. The Parliamentary lobby, a journalistic élite, gains privileged access to inside information in return for maintaining confidentiality. So enthusiasm for breaking the system of secrecy, subtly corrupting as it is, is weakened even among those who might be expected to be the foremost champions of freedom of information.

Civil servants are bound by the tightest of disciplines, and by a code so arcane that few members of the public know of its existence. Every civil servant in Britain must sign a declaration saying that he or she is aware of, and will comply with, the Official Secrets Act. The training and ethos of civil servants emphasize loyalty to ministers and to elected governments. Civil servants prepare answers to debates and Parliamentary questions so that, however non-political they may be in principle, much of their work involves defending the executive against the legislature. Their promotion and preferment depend upon the exercise of discretion and the practice of secrecy. There are no marks for civil servants determined to provide as much information as possible to the public.

In January 1985, the jury in the trial of Clive Ponting, a senior official in the Ministry of Defence who had sent documents without authorization to an MP, Tam Dalyell, found him innocent of charges under Section Two of the Official Secrets Act. Mr Ponting claimed that it was 'in the interests of the State' for him to disclose these documents, because ministers were systematically misleading Parliament and concealing the facts about the sinking of the Argentine cruiser, the *General Belgrano*. That verdict, reached in spite of emphatic directions on the law as he interpreted it by the judge, Mr Justice McCowan, destroyed whatever credibility Section Two retained. No rational Attorney-General, given also the earlier disastrous Official Secrets case concerning Biafra, would be likely to risk such a humiliation a third time.

The nature of the legislation that replaces Section Two has become of central importance to Britain's economic and political future. Will it replace the blunderbuss of the Official Secrets Act with some streamlined modern version, more effective in protecting the executive from scrutiny? Will it simply repeal Section Two, and replace it with a code of conduct for civil servants? Or will there be a major reform, providing a right to information, changing the burden of proof from the citizen to the executive, yet protecting the privacy of individual data?

The Interest Groups

There is another formidable force ranged against the disclosure of official information and its importance is rarely appreciated. British governments work closely with the great corporate powers, industry, the professions and the trade unions. Consultative structures in most government departments are based on private discussions with them. Very often, these bodies are themselves reluctant to agree to the disclosure of information. Firms and trade unions fear their competitors or rivals will gain advantage from information about their attitudes or plans. The professions jealously guard their prerogative of confidentiality. Information is about power, and all these groups have a corner in power they do not want to share. Even the expression of an intention to disclose information mobilizes opposition over a very wide front. Doctors' organizations have until recently been reluctant to let patients see their records. Teachers' organizations opposed parents who wanted to see their children's personal profiles, and for a long time resisted parents having access to information about schools. Manufacturers dislike publication of product tests or details about industrial pollution or waste. Shopkeepers resist the publicizing of prices. Pressure from groups such as these has led to an extension of confidentiality and secrecy beyond the confines of the Official Secrets Act. Over a hundred British statutes contain clauses that make unauthorized disclosure of information a criminal offence. In some instances, like the Census Act of 1920, the privacy of citizens is being protected. In many more, it is the interests of officials or organized bodies that lie behind these statutory restrictions.

British newspapers and British citizens, via a United States go-between, can seek information through the United States Freedom of Information Act, to which British firms trading with the United States have to conform. The *Sunday Times* made extensive use of the American legislation in its investigation of the Distillers' Company, the manufacturers of thalidomide. Other companies and other individuals have followed that lead.

The usual defence of the present system is that the government is accountable to Parliament, and Parliament defends citizens' liberties. The growth of Parliamentary select committees, which have the right to call for persons and papers, has certainly led to more information being made available by government departments. Some select committee reports have been perceptive and useful. But Parliament as a whole rarely debates select committee reports, nor is departmental legislation initially submitted to their informed scrutiny, so their influence is limited. It is easier for governments to get legislation through Parliament if MPs know little about it. Furthermore, select committees can breed cross-party relationships of mutual respect in which MPs agree on recommendations to make to government, or combine to criticize the executive's actions. The key to the executive's power in the United Kingdom – the 'elective dictatorship' of which Lord Hailsham once spoke – is control over information supported by Party discipline and the ability of the governing party through the Whips to push its legislation through.

Since 1979, the flow of official information in Britain has been reduced even further, to a trickle. Work on the Croham directive was suspended on the election of Margaret Thatcher's Government to office in May 1979, on the unconvincing grounds of economy. A new bill, the Protection of Information Bill, was introduced in 1979. It actually extended the definition of what constituted official information to new areas, and allowed a minister's certificate to be sufficient proof of a threat to national security. Fortunately, the bill was not proceeded with.

As the society of senior civil servants, the First Division Association, drily pointed out, 'the more secretive the government, the greater the risk of leaks'. Official secrecy and a free Press go ill together. British governments have been plagued by leaks in one field after another, from budgets and social security changes to Cruise missiles and the sinking of the *General Belgrano*. The leaks are pursued obsessively. Once the subject of inquiries within Whitehall, important leaks are now investigated by Scotland Yard's Serious Crimes Squad. In whole areas of public concern not conceivably related to national security, officials have been reminded that there must be no disclosures, and that proscription includes prison conditions or environmental hazards, with no conceivable implications for national security. Civil liberties have been threatened or destroyed in the name of national security – for instance, the abolition of the right of people working at the Government Communications Headquarters to belong to a trade union, or the tapping of private telephones which has until recently been authorized by the Home Secretary with no explanation being required and no reason being given.

British citizens have no legal right to official information. Until recently, they have had no access to records containing personal information either. To flourish, the information society needs safeguards for the individual too. Without such safeguards, people fear that computers will control their lives and abuse their privacy. The safeguards that now exist in British law have been forced on the Government by the need to comply with the verdicts of the European Court. Cases against the

British Government have in recent years far outnumbered cases against any other single government that recognizes the Court's jurisdiction.

One outcome of the need to conform to European conventions was the Data Processing Act, which gives individuals access to information held about them on computers. This legislation was reluctantly introduced because, without it, Britain would have been unable to ratify the Council of Europe's convention on data protection, and British data processing companies might then have been excluded from international data flows.

The Act, passed in 1985, requires that all data-bases kept for other than purely social or private purposes, or for personal accounts, be registered, and that the purposes for which the data-base is kept be explained. If individuals believe that data held about them is inaccurate or misleading, they can ask that the information be corrected, and if that is not done, they can complain to an independent Registrar who has a duty to investigate every such complaint. The task involved is enormous, since it is estimated that there are already some 400,000 data-bases in Britain held for commercial, political, personal and other purposes.

There are gaps in the Act. It does not cover manual records, partly because such a requirement would be impossible to enforce, and there will probably be some 'leakage' of information about individuals from computer to manual records. Information that bears on national security is exempted from the Act's controls; such exemptions must be authorized by a Cabinet Minister or by the law officers, the Attorney-General and the Solicitor-General. Exemptions cannot be challenged in the courts or anywhere else, any more than can ministerial classifications of official documents. This lacuna exists in all legislation, and can only be filled by a new Bill of Rights in which citizens can challenge ministerial decisions affecting their liberties in the courts. The Data Protection Act is nevertheless a long step forward, achieved by a group of persistent reformers in this country and supported by the Council of Europe in Strasbourg, whose principal concern is the protection of human rights in its twenty-one member-states. It is evidence of the embarrassing truth that British citizens living in an information society are driven to seek redress outside their own borders through laws and conventions made in other jurisdictions.

New technologies make the surveillance of individuals easy and cheap. Telephone tapping has in the past been expensive and labour-intensive, only worth undertaking in carefully selected instances, for instance to investigate those suspected of planning serious crimes, though governments of both Right and Left have not hesitated to use it. New microelectronic devices are capable of voice recognition, and can be instructed to record passages containing certain key words or names, excluding conversational dross. That makes authorized telephone tapping a much cheaper operation, and one that is hard to detect, though on the other hand the introduction of automatic telephone exchanges in place of manual ones makes unauthorized tapping more difficult.

Intermittently, evidence of the prevalence of telephone tapping floats to the surface; our threatened democracies are temporarily disturbed before the danger is once again dismissed. The Western world was duly shocked by the widespread use of telephone and wire tapping in the Nixon administration, brought to light by the investigation of the Watergate affair. It was not, however, a precedent. Under President Johnson prominent opponents of the Vietnam war were kept under surveillance, even though their organizations were legal and their protests constitutional. A furore erupted in the British Parliament following allegations early in 1985 that the telephones of leading figures in the Campaign for Nuclear Disarmament had been tapped, although no offence had been alleged against them.

Article 8 of the European Convention of Human Rights lays down a right to privacy. This was invoked in a recent case involving telephone tapping by the Metropolitan Police. In the British court, the vice-chancellor, Sir Robert Megarry, ruling against the plaintiff, declared that telephone tapping 'cries out for legislation'. It took until 1985 for legislation to come before Parliament, in the shape of the Interception of Communications Bill. The Bill, which became law in the same year, makes unauthorized tapping of telephones a criminal offence. The Home Secretary alone can authorize the tapping of telephones. Those who believe their telephones are being interfered with can complain to a special tribunal. There is also a Commissioner, who will oversee general policy on warrants and safeguards.

The Act tidies up a muddled and unsatisfactory situation, but, as in the case of the Data Protection Act, offers no appeal against the minister's decision. The Home Secretary can issue general as well as individual warrants for telephone tapping; warrants can be abused. In the case of the telephone tapping of individuals belonging to the Campaign for Nuclear Disarmament, the tapping had been carried out by way of a warrant from the Home Secretary to tap the telephone of a member of the CND Council who happened to be also a member of the Communist Party. The warrant was properly authorized, but it was used in a highly objectionable manner. A hurried and unsatisfactory inquiry by Lord Bridges followed the Parliamentary outcry. It revealed just how fragile a protection even the requirement for authorization is, though it is admittedly an improvement on the slapdash unauthorized tapping that has often occurred in the past.

The fragile balance between freedom and restriction of information is exemplified by recent events on both sides of the Atlantic. In Britain, the Official Secrets Act is under attack, and its critics want to emulate American legislation. In the United States, some authorities regard that legislation as dangerously liberal, and want to prevent disclosure of classified information without authority. The Central Intelligence Agency has been pressing for such disclosures to be treated as criminal actions, much on the lines of Britain's Official Secrets Act. Engagingly, the CIA proposal was itself classified as secret, but could not be protected because it had not been agreed by Congress.[3] Congress has traditionally been reluctant to agree to such legislation because it would inhibit debate on military questions. Ironically, the Nixon administration promoted a similar bill in the early 1970s. It would have made the disclosures that led to the Watergate investigation liable to criminal prosecution.

The Privatization of Information

Reluctance to disclose information to one's own citizens is bolstered by reluctance to exchange information with Community partners. Britain is not unique among European countries in this respect. European Community countries still pursue essentially national telecommunications policies and maintain barriers of incompatible regulations and standards between themselves. Progress in establishing a common European Community standard has been painfully slow. Telecommunications equipment was deliberately excluded from the harmonization of member countries' public purchasing, so that no European manufacturer has the research base or the operational scale to compete across the board with the Americans and the Japanese. It is a classic case of national greed jeopardizing the survival of the continent's industrial base. Each European country has some advanced area of which it is justly proud – viewdata in Britain, teletext in West Germany, packet switching in France. But the failure of European Community countries to adopt a common purchasing policy has left the field to the great international corporations and particularly to American-based multinationals.

Multinational data networks already operate extensively in banking and financial services. One example is SWIFT, which transfers funds electronically between over 500 banks engaged in international transactions. Major corporations are building up data-banks, and are buying in information for them, including lists of addresses useful for marketing. The manufacturers of microelectronics, particularly the great American-based multinationals like IBM and ITT are establishing communication networks using their own hardware. British Telecom, Europe's largest telecommunications company, proposed a joint venture with IBM to provide an interactive service for business, to be complemented by value-added services like electronic mail. This joint venture would have tied British Telecom into IBM's network architecture, known as SNA. It was vetoed by the British Government.

SNA is already immensely powerful. According to IBM, 16,000 networks have already been licensed within this particular systems architecture. As SNA grows, more and more companies will buy IBM computers and plug into IBM systems.

SNA is not the only systems architecture. British Telecom has its own national network, PSS. The user standards of PSS are based on those agreed internationally by European governments and others as the foundation for an open, non-commercial network system, OSI. It is an open system because any make of computer equipment can be used or made compatible with it. The trouble is that OSI requires governments and companies to reach agreement on technical standards, and that has proved to be a slow and difficult operation. In the end it will be accomplished, but by that time SNA, the IBM system, is likely to dominate the world of business information. While governments protect their secrets, information by-passes them, moving through private channels and controlled by private companies.

What is at stake is important: sovereignty. In a world where information moves freely across borders, national sovereignty has to be exchanged for national influence over those who shape international networks and systems. Five years ago, it looked as if the European Community might succeed in combining its resources to create a formidable European challenger in the telecommunications field. Despite the European Community's ESPRIT programme, that now seems unlikely: the Italians and the Dutch have linked up with AT&T, the British and West Germans with IBM. The battle to dominate the information society will be fought out by the Americans and the Japanese, with the Europeans as bag-carriers, split among themselves. OSI may provide a bridge between the private sector systems, but it is unlikely to be in operation for several years. The European Community's dependence on the great multinationals for information and communications in the new epoch is at least as significant a threat to the sovereignty of its member-states as the power of veto some insisted upon retaining under the Luxemburg compromise. Indeed, insistence on that power of veto has crippled the European Community and prevented it from developing a common industrial policy. In the information society, the Community's inability to unite has made Europeans into secondary actors on the world stage.

19 The Means of Surveillance

'...there are, in our own day, gross usurpations upon the liberty of private life actually practised, and still greater ones threatened with some expectation of success...'

John Stuart Mill, *On Liberty*, (1859)

Among the democracies, the largest surveillance operation of all is conducted by the United States National Security Agency, an obscure organization which, unlike the Central Intelligence Agency or the FBI, is rarely subjected to Congressional scrutiny. Despite its shadowy existence, the NSA boasts a formidable capacity for gathering information. Its installations can monitor virtually all communication links, including international telexes and telegrams. Its unmanned receivers are capable of recording through microwaves, and the agency's knowledge of cryptography enables it to unravel coded messages. Representatives of NSA have given national security as a reason for refusing to answer questions from members of Congress about its functions, which extend beyond national borders. Some of its most important information-gathering installations are outside the United States. The scale of its operations can be judged from just one example: the NSA monitored 2·5 million telephone calls between the United States and South America over a brief period in pursuit of an international narcotics ring.[1]

Surveillance for purposes genuinely concerned with the security of the state is all too easily extended to include political opponents as described in Chapter Eighteen. Nothing may happen to those whose letters are opened and whose telephones are tapped, but the atmosphere of intimidation and suspicion engendered by surveillance is inimical to individual liberty. It is a first step towards totalitarianism. 'Liberty', the Russian historian Solovyev wrote, 'grows in the interstices of the state.' Inefficient dictatorships leave a little room for liberty. Officials can muddle the records, or be bribed, or simply bend the rules. Some rebellious souls slip through the net. But the efficient dictatorship carries out the wishes of the rulers absolutely. That is why Nazi Germany, a state with meticulously compiled records on all its citizens, was so terrible a regime compared to Fascist Italy. In Germany no one was unknown; no one was spared.

The tapping of telephones and cables is not the only means of surveillance the computer renders both efficient and inexpensive. The multiplication of credit cards and computer booking systems means that a great deal of information may be gleaned about people's movements, spending habits and life-styles. Electronic funds transfer for personal transactions is certain to be widespread in advanced economies by the end of the century. What that means is that payments at supermarket and department store cash tills will be made by an electronic message to an individual's bank, crediting the shop and debiting his or her account, while recording details of the time, place and amount of the transaction. Cash and barter transactions are anonymous since nothing is recorded other than the amount owing. Once the bill is settled by cash, no record is normally kept. Electronic transfer will provide records of the time and place of transactions which, matched with other records held on computers, will permit a detailed picture to be drawn up of almost any individual. The absence of a requirement in North America and Britain for all citizens to hold identity cards will slow down the process of composing individual records, but will not prevent it. Computer matching of individual names and addresses on a number of different records remains feasible. Meanwhile, moves towards a common identity number continue. United States' servicemen are now often given the same service numbers as the numbers on their social security cards, while social security cards have been introduced for infant children.

Computer Matching

Record matching is undertaken not only for political purposes, but also for administrative convenience. American parents who fail to pay child maintenance to divorced or separated partners are now traced in a cooperative effort by state and Federal authorities through tax, social security and public service records. Sixty-two per cent are tracked down. Drivers' licences for 17–24-year-old drivers have been scanned to catch draft dodgers. The FBI, like the British police forces, is building up a computer record of crime and criminals which enables a person's previous criminal record in any state to be summoned up on a terminal in a matter of seconds. No longer can a record be forgotten or lost in the obscure corners of a decentralized police system. It is there, insistent, ever present, impossible to unload.

The bloodhound computer operates in the private sphere as well as the public one. In the United States, where there is no legislation protecting data about individuals, private agencies build up computer lists of names and addresses, often by purchasing them from companies who have used them for other purposes, like selling by post. They can then match these lists against others, such as credit ratings or court appearances. A computer record is being constructed of any tenant who has appeared before a court for non-payment of rent or to be evicted. Landlords pay for the information so that bad tenants can be barred from renting their property. The possibilities for abuse are endless; one obvious danger is the linking of records of offences to employment, making it difficult for young offenders ever to get a job.

Computer records are no better than the material fed into them. Many register faulty or misleading information. A good tenant may bring a rogue landlord to court for failing to do repairs or because the apartment is damp or infested. If the landlord retaliates with an eviction order, the tenant may be blacklisted for years to come. Inaccurate information about credit-worthiness may prevent someone getting a loan or being able to start a business. All this was true in the past, of course, but the link-up of local or individual information with national and international data-bases multiplies many times over the damage done.

The Persistence of History

There is a subtler danger too. The computer's capacity for summoning up records almost instantaneously, regardless of when or where the recorded event occurred, mean that individuals cannot escape their personal history. The prodigal son's prodigalities in a far-away land are forever recalled. A minor offence, a momentary slip, a dishonest action long repented will be as inescapable as one's shadow. Computer systems are without forgiveness and only forget if instructed to. Laws, of course, can ensure a person's rehabilitation. Even with such merciful laws, the premium on conformity is immense. We will instruct our children to have clean records rather than clean hands or pure souls. The price of kicking over the traces could be paid for a long time.

The long arm of modern information systems does not only reach back into history. It also reaches forward into the future. Computer matching of personal records already enables us to piece together someone's history. Computer profiling may make possible a reasonably accurate prediction of his or her future. For instance, it is possible to compare the characteristics of violent murderers or rapists with those of the general population. Indeed, past studies have suggested some correlation between violent crime and an additional Y chromosome in men. It is equally possible to identify every male baby born with an additional Y chromosome and to keep his name on a list of those at risk of behaving violently. This is a crude example, but the possible consequences are easy to spell out. Children could be labelled at birth by society's expectations as they are now by colour, class and sex. The burden will be worse than it is now, for the label will carry more detail, and will bear a spurious authority.

It would be facile simply to deplore the sophisticated surveillance mechanisms made possible by microelectronic technology. They do indeed pose a disturbing threat to personal freedom, yet paradoxically they protect it too. Organized crime and terrorism are children of advanced technological societies, the former because criminals too inherit the technology, the latter because such societies are complex, interdependent and highly vulnerable to unpredictable actions. There is a synergy between technology and terrorism that threatens the fragile, mutually supportive and balanced structures of civilization. If we are to sustain our societies against these new fields of force, democracies will have to construct a new framework. In Theodore Lowi's words, 'individual freedom [becomes] a matter of policy choice'.[2]

Safeguards and Structures

There is no contradiction in balancing the claims of privacy against those of access to information, since the information to be protected is different from the information to be provided. Information about identifiable individuals must be protected. Information about institutions, policies, categories and objects should be provided, subject only to national or international security rigorously defined. To abuse the term 'national security' is so tempting that classification should be subject to a tight definition, and to review by a body or individual wholly independent of the executive. Like the operation of freedom of information legislation, classification of information could be monitored by a committee of Parliament and Congress, or, perhaps better, by an independent agency or a constitutional court.

The individual citizen in the United States should have access to any information held about him or her, and should have the right to correct factual inaccuracies and to dispute subjective opinions, a right the citizen now has in Western Europe. Many citizens have no idea what is recorded about them, nor where it is kept, so it would be more attractive to require by law that records of individuals held by public authorities be regularly reviewed, say every three to five years, and print-outs of the personal information held on them be distributed as part of the process of review. Such a requirement would, however, be both very expensive and administratively difficult. A practical compromise would be to encourage voluntary organizations and others offering legal advice, citizen's advice bureaux and legal aid centres for instance, to tell people about their new rights and how to ensure that these rights are respected. Records could then be 'cleaned up'.

No one should have access to anyone else's personal record except on the 'need-to-know' principle, and each occasion should be noted. In no circumstances should information on individuals be allowed to be sold or transferred without the individual's permission. Information no longer needed for the purpose for which it was collected should be destroyed.

The Swedes have a system of data protection which establishes gateways between separate sets of official records, such as medical records and tax records. The sets cannot be linked together without specific permission, and the reason for requesting a linkage must be made known to and approved by an independent watchdog agency. From time to time the committee initiates computer 'searches' to make certain that the gates between data-bases are kept closed.

Two other safeguards should be added. In many European countries, including the United Kingdom, a person's record is cleared of crimes after a period of good behaviour, just as endorsements on a driving licence disappear after a period of driving with no offence being committed. The danger of being haunted by a record is greatest in the United States, where arrests are logged, even when a person is subsequently acquitted of any crime, and where there is no system of rehabilitation. Rehabilitation is a crucial factor in ensuring an individual's freedom in the computer age. It will not be enough to rely on being forgiven by neighbours and friends. Forgiveness, like individual freedom, becomes a policy choice. Individuals must be allowed to make a fresh start; their *alter ego*, the computer record, must therefore be started afresh too.

Technology may help to control itself. According to Theodore Lowi, the invention of a 'smart card' in France, in which a programmable microchip is embodied, makes it possible to record data on an individual in virtually unbreakable code. It might in addition be possible to record every occasion on which an individual's data was demanded and by which department or agency.

It is an illusion, however, to rely solely on a technological answer to these problems. The gulf between the technological capacity to destroy individual liberty and the complacent out-dated response of our elected institutions can only be bridged by the determination of free people to legislate safeguards.

20 Can Democracy Survive the Computer?

'What could be more obvious than the fact that, whatever intelligence a computer can muster, however it may be acquired, it must always and necessarily be absolutely alien to any and all authentic human concerns?'

Joseph Weizenbaum, *Computer Power and Human Reason*, (1976)

It is easy to forget how young, in the historical sense, universal suffrage is. Truly democratic political institutions came to maturity in the closing decades of the industrial epoch, that is to say, in the first half of the twentieth century. In those decades, the suffrage was extended in North America and in most of Western Europe first to all adult males and then to women. Political institutions showed vigour and imagination after a Second World War in which democracy's most formidable European antagonist was soundly defeated. Democratic organizations were rebuilt in Germany and Austria. The foundations of the European Community were laid. Throughout Western Europe welfare states were developed. Among the fruits of these efforts were stable societies and the elimination of dictatorship from the Western part of the European continent, as Greece, Portugal and Spain came into the European democratic fold.

The political institutions of democracy have not shown a similar capacity to comprehend or to shape the new epoch, the technological revolution based on the computer. Popular democracy was born of the industrial revolution and of mass elementary education, which between them produced an organized industrial working class and an organized professional and managerial class. Institutions were created or reformed to provide means through which their opinions and wishes could be expressed; regular elections to national and local legislatures and authorities, the accountability of the executive to elected men and women, the narrowing of inequalities and the provision of publicly funded services enabling everyone to participate in the political process. The new epoch brings different patterns of work and different relations at the workplace. It renders irrelevant the occupational delineations and class patterns of the past and requires that the majority of the population be highly educated. The implications for the political process are every bit as profound as they were in the transition from feudal agriculture to industrialization.

Information Flow

Computer systems have obvious impacts on democratic political institutions. The first is the ready availability of vast quantities of information. Cable and earth satellite systems make possible an astonishing range of choice of television programmes, teletext, videotext and so on. Millions of homes in North America and Western Europe can already select from scores of television channels, showing programmes for every taste. Events from all over the world are brought on to the screen as they happen. Individuals can compose a programme of entertainment and information to suit their own wishes, and can view, thanks to video-recorders and teletext, at a time chosen by themselves. The constraints of scheduling and transmission have been loosened. Any citizen who wants a lot of information on a particular subject, a political issue for instance, can learn a great deal very easily. The constraints on information are no longer technological. They are political and commercial, and deliberately imposed because those in powerful positions want to keep information in their own hands. A free flow of information restricted only by the need to ensure the safety of the state and the privacy of individual citizens is a *sine qua non* of the democratic process in the new epoch. Previous chapters have already spelled out some of the legislative and administrative measures required.

Storage and Retrieval

The second obvious impact of computer systems on democratic societies, the cheapness and ease they bring to the collection, storage and retrieval of data about individuals, has already been discussed. The cumbersome, labour-intensive and space-wasting business of surveillance is transformed into a system that is capital-intensive, uses flexible and inexpensive equipment, and needs very little storage space. Once details of a population (or part of it) are on computer, it is relatively simple to keep them up to date and to produce endless new information by cross-referencing data-bases. Correcting individual data, which has to be done manually, is by contrast tedious and costly. It only happens if legislatures insist. They may be opposed by governments who tell them it is inconvenient and by civil servants who tell them it is expensive and unnecessary. However, if democratic institutions are to survive and flourish in the new epoch, statutory protection of privacy and the right of access for individuals to the data held about them are minimal prerequisites.

Interactivity

New technology makes possible visual interactivity (two-way communication) over a distance, just as the telephone made aural interactivity over a distance possible. But the technology of teleconferencing is in its early days, and fairly expensive. It will be some years yet before people chatting over a private telephone will be able to see one another, and longer before viewers will be able to participate in a programme made many, many miles away. Electronic mail and teletext, on the other hand, are already well established. Fibre optics and cable permit instantaneous responses to information that is visually conveyed, and are already widely used in business.

In a different sense, interactivity between presenters and audiences is a well-known feature of entertainment and current affairs programmes, both on radio and television. Hours of radio are devoted to phone-in programmes on every subject under the sun. Audience participation programmes range from competitive games to discussions of political and social issues.

Two particular programmes may help us to predict how interactive systems could shape the political process. The first is a long-standing BBC radio series, *You, the Jury*. A topical political controversy is chosen for debate, and the audience is asked to indicate its support for one side or the other, before any debate takes place, by pressing the appropriate button. A debate is then held, in which the main speaker for each side calls a number of expert witnesses. At the conclusion of the debate, a second vote is taken. The second, post-debate vote, is often very different from the first; the audience has responded to the arguments, and is influenced by them. The other significant programme was the series produced by Granada Television during the British General Election campaign in May and June 1983. A panel of people composed to reflect the characteristics of the entire British population according to age, income, region and race was assembled by the television company. The panel met on several occasions during the election campaign. Its members listened to leading figures in the main political parties discuss the most important election issues, such as unemployment and law and order. Members of the panel voted before the debate for the political party they regarded as best on the particular issue, and then voted again after the debate. It is hard to believe that these widely watched programmes had no influence on the result of the election.

The Instant Referendum

The step from such programmes to what some have called 'the electronic lyceum' is not a long one. In some countries, interactive systems already reach a substantial proportion of the population. In the Netherlands, for instance, two thirds of homes are cabled. In other densely settled European countries, cabling is likely to spread quickly. Even in the United States, 20 per cent of households are cabled, and half of those have interactive capability. In Britain, France and West Germany, teletext and viewdata systems are widespread, enabling viewers to respond immediately to news of events, and bringing teleshopping, telebanking and telebooking into daily use. There will be no technical difficulties therefore about instantaneous referenda. A plebiscitary democracy will be feasible, although it will lack the opportunities for discussion and debate of a direct democracy, like that of the ancient Greeks (always excepting the unenfranchised women and helots).

There are large objections, however, to canvassing electors' views through interactive systems, other than on a sample basis. Most electors possess no such system. Many have little chance of acquiring one in the present century. Cable companies go where the money is, to the prosperous regions of a country, and to the better-off towns and suburbs in those regions. Rural areas, inner cities and depressed regions are at the back of the queue. So are poor countries. A direct democracy based on cabling would be a plutocracy. Earth satellites, cheap and moving rapidly into new markets, are beginning to reach rural areas – plaintive dishes turned towards the sky are blooming all over the farmlands of Canada and the United States – but neither cable nor earth satellites will give priority to the poor over the rich, to the slums over the suburbs. A teledemocracy based on instant referenda would be more inequitable than the traditional representative form.

There is another limitation inherent in the technology itself. An interactive system cannot permit more than a limited expression of views: 'I agree strongly; I tend to agree; I don't know; I tend to disagree; I disagree strongly'. The subtler shades of agreement and disagreement, for instance a reservation on one point, a willingness to be persuaded, a doubt about the way a question is formulated, are sacrificed to the need for a simplified and limited range of choices. The Qube system in Columbus, Ohio, one of the earliest interactive cable systems anywhere, could convey only a very limited set of reactions to television programmes, and has been little used. Even if viewers do register an opinion, difficulties remain. Will opinions be registered after a programme on a political issue has been shown? If so, opinions are likely to be greatly influenced by the presentation of that programme, as *You, the Jury* shows. In the United States, where political and current affairs programmes can be sponsored by interested parties, instant referenda might be held on individual issues immediately after a highly slanted programme. An instant referendum on capital punishment or on abortion could be swayed one way or another by the content of the programme preceding the vote. There is an analogy with opinion polls, which often reflect people's short-lived reaction to some particular recent event.

It would be surprising, therefore, if those elected to Parliament or Congress agreed to be bound in any way by electronic referanda. But that is not the end of the matter. Instant referenda will have immense public appeal once a large number of households have been reached by interactive systems. They will be public opinion polls in glorious technicolour. We will be able to hear people's reasons for voting as they do, and we will know their verdict on the issues before them immediately. The potential of such an instrument for bringing pressure to bear on elected politicians is so great that it is bound to be used. How should Congressman X vote on the MX missile? How should Ms Y, MP, cast a free vote on the legal limits on abortion? On any issue of great public interest which can be expressed as a simple choice, the instant referendum will be added to the opinion poll as a way of influencing politicians' decisions.

At a more fundamental level, electronic referenda could by-pass the institution of representative democracy on which all modern democracies are based – the election of men and women by their fellow-citizens to represent them at every level of government. Representative democracy depends on the representatives using their own judgement on behalf of their electors, and being accountable to them at intervals for what they have decided to do. Representatives should weigh in the balance not only their own popularity with their electors, and the pressures they may collectively or individually bring to bear, but also the common good of the nation, and even of humanity. Edmund Burke produced the classic definition of Parliament as a representative assembly:

Parliament is not a congress of ambassadors from different and hostile interests; which interests each must maintain, as an agent and advocate, against other agents and advocates; but parliament is a deliberative assembly of one nation, with one interest, that of the whole; where, not local purposes, not local prejudices ought to guide, but the general good, resulting from the general reason of the whole. (Speech to the Electors of Bristol, 1774)

Representative democracy, so eloquently extolled by Burke, is coming under great strain. Compulsory education has produced a better-informed electorate, and one that can be mobilized into supporting particular interests and causes. The new technologists are enabling pressure groups to organize opinion quickly and with far-reaching consequences.

Direct Mailing

Direct mailing is a technique made possible by the new technologies, in this case by word-processors. It has been developed into a highly sophisticated technique by several American pressure groups, mainly on the political Right, in particular those associated with the Reverend Jerry Falwell and the so-called 'Moral Majority'. Direct mailings aimed at members of Congress have changed the whole tide of opinion on some political issues, like the proposed Equal Rights amendment to the US Constitution, and abortion by choice. The word-processor makes it possible to dispatch tens of thousands of letters, all personally addressed to named individuals, and to keep track of replies. It is a simple and devastating political weapon. Direct mailing combined with public opinion expressed in instant referenda could determine the outcome of many political controversies, and could make independence of mind and judgement a perilous attribute in an elected politician.

The fragmentation of broadcast radio and television into individual 'menus' assists the fragmentation of politics into single issues, a disturbing recent development in politics. Direct mailing and instant referenda also encourage this single-issue trend. It is more difficult to adapt them to a policy spectrum or a party platform where the choice depends on the balance struck in the voters' minds after they have listened to arguments during an election campaign

The Orwellian Nightmare

Since George Orwell's terrifying evocation of the future in *1984*, technologies able to control information and communications have been feared as seedbeds of totalitarianism. The potential certainly now exists for sealed-in prison societies in which humans become helots, their every word and gesture recorded and observed. Nor is there any escape, even in one's own cell or room. The nooks and crannies of older tyrannies offer no hiding-places now. Freedom, as Theodore Lowi says, is now a policy decision. If totalitarianism comes, it will be because the citizens of democracies forget that liberty demands eternal vigilance. Totalitarianism is not, however, the only danger. The other is chaos, a political system ripped apart by interest and pressure groups each pursuing its own ends, each unwilling to sacrifice those ends to a common good of which it is only dimly aware.

Like direct mailing and instant referenda, computer profiling can be effectively mobilized by pressure groups. The technique enables an interest group to define a target audience with great precision, dependent only upon its ability to get hold of adequate data. It is already easy to target electors according to occupation, house and car ownership, and neighbourhood. Information on educational attainment and voting habits can be built up over a period. Health, crime and tax records are harder to come by, but are not inaccessible, given a friendly contact. Every year such a data-base of electors becomes more valuable to a pressure group. They can profile, for example, all women aged between eighteen and forty in better-off cities and suburbs for a campaign on abortion. They can profile car-owners in a campaign against higher taxes on petrol, or gun-owners to oppose gun controls. The organization of politics is becoming very sophisticated indeed, after a century in the horse and cart age.

Computer profiling of electors helps incumbent elected officials as well as pressure groups. Incumbents have much easier access to data. They may be able to lean on officials for sources. They know their own state or constituency. They know which electors they want to target. It is going to be very difficult to break into politics without the backing of powerful pressure groups or of party machines where they still operate, though they are less effective than they used to be.

Parties can, of course, use the new techniques too. Lists of members and supporters filed on a computer can be mobilized to help in elections or enlisted for a particular campaign, taking the location and occupation of electors into account. Local parties can be linked by earth satellite to regional and national headquarters. Campaigns can be conducted from the centre; in theory at least, the energetic muddle that now characterizes many political campaigns will disappear.

The Devolution of Power

Despite these techniques, national political parties are unlikely to become stronger. Like highly centralized political institutions, they are out of sympathy with the centrifugal forces of the new epoch. Such institutions are inappropriate to economies in which local enterprise and community initiative are powerful engines for growth and innovation. They do not fit well with teamwork and partnership in industrial relations, nor with the local and regional networks encouraging mutual help among businesses, social services and local authorities. Nor will there be a political network of links *between* those individuals and communities, whatever measures centralized political institutions may implement to ensure access for citizens both to computers and to official information, and to protect individuals against the abuse of computer records.

For reasons of security, prominent politicians are retreating from the pavements to the television studios: being good on the 'box' is all-important. But electors hunger for human contact with those who govern them. They want to ask questions and offer opinions. Instant referenda will provide at best a poor and contrived substitute for open political meetings.

Part of the answer to these developments lies in devolving decision-making to the lowest level of authority capable of making a particular decision. The existence of tenants' groups managing housing estates, neighbourhood committees concerned with the local environment, self-help organizations for people with particular needs or problems, and statutory and voluntary support to enable the elderly to live independent lives in the community is evidence of a sense of independence and self-awareness at a local level. People want to shape their own lives. But they also want to contribute to, and be part of, a community. Many people dislike a heavy-handed state promulgating rules and regulations. But many people recognize too that there are vulnerable members of any community, who cannot be left to drown in the blind operation of market forces.

Power is beginning to be devolved. In the United States, the Federal Government has retreated from education, welfare and employment, while the states have stepped in, raising state budgets two and a half times over in ten years. Cities and districts have gone out to encourage new businesses and new jobs, and have sponsored schemes to improve education and training. The same is true of the British economy, though legislative measures to curb local government autonomy run directly contrary to the current of the new epoch. Even centralized France has abandoned prefectures and created a system of regional government.

Debate and discussion in a democracy can lead to an awareness of the common good, and a willingness to accept some qualification of individual interests to achieve it. The danger of fragmentation, and of highly organized pressure groups on single issues, is that this necessary process of bargaining and compromise becomes impossible. Representative government turns into a frustrating attempt to reconcile the irreconcilable. Devolution of power offers a way out of this impasse. Cable and satellite systems may fragment national politics into single issues, but they are likely to enrich discussion of local matters, as local radio has done. Cable makes television more local, and at the local level politics will be illumined by information and debate on issues which rarely if ever get time or space on national or regional programmes. The quality of local decision-making should be improved. The more decisions that can be made locally, therefore, the better for society. The conclusion to be drawn from the fragmentation of national politics, the development of local media, the vigour of local economies and the emergence of a better-informed electorate is that government should be decentralized, each decision being taken at the lowest level at which it can be effective. Pressure groups cannot easily distort the perception of what is good for the community if that community is local and well known to those who reach the decisions. At this level, the fragmented interests can be reconciled, in some cases by local referenda.

At national level, where the communications revolution heightens awareness of single issues, and where electronic referenda will focus the already powerful impact of opinion polls on political parties, it may become necessary to submit certain issues to national referenda. The distinction might be between major constitutional matters, on which referenda would be held, and all other issues. The precedents in the United Kingdom of the 1975 referendum on membership of the European Community and the regional referenda on devolution to Scotland and Wales conform to that distinction.

It needs to be said loud and clear, however, that representative democracy will be destroyed if referenda become the usual way of determining decisions on important issues. There is no practical alternative to representative democracy in large and complex countries. Decentralization of decision-making and devolution of power to the regions or states will reduce the load on central government, and enable individual citizens to have more influence, but cannot replace the role Parliaments and Congresses are meant to perform.

The communications revolution tends not only to fragment political parties and enhance coverage and awareness of local issues, but also to make national borders irrelevant. As was pointed out in Chapter Sixteen, shortwave radio and earth satellites make it difficult to police the movement of information across boundaries. Totalitarian countries will have to build roofs as well as walls, and governments of all countries will find that their objectives can only be reached by international agreements and common policies, as is happening already in the economic and financial fields. The nation-state, which has dominated the history of the last two centuries, is being subjected to intense pressures to yield power in both directions, to the people below and to the international institutions above.

21 Who Will Make the Decisions?

'Between those happenings that prefigure it
And those that happen in its anamnesis
Occurs the Event, but that no human wit
Can recognise until all happening ceases '

W. H. Auden, *Homage to Clio* (1960)

The process of policy-making in Western societies is complex and secretive. Politicians and administrators prefer it to be secretive, because they are then protected from outside pressures. Secrecy also makes them feel more important. It is complex because so many different interests, as well as public opinion and the opinions of legislators, have to be weighed in the process. The products of policy-making, bills, White Papers, directions or circulars, are often arcane, or even incomprehensible.

Politicians pride themselves on belonging to a race of amateurs, men and women who learn on and from the job itself. What they bring to the democratic process is common sense, an awareness of how people feel and, at best, wisdom and judgement. Those expert in fields outside politics – businessmen/women, trade union leaders, scientists and academics – do not often shine as politicians. They lack sympathy for the paradoxical mixture of the rational and the emotional, the visionary and the self-interested, that gives politics its excitement and its zest.

How will computer systems fit into this alien world of political decision-makers? In some policy areas, computer simulations and computer systems are already widely used. No Chancellor of the Exchequer or Secretary of the Treasury nowadays would fail to try out that year's budget proposals on a computer model of the economy. The Chancellor's opponents do the same with their alternative policies. Computer models have become so important that politicians now shop among them for the one that produces the forecasts they prefer. Simulations are not restricted to the economy; ministers and their advisers can project the consequences of their decisions on student numbers or energy demand or traffic congestion. There is no difficulty in forecasting or simulating the consequences of one variable, given a certain set of assumptions. The argument, and the judgement, are about the assumptions themselves. It is a central question to which I shall return.

Expert Systems

Expert systems, computer programs which embody the rules of thumb of one or more experts embodied in a series of 'if ..., then ...' propositions, are already being used to help human experts. The knowledge of the expert is built into a program by a knowledge engineer skilled in the design of questions and answers which make plain the inferences and heuristics human experts rely upon. That is why such programs are 'knowledge-based'. Expert systems can be asked to explain themselves, that is to say to reveal the steps by which they reach any particular conclusion, and that is why the adjective 'intelligent' qualifies the description 'knowledge-based systems'. Intelligent knowledge-based systems, otherwise known as expert systems, have been used for the diagnosis of disease, the examination of chemical structures, the discovery of mineral deposits and the design of bridges. Those that have been successfully used have been in limited domains, that is, subject areas with clearly defined limits, and have been based on a set of rules or a theory that has been thoroughly tested in practice. Doctors seeing many cases of a particular disease or engineers designing buildings for different conditions work out rules of thumb that are moderated in the light of experience. They apply common sense to professional knowledge, thereby saving themselves a great deal of time and effort.

Expert systems may have a role in politics. At Imperial College, London, Professor Robert Kowalski and his colleague Marek Sergot have managed to embody substantial parts of the British Nationality Act, 1981, a very complex and opaque piece of legislation, in a logical form that can be run on a microcomputer, answering many of the difficult questions those affected by the Act might ask. Computational logic could, Kowalski argues, help to determine the logical consequences of legislation before it is approved. In other words, a bill before Parliament or Congress could be analysed in advance of being enacted; the computer program that shows the rules behind the bill and the consequences of those rules could be made available to legislators on the committee dealing with the bill, so that its meaning would be clear both to them and to the public. Existing laws can be made more 'transparent' by being embodied in expert systems which can tell the inquirer how he or she is affected by them. The experiment of providing computer programs for DHSS (social security) offices which describe on a simple question and answer basis what benefits a person is entitled to has already been mentioned. Such programs would be excellent *aides-mémoire* for Members of Parliament, social workers, advice bureaux and legal aid centres, because of their capacity to hold large quantities of accurate information and because they can explain their replies. Expert systems could be valuable in helping inexperienced people taking up political office to comprehend legislation in their own fields of interest.

Once outside a domain where the underlying rules are widely agreed upon and accepted as objective, or where an existing law is being analysed, an expert system can embody values in a covert way. Economic models differ in their outcomes because of the subtly different assumptions embodied in them. Economic expert systems and others in the social sciences are bound to reflect the values of the expert whose knowledge is embodied in them, be it Maynard Keynes or Milton Friedman. Because the outcomes of computer programs often resonate with a spurious authority not accorded to the advice directly offered by human beings, there are dangers in using expert systems in those policy areas where politicians need to make value judgements, unless the values are explicit.

There are a number of ways in which democratic societies can come to terms with expert systems. The phrase itself, which is unfortunate, loses some of its authority once it is recognized that expert systems are neither infallible nor, in any area where value judgements must be made, objective. As with conventional computer software, familiarity is important. Simple models of expert systems should be provided to schools along with other education programmes. Students will soon try to write their own. Public libraries and advice bureaux should have expert systems which can explain those laws which affect many members of the public. There is likely to be a large demand for programs on social security, housing and rent acts, and aspects of law. Well-constructed expert systems in which the knowledge of experts is communicated to the public are likely to have substantial sales. Apart from legislation, advice on investments, property and pensions look like promising candidates for expert systems. Several pioneering companies are moving rapidly into the field, and multiplication many times over of present sales is likely to occur in the next five years.

Governments will not be able to ignore the challenge expert systems pose. Those challenges relate first to expert systems providing advice to the public, and second to expert systems used to assist decision-making, including in government itself.

Licensing and certification

For many expert systems available for sale, neither licensing nor certification would be appropriate. *Caveat emptor* remains good advice in the market-place, provided the buyer knows what he or she is doing. Expert systems on house-buying, personal investment or casting horoscopes pose no more problems than do books. Medical expert systems fall into a different category, since they can be used to diagnose illnesses and suggest forms of treatment. Their development has been delayed in the United States by the concern of pharmaceutical companies that they might be sued in the courts if a patient died because an expert system was shown to be wrong, or if the advice obtained from the expert system was misapplied. The opposite danger is that a doctor might be sued for failing to follow advice available from an expert system.

The framework in which expert systems are developed is likely to be a spectrum ranging from, at one end, no regulations at all to, at the other, certification in the case of 'life and death' systems. Within that spectrum are many alternative models. Knowledge engineers and systems designers might accept a code of conduct, and promote a quality kitemark for programs produced in conformity with the code. Public sector bodies, such as public libraries, schools and colleges, and health authorities, might themselves indicate the expert systems they found most useful, after consulting the relevant professional bodies. But regulation and self-policing is less important than preventing monopolies of either suppliers or experts or both. Expert systems will flourish best, and will threaten open societies least, if the climate is one of competitive plurality. Where value systems are embodied implicitly or explicitly, competition is essential. Indeed, there are few areas of the market where strong anti-trust legislation is more important. For there is a danger of embodying in expert systems the currently fashionable conventions, and then finding it difficult to move away from those conventions. Up-dating alone will not alter the assumptions on which a system is founded. For instance, in health care, expert systems might leave forms of treatment based on alternative medicine out of account. Economic expert systems and management expert systems are likely to be based on a conventional wisdom that does not endure. Competition among several suppliers, including divergent ones, and a healthy scepticism based on familiarity with knowledge-based systems from schooldays are the best protections for society against the threat of a stultifying intellectual conformity.

Like the other instances of new technology described in this book, expert systems are capable of conferring immense benefits on society. As *aides-mémoire* to doctors, engineers, managers and legislators, they should improve the quality of the decisions made because they contain relevant and sometimes rare information, and because they lay bare the meaning and the consequences of a decision. In the domains where the rules command a wide consensus, such as science and engineering and to a lesser extent medicine, expert systems multiply the scope and extend the reach of outstanding human authorities. It is not fanciful to imagine doctors in the western provinces of China or paramedics in Tanzanian villages having access to the finest medical expertise available anywhere in the world. The quality of engineering, irrigation, land management and agriculture could all be improved at low cost; indeed Third World countries in consultation with voluntary organizations might themselves want to sponsor expert systems they believed to be relevant to their needs.

Much depends on choosing the expert or experts; much also depends on the role of the human being who uses the expert system for advice. Too many experts from the West and the Soviet bloc have done great damage to the Third World by advocating huge prestige projects and inappropriate capital-intensive agriculture which have undermined indigenous rural communities and landed developing countries with heavy debts. Expert systems commercially promoted and embodying the heuristics of experts from advanced industrial countries might do even more extensive harm, not least because of the respect in which many people hold computer systems, which could mean that advice in the form of an expert system was accepted without question.

If expert systems are used to complement human advisers, they are less likely to be followed in situations for which they are not appropriate. The 'human in the loop' liaises between the system and the situation, bringing in elements of judgement and intuition the system's designers could not have incorporated; the more complex the situation, the more important the catalytic role.

There are some situations, however, where the human user and decision-maker may be by-passed – where, in the jargon, the human is programmed out of the loop. It is in areas where the decision-making time is shrinking to a shorter period than is required for human deliberation that artificial intelligence and its product, the expert system, is being looked to, not just to assist decisions, but to make them.

Command and Control Systems

Computer systems (though not necessarily expert systems) are indispensable to decision-making in highly complex areas, or in areas where the time to make decisions is short. Defence policy meets both descriptions, and, as one would expect, the command, control and communications structures of the military are heavily reliant on computers. Political control is still in the hands of elected politicians, at least in constitutional theory, but the shrinkage of time in which to make decisions challenges the practicality of that theory. Surveillance and detection of other countries' military dispositions are largely conducted by remote-controlled devices, especially by satellites. Early warnings of hostile or potentially hostile actions are given by radar systems that are computer-controlled.

Computer systems do inspire respect, but they are not faultless. Blood-curdling stories circulate among computer professionals about near-misses between aircraft controlled by ground computers, and about the occasions when the North American missile defence system has been falsely alerted as a result of computers malfunctioning. In one famous case in 1960, the rising moon was mistaken for an enemy attack. In every instance so far, the error which led to the false alarm has been corrected by a human being in time. What needs repeating over and over is that computers are no more infallible than the human beings who make and programme them.

The possibility of a mistake or a malfunction makes responsible leaders hesitate when they are asked to entrust decisions entirely to computers. Yet the most important decision of all, whether or not to launch nuclear weapons, becomes more dependent on computerized systems with every advance in military technology. The companion to the huge research programme into President Reagan's Strategic Defense Initiative is a smaller programme called the Strategic Computer Initiative. This programme will finance work on the elaborate and sophisticated computers necessary to control defensive systems in space. Such systems, if they prove technically possible, would allow only a minute or so for a decision on how to respond to a missile attack. No conventional political process of decision-making could take place in so short a time. So every possible condition, factor and circumstance must be written into a control program. Current estimates are that such a program would exceed by a factor of ten the most complex programs now being written. Furthermore, no single expert could devise the whole of such a program; it would require many authors. And once there are many authors, no single person understands or can explain the computer's conclusions.

Does that matter? Computers calculate much faster and much more accurately than humans do. They can store millions of bits of data, and can retrieve any one of those bits on the instant. The intelligent computer of the future will be able to operate along parallel lines of logic, and will simulate human styles of thinking, inferences and rules based on experience, to speed up and simplify its conclusions.

The Limits of Technology

And yet no expert system and no computer program, however sophisticated they may be, can predict the unpredictable. Humans under stress behave in unpredictable ways. As defeat in the Second World War approached, Hitler chose a wholly irrational policy, preferring the destruction of Germany in some awesome Götterdämmerung to its survival after an Allied victory. Stalin ended his life in a paranoiac pursuit of his enemies, real or imagined. President Nixon agreed to the falsification of the computer records of bombing raids against neutral Cambodia in March 1969, so that the computer records themselves showed that the raids had taken place in Vietnam.[1]

Judging how human beings will respond to events, which includes envisaging their emotional state and knowing something of their history, is one element of political wisdom. Systems designers may work at a whole range of variables and base their predictions of a political leader's behaviour on a detailed and exhaustive assessment of the strategy and interests of the leader and his or her country. But human beings, even political leaders, do not act wholly according to a rational calculus. Men and women have always disappointed economists by failing to act as economic operators, intent on maximizing their returns. Anyone experienced in politics knows that sentiment, intuition and personal experience play a central role in the making of decisions. Fears, emotions, trust and distrust all lie outside the realms of calculation and logic inhabited by the computer, and outside the realm of artificial intelligence too. Artificial intelligence is not human intelligence in the fullest sense of those words. The intelligent computer may deduce, induce, work through logical sequences, 'see' and 'touch' objects and rearrange them. In that sphere of intelligence it could be of great benefit to human beings. But computers, however 'intelligent', cannot make value judgements. They cannot appreciate music, fall in love, make friends, or feel wonder at a spring flower. Theirs is the domain of birth rates and body counts, of gigavolts and megadeaths. The world of emotion, sensory experience and belief is closed to them.

That is why human beings must not entrust the final decision on whether or not humanity survives to a computer, however 'intelligent'. To do so is the ultimate betrayal of Man, 'the measure of all things' according to the great mathematician Pythagoras in civilization's shining youth. To yield power over our survival as a species to the machine-god is to pursue the technological imperative to the point of insanity. The world's leaders should reject systems that take human decision-makers 'out of the loop'. It is highly improbable that a space-based defence system will ever be impermeable, and even if it were it offers no protection against earth-hugging missiles or nuclear weapons smuggled across borders by terrorists. That such a system should be run by computers, which cannot possibly accommodate all the conceivable combinations of accident, error, misjudgement, malfunction or plain misunderstanding that might constitute a crisis and would influence the decision about what is an appropriate response, compounds the danger. It is enormously important to reverse the arms race before a new escalation into space. Only the frail and compromised anti-ballistic missile treaty bars the way to such an escalation, and it must be honoured and reinforced. The Soviet Union's strictures on the Strategic Defense Initiative would be more convincing if it opened up the phased radar installation at Krasnoyarsk to inspection, and thereby underlined its own commitment to the Treaty.

It is vital that human beings be put back into the loop at every stage of the relationship between the Great Powers. A structure of consultation – joint emergency centres, better hotlines between Moscow and Washington, regular meetings between the military and the scientists on both sides and mutually agreed ways of dealing with accidents or errors – is the human corollary of the command and control systems of each separate superpower. It is given far less attention and a much lower priority than they are. Our survival probably depends upon it.

Conclusion

For centuries, Western civilization has admired rational intelligence. In our own century, that admiration has narrowed into an obsession with what can be quantified. Numeracy is the alphabet of mathematics, engineering and the physical sciences; it has given us computers and calculators, and the power to destroy the world.

In pursuit of what is quantitative, social scientists have accumulated statistics and undertaken surveys to such an extent that they have come close to losing sight of the real human beings who are at the heart of social science. Even in politics, which is all about governing human communities, a certain embarrassment with the awkwardness and idiosyncrasy of human beings drives politicians into talking in abstractions. People are subordinated to policies. As the first part of this book attempts to show, economic ideology has been adhered to in Britain, West Germany and elsewhere without any acute consciousness of the cost unemployment levies in human self-respect. Perhaps there will not be enough work by the end of the century to provide everyone with a full-time job, in which case hours will have to be cut and work shared out. But we are nowhere near running out of work in the mid-1980s. It is the political will to make employment the top domestic priority that is lacking, and not only on the part of governments. Education and training systems cherish institutional divisions and academic snobberies which are obstacles to more people fulfilling their talents and capabilities. Technology is adopted because it brings prestige and makes money, without regard to the damage its unconsidered application may do to traditional societies and fragile environments. This book is about that too, about the way the old epoch of the Industrial Revolution imposed itself on relations between management and workers, machines and people, and about the danger that we may repeat that experience in the new epoch of information technology.

Appropriate Technology

A different sort of technological revolution from the first Industrial Revolution is possible, and it is based on the husbanding of the earth's resources of land, water and minerals. Warning of the violence done to the environment by industrial techniques based on heavy exploitation of fossil fuels, and concerned with the consequences for future generations, Fritz Schumacher and his followers evolved the idea of what they called 'appropriate technology'. Appropriate technology is primarily directed at the less developed Southern Hemisphere, rich in labour, poor in capital, but has increasingly been advanced as a sustainable alternative technology for the Northern Hemisphere as well. Appropriate technology develops methods for conserving energy in preference to further increasing supplies (except from 'friendly', reusable sources like wind and water). It is concerned about the dependence of high-yield modern agriculture on hydrocarbon-based fertilizers, pesticides and ranch-type farming with their destructive impact on the environment. It seeks to scale down technology to the needs of existing human communities, villages and small towns, rather than increasing the scale of human settlements to match advanced industrial technologies. Recycling of materials and refurbishment of existing structures are important to its human-centred approach.

Schumacher pioneered a quiet revolution in thinking about technology. He asserted that technology could be harnessed to human ends. Small-scale irrigation schemes and local power generators could transform the lives of villagers in Asia or Latin America, without their being compelled to move to factories in the sprawling cities. Local manufacture of bricks or tiles or cement would provide jobs, whereas centralized manufacture would use scarce capital and might depend upon expensive imports. Schumacher was not prepared to adopt the most advanced technology regardless of whether or not it would improve the lives of people living in a particular society. He believed that technology could destroy the fabric of some societies, including traditional communities and family relationships. The question he wanted an answer to was whether a particular technology would benefit people, or how it might be made to do so.

No political system should treat people as instruments or as components in a social mechanism. Totalitarian and command systems are mechanistic and instrumental. The decisions they make turn on administrative efficiency and not on ethical values. So it becomes possible to ask how to gas Germany's Jews, or how to burn the largest possible number of civilians in Dresden or Hamburg. When people are turned into numbers, such decisions become rational abstract calculations, bearable to make. It is a process that is particularly marked in the field of defence.

In his book *Computer Power and the Human Reason*, Joseph Weizenbaum writes:

Computers can make judicial decisions, computers can make psychiatric judgements. They can flip coins in much more sophisticated ways than can the most patient human being. The point is that they *ought* not to be given such tasks. They may even be able to arrive at 'correct' decisions in some cases – but always and necessarily on bases no human being should be willing to accept. There have been many debates on 'Computers and Mind'. What I conclude here is that the relevant issues are neither technological nor even mathematical; they are ethical. They cannot be settled by asking questions beginning with 'can'. The limits of the applicability of computers are ultimately statable only in terms of oughts. What emerges as the most elementary insight is that, since we do not now have any ways of making computers wise, we ought not now to give computers tasks that demand wisdom.[1]

Political decisions in a democracy should be about the quality of society and the fulfilment of people's hopes and aspirations. Mutual generosity should be nurtured and the power of love be respected. Computers cannot make us either wise or good. No technological fix will bring us peace or liberty, tolerance or salvation.

Notes

Part I
Rough Passage

Chapter 1: The Dole Queues Lengthen

1. Manpower and Social Affairs Committee, Working Party on Employment, *Employment Outlook*, chapter 6, 'Unemployment and Economic Hardship', Paris, OECD, 1984.

2. ibid.

3. The basic six months' programme of unemployment benefit is financed by employers at the state level, with the rates laid down by Federal law. In 1975, during the administration of President Ford, federally funded Extended Benefits (FEB) and supplemented benefits (FSB) were payable up to the sixty-fifth week of unemployment. Except for the few instances detailed below, Federal programmes of extended benefits have now been virtually eliminated.

4. *The New York Times*, 27 February 1985.

5. Hendry, L.B., Raymond, M., and Stewart, C., 'Unemployment, School and Leisure: An Adolescent Study', Department of Education, University of Aberdeen, 1981.

6. Hartnoll, R., Lewis, R., Mitcheson, M., and Bryer, S., 'Estimating the Prevalence of Opioid Dependence', *Lancet*, 26 January 1985.

7. 'Drug Abuse', Merseyside Drugs Education, Training and Research Unit, July 1984. The plight of the young unemployed in Merseyside is sensitively analysed in Ridley, F.F., 'View from a Disaster Area: Unemployed Youth in Merseyside', *Political Quarterly*, vol. 52, January 1981.

8. BBC *Newsnight* report, 27 November 1984.

9. *Social Trends*, Central Statistical Office, London, January 1985.

10. Moser, K.A., Fox, A.J., and Jones, D.R., 'Unemployment and Mortality in the OPCS (Office of Population Censuses and Surveys) Longitudinal Study, 1971–81', *Lancet*, 8 December 1984.

11. Figures from House of Commons sources confirmed by Sinfield, Adrian, and Fraser, Neil, *The Real Cost of Unemployment*, a special paper for BBC North East, Department of Social Administration, University of Edinburgh, March 1985. Sinfield and Fraser arrive at a national cost of unemployment to the Exchequer of £20 billion.

12. Burtless, G., 'Why is Insured Unemployment So Low?', *Brookings Papers on Economic Activity*, no. 1, 1983.

13. According to Scott McDonald, President of the Interstate Conference of Employment Security Agencies, in evidence to the House Ways and Means Subcommittee on Public Assistance and Unemployment Compensation, 12 September 1984, reported in *Employment and Training Reporter*, 26 September 1984, Washington DC, Manpower Inc.

Chapter 2: Unemployment: Why Does Society Acquiesce?

1. Whitman, M.V.N., *American and European Perspectives on Unemployment: Cyclical and Structural Aspects*, Seventh Annual Marion O'Kellie McKay Lecture, University of Pittsburgh, April 1983.

2. 'Jobless Too Placid', *Economist*, 4 December 1982.

3. *Economic Outlook*, OECD, July 1984.

4. *Policies for Recovery*, Cambridge Econometrics, December 1981.

5. Norman, Peter, 'A Continent Stews in Its Own Economic Juice', *Wall Street Journal*, 20 April 1983.

6. 'Can Europe Catch Up?', *Forbes Magazine*, 4 July 1983.

7. Tobin, James, 'Unemployment in the 1980s: Macroeconomic Diagnosis and Prescription' in (ed.) Pierre, A.J., *Unemployment and Growth in the Western Economies*, New York, Council on Foreign Relations Inc., 1984.

8. Britain's ambivalent attitude towards modern industrial society and a tradition, which can be traced back to the middle of the nineteenth century, of hostility, pervasive then among the middle and upper classes, to industrialism and economic growth is imaginatively explored in Wiener, Martin J., *English Culture and the Decline of the Industrial Spirit, 1850–1980*, Cambridge University Press, 1981.

Chapter 4: Incomes Policy

1. Layard's ideas on an inflation tax are worked out in Layard, Richard, 'Is

Incomes Policy the Answer to Unemployment?', *Economica*, August 1982, and in Layard, Richard, *More Jobs, Less Inflation*, London, Grant McIntyre, 1982. See also Meade, James E., *Wage-Fixing Revisited*, the revised text of the Fourth Robbins Lecture delivered at the University of Stirling, Institute of Economic Affairs, 1985.

2. Weitzman, Martin L., *The Share Economy: Conquering Stagflation*, Cambridge, Massachusetts, Harvard University Press, 1984.

3. 'Can Europe Catch Up?', *Forbes Magazine*, 4 July 1983.

Chapter 5: The Information Technology Revolution

1. *A Survey of Technological Innovation in Japanese Firms*, Japanese Ministry of Labour, November 1982.

2. *The Microelectronics Revolution and Labour-Management Relations*, a summary of the *White Paper on Industrial Relations*, Japan Productivity Centre, 1982.

3. Figures from Yonemoto, K., *Robotisation in Japanese Industries: Socioeconomic impacts by Industrial Robots*, Japanese Industrial Robot Association, October 1983.

4. ibid.

Chapter 6: Japanese Attitudes

1. JEWU–Denki Roren, 'Surveys on the Impacts of Microelectronics and our Policies towards Technological Innovation', Paper for the Fourth I M F World Conference for the Electrical and Electronics Industries, October 1983.

2. ibid.

3. ibid.

4. Kuwahara, Yasuo, 'Creating Jobs in High-Technology Industries', Paper submitted to the O E C D Conference on Employment Growth in the Context of Structural Change, February 1984.

5. Japanese Ministry of Labour Survey, op. cit.

Chapter 7: Great Britain: Irreversible Decline?

1. Northcott, J., and Rogers, P., *Microelectronics in British Industry: The Pattern of Change*, London, Policy Studies Institute, 1985.

2. 'Capital Investment Level with Japan', *Economist*, 17 December 1983.

3. *The Human Factor – The Supply Side Problem*, Information Technology Skills

Shortages Committee, First Report, Department of Trade and Industry, 1984.

Chapter 8: Jobs for the Future

1. Colombo, U., 'Jobs of the Future', translated from 'Dove nascono i mestieri degli anni '90', *Sole 24 Ore*, 7 October 1983.

2. Leontief, W., and Duchin, F., 'The Impacts of Automation on Employment, 1963–2000', Abstract and Executive Summary of Final Report, Institute for Economic Analysis, New York University, April 1984. The results of this study are at time of writing to be published in 1985 by Oxford University Press as Leontief, W., and Duchin, F., *The Future Impacts of Automation on Workers*.

3. *Wall Street Journal*, 9 August 1983.

4. Jonscher, Charles, 'Information Resources and Economic Productivity', *Information Economics and Policy*, vol. 1, no. 1, 1983.

5. Figures based on the United States Bureau of Labor Statistics, 1984.

6. Jenkins, Clive, and Sherman, Barry, *The Collapse of Work*, London, Eyre Methuen, 1979.

7. Jonscher, op. cit.

8. Jonscher, Charles, 'Telecommunications and the Economy' (December 1982) and 'A Study of Telecommunications and the Economy – The Policy Implications for BT. Executive Summary' (March 1983). Unpublished studies carried out by Communications Studies and Planning International.

Chapter 9: The Intelligent Computer: A Threat to the Professions?

1. *Preliminary Report on Study and Research on Fifth-Generation Computers, 1979–1980*, Japan Information Processing Development Centre, Tokyo, 1981.

2. Unpublished Department of Health and Social Security report, conducted by the Research Institute for Consumer Affairs. Reported in the *Guardian*, 13 August 1984.

3. 'Computers and the Disabled', *The Times*, 15 April 1985.

Chapter 10: Can Small Business Create Jobs?

1. Birch, David L., 'The Job Generation Process', *MIT Program on Neighborhood and Regional Change*, Cambridge, Massachusetts, MIT, 1979.

2. Armington, Catherine, and Odle, Marjorie, 'Sources of Recent Employment

Growth, 1978–80', *Business Microdata Project*, The Brookings Institution, March 1982. Their argument is summarized in 'Small Business – How Many Jobs?', *The Brookings Review*, Winter 1982.

3. Birch, David L., and MacCracken, Susan, 'The Small Business Share of Job Creation: Lessons Learned from the Use of a Longitudinal File', *MIT Program on Neighbourhood and Regional Change*, Cambridge, Massachusetts, MIT, November 1982.

4. Teitz, Michael B., Glasmeier, Amy, and Svensson, Douglas, 'Small Business and Employment Growth in California', working paper of the Institute of Urban and Regional Development, University of California, Berkeley, March 1981.

5. Tauzell, John, 'Survival of Minnesota New Businesses, 1977–1980', *Review of Labor and Economic Conditions*, Minnesota Department of Economic Security, Second Quarter 1982.

6. Birch, David L., 'Who Creates Jobs?', *The Public Interest*, Fall 1981.

7. Teitz, Glasmeier and Svensson, op. cit.

8. Armington and Odle, op. cit.

9. Birch, 'Who creates jobs?', op. cit.

10. Quoted by Moreton, A., 'Regional Development', *Financial Times*, 25 January 1985.

11. Ganguly, P., and Povey, D., 'Small Firms Survey: The International Scene', *British Business*, 19 November 1982.

12. *Changing Employment Patterns: Where Will the New Jobs Be?*, National Economic Development Council, London, 28 November 1983.

Chapter 11: New Patterns, New Possibilities

1. *Employment Growth and Structural Change*, Paris, OECD, 1985. Papers based on inter-governmental conference held in February 1984 under the auspices of the Manpower and Social Affairs Committee.

2. Dizard, J., 'Europe Rediscovers the Entrepreneur', *Fortune*, 3 October 1983.

Chapter 12: Information Networks for Small Business

1. Northcott, and Rogers, op. cit.

2. Leontief, W., 'The Distribution of Work and Income', *Scientific American*, vol. 247, no. 3, September 1982.

Chapter 13: The Bootstrap Economy

1. *Technology, Innovation and Regional Economic Development: Encouraging High-Technology Development*, Background Paper 2, Washington DC, United States Congress, Office of Technology Assessment, February 1984.

Chapter 14: Regional Policy

1. Kuwahara, op. cit.

2. ibid.

3. Figures derived from the Chartered Institute of Public Finance and Accountancy.

4. Cambridge Econometrics Ltd, op. cit.

Part II
A New Epoch

Chapter 15: The Skills Crisis

1. IMS Computer study for NEDO, 1983.

2. Northcott, J., Rogers, P., Knetsch, W., and Lestapis, B. de, *Microelectronics in Industry. An International Comparison: Britain, Germany, France*, Policy Studies Institute and Anglo-German Foundation, January 1985.

3. Goldsack, S.J., and Dalbeck, E., 'Jobs in the Software Industry'. Unpublished survey, Imperial College, May 1983.

4. CBI Industrial Trends Survey, June 1984.

5. Atkinson, A.D., *Manpower Needs and Demographic Trends in the UK*, IMS, January 1985.

6. Carnegie Foundation study.

7. *The National Journal*, 11 February 1984.

Chapter 16: Education: The Determinant of Tomorrow's Success

1. *The Times*, 25 January 1985.

2. 'Microcomputers in Secondary Schools', a summary of a postal survey conducted jointly by the BBC and the Department of Education and Science's Microelectronics Education Programme, 1984.

3. ibid.

4. Quoted in *People and Productivity: A Challenge to Corporate America*, New York Stock Exchange, November 1982.

5. Snow, C.P., *The Two Cultures and the Scientific Revolution*, Cambridge University Press, 1959.

6. Evans, Norman, *Access to Higher Education: Non-standard Entry to CNAA First Degree and DipHE Courses*, CNAA Development Services, August 1984.

7. The Open University, the most radical and successful innovation in education for many years, is itself threatened. It suffered a small budgetary cut every year from 1980, in spite of an increase of 10 per cent in the student population. In 1984, much larger cuts, £13·2 million over three years, were proposed. These cannot be absorbed without major and damaging changes. For a country that so badly needs to increase the skills and knowledge of its population, such policies are incomprehensible.

Chapter 17: Men, Machines and Management

1. Taylor, F.W., *On the Art of Cutting Metals*, American Society of Mechanical Engineers, Third edition, 1906. Taylor's *Principles of Scientific Management* (1911) is the most complete expression of his philosophy. For a modern assessment of Taylor's work, see Nelson, Daniel, *Frederick Winslow Taylor and the Rise of Scientific Management*, University of Wisconsin Press, 1980.

2. Rosenbrock, H.H., 'Final Report on Senior Fellowship, 1979–83', February 1984.

3. Japan Productivity Centre, op. cit.

4. ibid.

5. ibid.

6. *A Survey on Labour Union Activities in the 1980s in Japan*, Japan Industrial Relations Research Association, March 1983.

7. Japanese Productivity Centre, op. cit.

8. Northcott, Rogers, Knetsch and Lestapis, op. cit.

9. Japanese Ministry of Labour Survey, op. cit.

10. JEWU–Denki Roren, 'Surveys on the Impacts of Microelectronics and our Policies towards Technological Innovation', op. cit.

11. In an interview with the Japanese Social Democratic Party executive committee, February 1984.

12. Japanese Ministry of Labour Survey, op. cit.

Chapter 18: The Information Flow: Access and Control

1. Quoted in Dresner, Stewart, *Open Government: Lessons from America*, Outer Circle Policy Unit 1980.

2. *The Civil Service* (Chairman: Lord Fulton), HMSO, 1968.

3. Burnham, David, *The Rise of the Computer State*, New York, First Vintage Books, 1984.

Chapter 19: The Means of Surveillance

1. Burnham, op. cit.

2. Lowi, Theodore, 'The Third Revolution Revisited', an unpublished paper, Cornell University, 1984.

Chapter 21: Who Will Make the Decisions?

1. Shawcross, William, *Sideshow: Kissinger, Nixon and the Destruction of Cambodia*, London, André Deutsch, 1979.

Conclusion

1. Weizenbaum, J., *Computer Power and Human Reason: From Judgement to Calculation*, New York, W. H. Freeman & Co., 1976 (and Penguin Books, 1984).

Index

MORE ABOUT PENGUINS, PELICANS, PEREGRINES AND PUFFINS

For further information about books available from Penguins please write to Dept EP, Penguin Books Ltd, Harmondsworth, Middlesex UB7 0DA.

In the U.S.A.: For a complete list of books available from Penguins in the United States write to Dept DG, Penguin Books, 299 Murray Hill Parkway, East Rutherford, New Jersey 07073.

In Canada: For a complete list of books available from Penguins in Canada write to Penguin Books Canada Ltd, 2801 John Street, Markham, Ontario L3R 1B4.

In Australia: For a complete list of books available from Penguins in Australia write to the Marketing Department, Penguin Books Australia Ltd, P.O. Box 257, Ringwood, Victoria 3134.

In New Zealand: For a complete list of books available from Penguins in New Zealand write to the Marketing Department, Penguin Books (N.Z.) Ltd, Private Bag, Takapuna, Auckland 9.

In India: For a complete list of books available from Penguins in India write to Penguin Overseas Ltd, 706 Eros Apartments, 56 Nehru Place, New Delhi 110019.

THE PENGUIN ENGLISH DICTIONARY

The Penguin English Dictionary has been created specially for today's needs. It features:

* More entries than any other popularly priced dictionary
* Exceptionally clear and precise definitions
* For the first time in an equivalent dictionary, the internationally recognised IPA pronunciation system
* Emphasis on contemporary usage
* Extended coverage of both the spoken and the written word
* Scientific tables
* Technical words
* Informal and colloquial expressions
* Vocabulary most widely used *wherever* English is spoken
* Most commonly used abbreviations

It is twenty years since the publication of the last English dictionary by Penguin and the compilation of this entirely new *Penguin English Dictionary* is the result of a special collaboration between Longman, one of the world's leading dictionary publishers, and Penguin Books. The material is based entirely on the database of the acclaimed *Longman Dictionary of the English Language*.

1008 pages	051.139 3	£2.50 ☐

PENGUIN REFERENCE BOOKS

☐ *The Penguin Map of the World* £2.50

Clear, colourful, crammed with information and fully up-to-date, this is a useful map to stick on your wall at home, at school or in the office.

☐ *The Penguin Map of Europe* £2.95

Covers all land eastwards to the Urals, southwards to North Africa and up to Syria, Iraq and Iran * Scale = 1:5,500,000 * 4-colour artwork * Features main roads, railways, oil and gas pipelines, plus extra information including national flags, currencies and populations.

☐ *The Penguin Map of the British Isles* £1.95

Including the Orkneys, the Shetlands, the Channel Islands and much of Normandy, this excellent map is ideal for planning routes and touring holidays, or as a study aid.

☐ *The Penguin Dictionary of Quotations* £3.95

A treasure-trove of over 12,000 new gems and old favourites, from Aesop and Matthew Arnold to Xenophon and Zola.

☐ *The Penguin Dictionary of Art and Artists* £3.95

Fifth Edition. 'A vast amount of information intelligently presented, carefully detailed, abreast of current thought and scholarship and easy to read' – *The Times Literary Supplement*

☐ *The Penguin Pocket Thesaurus* £1.95

A pocket-sized version of Roget's classic, and an essential companion for all commuters, crossword addicts, students, journalists and the stuck-for-words.

PENGUIN REFERENCE BOOKS

☐ *The Penguin Dictionary of Troublesome Words*   £2.50

A witty, straightforward guide to the pitfalls and hotly disputed issues in standard written English, illustrated with examples and including a glossary of grammatical terms and an appendix on punctuation.

☐ *The Penguin Guide to the Law*   £7.50

This acclaimed reference book is designed for everyday use, and forms the most comprehensive handbook ever published on the law as it affects the individual.

☐ *The Penguin Dictionary of Religions*   £4.95

The rites, beliefs, gods and holy books of all the major religions throughout the world are covered in this book, which is illustrated with charts, maps and line drawings.

☐ *The Penguin Medical Encyclopedia*   £4.95

Covers the body and mind in sickness and in health, including drugs, surgery, history, institutions, medical vocabulary and many other aspects. Second Edition. 'Highly commendable' – *Journal of the Institute of Health Education*

☐ *The Penguin Dictionary of Physical Geography*   £4.95

This book discusses all the main terms used, in over 5,000 entries illustrated with diagrams and meticulously cross-referenced.

☐ *Roget's Thesaurus*   £2.95

Specially adapted for Penguins, Sue Lloyd's acclaimed new version of Roget's original will help you find the right words for your purposes. 'As normal a part of an intelligent household's library as the Bible, Shakespeare or a dictionary' – *Daily Telegraph*

A CHOICE OF PENGUINS

☐ **The Complete Penguin Stereo Record and Cassette Guide**
Greenfield, Layton and March £7.95

A new edition, now including information on compact discs. 'One of the few indispensables on the record collector's bookshelf' – *Gramophone*

☐ **Selected Letters of Malcolm Lowry**
Edited by Harvey Breit and Margerie Bonner Lowry £5.95

'Lowry emerges from these letters not only as an extremely interesting man, but also a lovable one' – Philip Toynbee

☐ **The First Day on the Somme**
Martin Middlebrook £3.95

1 July 1916 was the blackest day of slaughter in the history of the British Army. 'The soldiers receive the best service a historian can provide: their story told in their own words' – *Guardian*

☐ **A Better Class of Person** **John Osborne** £1.95

The playwright's autobiography, 1929–56. 'Splendidly enjoyable' – John Mortimer. 'One of the best, richest and most bitterly truthful autobiographies that I have ever read' – Melvyn Bragg

☐ **The Winning Streak** **Goldsmith and Clutterbuck** £2.95

Marks & Spencer, Saatchi & Saatchi, United Biscuits, GEC . . . The UK's top companies reveal their formulas for success, in an important and stimulating book that no British manager can afford to ignore.

☐ **The First World War** **A. J. P. Taylor** £3.95

'He manages in some 200 illustrated pages to say almost everything that is important . . . A special text . . . a remarkable collection of photographs' – *Observer*

A CHOICE OF PENGUINS

☐ *Man and the Natural World* Keith Thomas   £4.95

Changing attitudes in England, 1500–1800. 'An encyclopedic study of man's relationship to animals and plants . . . a book to read again and again' – Paul Theroux, *Sunday Times* Books of the Year

☐ *Jean Rhys: Letters 1931–66*
Edited by Francis Wyndham and Diana Melly   £3.95

'Eloquent and invaluable . . . her life emerges, and with it a portrait of an unexpectedly indomitable figure' – Marina Warner in the *Sunday Times*

☐ *The French Revolution* Christopher Hibbert   £4.50

'One of the best accounts of the Revolution that I know . . . Mr Hibbert is outstanding' – J. H. Plumb in the *Sunday Telegraph*

☐ *Isak Dinesen* Judith Thurman   £4.95

The acclaimed life of Karen Blixen, 'beautiful bride, disappointed wife, radiant lover, bereft and widowed woman, writer, sibyl, Scheherazade, child of Lucifer, Baroness; always a unique human being . . . an assiduously researched and finely narrated biography' – *Books & Bookmen*

☐ *The Amateur Naturalist*
Gerald Durrell with Lee Durrell   £4.95

'Delight . . . on every page . . . packed with authoritative writing, learning without pomposity . . . it represents a real bargain' – *The Times Educational Supplement*. 'What treats are in store for the average British household' – *Daily Express*

☐ *When the Wind Blows* Raymond Briggs   £2.95

'A visual parable against nuclear war: all the more chilling for being in the form of a strip cartoon' – *Sunday Times*. 'The most eloquent anti-Bomb statement you are likely to read' – *Daily Mail*

A CHOICE OF
PELICANS AND PEREGRINES

☐ *The Knight, the Lady and the Priest*
   Georges Duby £5.95

The acclaimed study of the making of modern marriage in medieval France. 'He has traced this story – sometimes amusing, often horrify-ing, always startling – in a series of brilliant vignettes' – *Observer*

☐ *The Limits of Soviet Power* **Jonathan Steele** £3.50

The Kremlin's foreign policy – Brezhnev to Chernenko, is discussed in this informed, informative 'wholly invaluable and extraordinarily timely study' – *Guardian*

☐ *Understanding Organizations* **Charles B. Handy** £4.95

Third Edition. Designed as a practical source-book for managers, this Pelican looks at the concepts, key issues and current fashions in tackling organizational problems.

☐ *The Pelican Freud Library: Volume 12* £4.95

Containing the major essays: *Civilization, Society and Religion, Group Psychology* and *Civilization and Its Discontents*, plus other works.

☐ *Windows on the Mind* **Erich Harth** £4.95

Is there a physical explanation for the various phenomena that we call 'mind'? Professor Harth takes in age-old philosophers as well as the latest neuroscientific theories in his masterly study of memory, perception, free will, selfhood, sensation and other richly controver-sial fields.

☐ *The Pelican History of the World*
   J. M. Roberts £5.95

'A stupendous achievement . . . This is the unrivalled World History for our day' – A. J. P. Taylor